Driven By Destiny

Dream Book

Dr. LaVerne Adams

Driven by Destiny: Dream Book

ISBN-13: 978-0-9822088-3-0

Printed in the United States

Photography – Phil Jackson, Shootworks
Cover Design/Interior Design – Kimberly Martin, Jera Web Creations
Publicity and Marketing – Veda Brown, BGPromo
Web Design – Gustavo DaCruz, Pixalies
Publishing Coaching – Patrick Snow, Patrick Snow Group

Library of Congress Registration Number: TXu-1-657-953

Dedication

This book is dedicated to my son
Warren,
who is discovering everyday
what it means
to be driven by destiny…

What people around the world are saying about *Driven by Destiny:*

I had the privilege of meeting this giant of a woman. I realized in an instant that here was someone whom God had hand-picked for His Glory to share His Word across the nations. She is a dynamic woman who leads with great aplomb. In her resourcefulness she gets things done through people who are likewise Kingdom minded. For several years she has been empowering and motivating others into their life's destiny. As you read this powerful work — walk alongside of her on her journey to the higher life. — **Joan McClou, Author, Seasons of a Mended Heart, Cape Town, South Africa**

It's very clear that this writer is a Kingdom Anointed Servant of God, one who is driven by destiny, and has a strong anointing and a passion to pursue the will and purpose of her God. As she does so, she helps to unlock the destiny and purpose of God in the lives of all of her readers. Divine destiny, anointing and revelation, is revealed on every page and in every chapter. Each chapter always opens with a life changing, thought provoking message. Dr. LaVerne motivates the reader to think, take a moment to reflect and to recommit to their lives to God. This book is a divinely ordained manuscript for living that will change and realign each reader, taking them through their destiny page by page, reminding them of their past present and future. It has been a tremendous blessing to my soul. God bless you Dr. LaVerne and cause you to succeed beyond your divine expectations. — ***Apostle Lucille Baird, Pastor, Mt. Zion's Missions International Barbados, West Indies***

Driven By Destiny is an invitation to inner growth. Both compelling and welcoming, it seems to dialogue with the reader while it guides him through the path of self-discovery and seek for success. Within its pages you won't find magical answers, but you'll be challenged with the right questions to put the missing pieces of your life in their place.

De la Mano del Destino, por la Dra. LaVerne Adams, es una invitación al crecimiento personal. Convincente, a la vez que afable, el texto mismo parece dialogar con el lector mientras lo guía por el camino del autodescubrimiento y la búsqueda del éxito. Entre sus páginas usted no encontrará repuestas mágicas, mas será retado con las preguntas correctas para poner en su lugar las piezas de su vida que no calzan. — **Andres Viales Lopez, Director, Cultural Center for Latin American Studies, Heredia, Costa Rica**

"Hard to believe that there is a destiny or that our stories have been already written. I use to think that every step in life creates the path and make the way. In Dr. LaVerne Adams' book, we find a new definition of destiny, in which we can create the path at every step. But this is also in the amazing mind of God which provides sense to our existence and lives. Therefore, destiny is not a path made or a way already created but a life to live with a sense of the amazing dreams and love of God the Creator, the redeemer and the guider of our lives." — **Obed Arango, Executive Director of Centro de Cultura, Arte, Trabajo y Educación (CCATE) US & Mexico**

As I read this book, I found it to be practical yet very thought-provoking. It is down to earth and the openness of the testimonies of her journey to life only proves the freedom that she has attained which no doubt has contributed to the reaching of her destiny. The book touches my heart as it was written from very cores of her heart. It has lifted my spirit personally and has encouraged me to look deeper into my heart and review my own thought patterns. It presented to me a sense of urgency if I want something better to happen in my life. It is life-changing. It helps one to discover that the best in life that is yet still ahead of us and urges us to be discerning, disciplined, determined and willing to submit to what God has in store for us-- which is far better than what we have planned ourselves.

I believe this book will help many to find more meaning in their lives as they follow the practical life guidelines to discovering and mastering the secrets of success and finding their destiny in life. Dr. Adams has truly reached the objective of presenting the tools to help readers get in touch with themselves to help bring to fulfillment to their dreams. — **Rose Mipiri, Manilla, Philippines**

Theorist Jean Piaget (1896-1980) gave humanity the stages of cognitive development, Eric Erikson (1902-1994) presented a model of the psychosocial stages of human development, Lawrence Kohlberg (1927-1987) outlined the stages in the development of moral judgment and now, Dr. LaVerne Adams, in similar academic structure has presented 'Driven by Destiny', as an holistic perspective on the spiritual stages of human development and beyond.

With intellectual craftiness Dr. Adams objectively combines her personal experiences, expertise and knowledge in diverse fields from architecture to theology to present what can only be considered an S.P.S or a Spiritual Positioning System for life, as opposed to the G.P.S. This is a must have for any serious seeker of destiny and spiritual growth, and a definite collector's item for any library. — **Bernard Marshall, Director, Strictly Kingdom Empowerment Center, Arima, Trinidad**

I'm just so grateful that I'm learning what it's like to be aligned with my destiny. I thank you so much for being that midwife in my life to birth what God has designed for me to do. You have shown me how to prepare a new mental diet, how to plan with purpose as well as how to do life differently. I have learned that when I walk in the destiny that God has designed, there is a joy like no other. I see in your smile and I hear it in your heart when we talk.

Your life is a great example of a woman who has been divinely designed to walk in her destiny. You actually get it! And I thank God that when you got it, you didn't keep it; instead you shared it! As my life coach you have poured into me and so many other women until our cups can't help but to overflow with joy about what walking in our destiny can do! God gets the glory when others meet you because your obedience has been my inspiration to trust God and walk right into my destiny. When a woman walks in her destiny, she will live her life like it's golden; just the way I'm watching Rev. Adams live her life! — **CeCe McGhee, Radio Show Host, Praise 103.9 FM, Philadelphia, Pennsylvania, USA**

Cuando nos encaran y retan nuestros grandes sueños y propósitos de vida, somos asaltados por la falta de fe, temores, obstáculos, dolor, y siempre requiere esfuerzo. Mas Dios nos pone a disposición su ayuda, la pasión y los recursos para lograrlo. He evidenciado que la Dra. LaVerne ha recibido el llamado, la unción y autoridad para enseñar y exhortar al respecto, y de una forma única contagiar el gozo de avanzar hacia la meta y descubrir las maravillas que están para nosotros en el camino. Te invito a dejarte ayudar animar durante tu propia travesía y dejarte enseñar cómo disfrutarlo.

When our big dreams and life purposes confront and challenge us, we are assaulted by a lack of faith, fears, obstacles, pain. This always requires effort. But God offers us his help, the passion and resources to achieve it. It is evidenced that Dr. LaVerne has received the calling, anointing and authority to teach and encourage in this regard, and a unique way to spread the joy of working towards the goal and discover the wonders that are for us on the road. I invite you to let this book help drive your journey and let you teach how to enjoy it. — **Mireya Farris, Director of Zapatos Nuevos, Caracas, Venezuela**

Acknowledgments

One can never truly accomplish anything meaningful without the help of trusted, competent people who support your vision and dreams. I am truly blessed because of the people who make a difference in the world and whose ministry personally impacts my life. There have been several people who have significantly helped to shape the course of my destiny. I have come to realize that God sends people to cooperate with Him in the fulfillment of one's destiny. Without them, much of my destiny would not be realized.

Dr. Mark Chironna has been an invaluable mentor, life coach, and friend. His brilliant style of ministry has not only challenged me to reshape my inner world which has tremendously impacted the unfolding of my divine destiny. Because of his caring visionary approach, I see with clarity a phenomenal future filled with endless possibilities and abounding potential.

The prophetic ministry of Dr. Chuck Pierce has literally transformed my existence in some very practical ways. His prayer focuses and timely prophecies helped me to cycle out of dysfunctional patterns and make strides toward my apostolic and prophetic calling to the nations. In addition, we are honored that Cathedral of Praise Community Church, where I have served as the senior pastor since 1997, is recognized as a "Church of Zion." This connection with Glory of Zion International strengthens our resolve to actively see the powerful prophetic flow of deliverance transform people's lives to help them reach their fullest potential and expand God's kingdom. This significant connection is also vital to helping me realize the magnitude and international scope of my destiny.

I thank God for prayer general Dr. Cindy Trimm, who I am privileged to call friend. By God's divine design she was brought into my life as a catalyst to move me into a realm of power and faith that delivered me into a deeper dimension of my divine destiny. Her brand of ministry has catapulted me into a greater sense of strength and purpose. As an ambassadorial mouthpiece for God, Dr. Trimm's dynamic style, cutting-edge prayer strategies, and kingdom technologies has profoundly aligned me to take dominion and prosper in every area of my life. Because of her unique passion to see me empowered to reach my fullest potential my life is royally positioned as a resource that advances the establishment of the Kingdom of God.

I am grateful to be connected to the astounding ministry of Bishop David Evans, of Bethany Baptist Church and the Abundant Harvest Fellowship of Churches, whose mandate for excellence abounds in every area of this ministry. I am particularly impressed with his passion for souls, which has drawn over 27,000 into his church membership, which is contagious! Through his ministry, I gain leadership and fathering in a way that advances me toward my purpose and destiny like never before. This connection has proved productive for ministry as I am mentored and exposed to more effective models for ministry, higher levels of kingdom enterprise, and greater levels of ministry success.

Patrick Snow, my publishing coach, whose advice has helped me to take my writing projects and publishing to the next level. He is a wealth of knowledge and a ball of enthusiasm.

To Rochelle Melander, who helped to me jumpstart writing my dissertation project, has once again offered invaluable assistance and has helped to edit this manuscript.

And to Mr. Tony Magee, The Destiny Doctor®! You have inspired me in ways that are beyond the imagination. You are truly an inspiration and master motivation I am so glad that destiny has brought us together to help people all over the world discover how to be their best selves.

And, finally, I thank God for Dr. Rick Warren, who by divine providence just happened upon one of my articles in the *African American Pulpit*, while preparing to be the first Caucasian preacher at the Ebenezer Baptist Church in Atlanta on Dr. Martin Luther King's Day 2009. His prompting to reach out to me for counsel further affirmed my calling and destiny as a spiritual advisor to great people. Ours is truly a divine connection as I have always been impressed with his ministry and literary work. And now our destinies have been miraculously aligned and driven with purpose.

Special thanks to the Cathedral of Praise Community Church and the International Kingdom Strategy Center, who are the most beautiful community of people that I have ever met in my life. I thank God for the privilege of being called your pastor. And to all of those who call me Coach and allow me to speak into your lives to help you draw on your own personal power to attain the success that is deep within you, thank you!

Foreword

If you want to know your destiny, you must begin with God. We were born for his purpose; yet, many of us stay puzzled about the destiny God has planned for us. That's because we typically begin at the wrong starting point—ourselves. We ask self-centered questions like, 'What do I want to be?' 'What should I do with my life?' 'What are my goals, my ambitions, my dreams for my future?'

But focusing on ourselves will never reveal our life's purpose. In her book, *Driven By Destiny*, Dr. LaVerne Adams provides a very practical plan for not only determining what your God-given destiny is, but also provides a way to help move you forward in fulfilling your destiny.

Part of your destiny is to become like Jesus, but you cannot reproduce the character of Jesus on your own strength. This book will help you understand how you must cooperate with the Holy Spirit's work of developing the character of Christ in you. It is a strong reminder that, although your own effort has nothing to do with your salvation, it has much to do with your spiritual growth.

We are to *make every effort* in our growth toward becoming like Jesus. We don't just sit around and wait for it to happen, but as LaVerne methodically shows, we are to very deliberately let go of old ways of acting; we are to actively work with the Holy Spirit in changing the way we think; and we are to consistently "put on" the character of Christ by developing new, godly habits.

Rick Warren, Pastor of Saddleback Church, San Diego California
Author of *The Purpose Driven Life*

Prologue

Quantum scientists have now confirmed what the Bible revealed to us centuries ago, that there are parallel worlds and "portals" that give us access to them all. Dr. Adams takes us on a scholarly journey and offers us a destiny altering practical guide to discovering and mastering the secrets for success, happiness, and prosperity. Her passion for educating and empowering the masses bleeds through every page as she skillfully excavates the mysterious realm of the spirit concerning the elusive topic, "Destiny". In my younger years I used the word destiny synonymously with the word purpose until I realized that they were not one in the same. Now I know that my purpose was pre-determined by God, while my destiny is determined by me. Your destiny is determined the moment you make a decision. In other words, God determines your purpose but you determine your destiny. Destinies are decision oriented, and as such you are always only one decision away from living the life of your dreams.

Dr. Adams writings are very thought provoking. Her transparency and candor mixed with humility makes her inspirational writing style inviting, practical, and spiritually motivating. In a world that is crying out for assistance and leadership, where fear and the grueling tasks of making a living has immobilized and handicapped the creativity within the masses, and stifled their ability to hope and dream for a better future, this book can be used as catalyst for change with Dr. Adams, the author, its agent. If you exist amongst the masses, this book will under gird your efforts in breaking away from the mundane, freeing your mind from self-imposed limitation and ultimately demolishing the chains that threaten to keep you bond to a life of misery. Read this book for it can positively change your life for the good. Dare to leave your past behind and travel through the dimensions of opportunity, purpose and destiny into a brilliant future.

Dr. N. Cindy Trimm, CEO,
Cindy Trimm International & World Summit on Prayer
Author of *Commanding Your Morning*

Preface

Just the mention of the word *destiny* evokes a wide spectrum of thoughts and feelings for us. On the one hand, if we believe that we are called to live on the edge of adventure, we respond to the hearing of that word with a sense of commitment to both its mystery and its unfolding. The word evokes the creative and more intuitive part of our nature to sense intangible things that have the potential of becoming tangible. Something in us senses great bliss in going after that which we believe is intended for us, the powerful pull of the yet-to-be-fulfilled future awaiting us. We count the cost and believe it is worth the risk of pursuing, and so with confidence and faith, we run after destiny in hopes of apprehending it and even fulfilling it.

On the other hand, some of us may feel less enticed to run after *destiny* because our journey has taught us that the things we tend to run after the hardest often evade our grasp and are quite elusive. We may prefer the less mysterious, and perhaps more reliable approach of logic and reasoning, which requires wise decision making and a careful evaluation of all the options and opportunities that are presented to us on a daily basis. After all, the choices we make determine the outcomes we get. In that, there are many *destinies* possible for us in many situations because of the number of options available for us to choose from. The real lesson then is to learn to choose wisely.

Between these two seemingly opposite poles lies a broad spectrum of possibilities of response and reaction to the word *destiny*. One's DNA, one's ethnic background, one's culture, one's personal history, one's environment, and the sum total of one's life experience will have shaped that response at any given moment. One's life experience encompasses the fullness of everything one has ever thought, felt, said, and done. In addition, we all have deep mental models of how we believe the world works. Some of those models are so embedded that they operate in us at unconscious levels beyond immediate awareness yet always exerting profound influence on our choices as well as our outcomes.

Merriam-Webster's Collegiate Dictionary defines *destiny* as "a predetermined course of events often held to be an irresistible power or agency". The dictionary then invites you to consider *fate* as an apt synonym, as *fate* implies that *destiny* is "the will or principle or determining cause by which things in general are believed to come to be as they are, or events as they do". For the destiny "purist" fate is not the same because there is no room for personal will, or free human agency to play a part in it, it simply is what it is. Something deep within us wants to believe that we have some modicum of control over the events of our lives, and with all the recent revival of interest in what metaphysics has taught for years as "the law of attraction", millions are being swept up into the momentum of believing that they are the ultimate creators of their reality.

A number of years ago I was watching a late-night talk show, and the now late Ray Charles was on as a guest. The host asked if Ray believed in a personal God. Ray said something that struck me. I will paraphrase as best as I can remember. He said something to the effect of, "When I LOOK around and SEE all the order and design in the universe, I have to concede that there is a Supreme Being." (Forgive me Ray if I have not quoted you exactly correctly). I marveled at that answer because a blind man used visual terms to describe a reality he could not SEE with physical eyes. He had developed a "sense" of sight because of his handicap.

Perhaps that is a healthy place to live when it comes to the issue of *destiny*, wherever we fall on the spectrum of what our response to the concept is, whether we live on the high seas of adventure and thrive on the unknown and what emerges from it, or we seek to control as much of life as we can because we don't want the unexpected to upset our apple cart. Somewhere in all of this wide spectrum of what we have the potential of influencing, and what unknown factors have the potential of influencing us, we all have one common factor: we are all human beings, which means at least to some degree that are subject to weakness, frailty, and limitation. In other words, we don't know it all, and we can't control it all. Not only that, we didn't make it all!

So where does that leave us? We would all do well to sit in for a series of meetings with recovering alcoholics, recovering chemical abusers, recovering gamblers, and any other recovery programs out there for any other addiction. One of the primary lessons learned in recovery is the need to give up the illusion of control. Forget controlling events they say, "we can't even control ourselves". Whenever I hear someone in recovery talk about giving up the illusion of control I smile and give a hearty internal laugh because a deeply spiritual and theological truth is being acknowledged: we have to stop playing God and start becoming human.

So where does that leave us then in terms of *destiny?* Hopefully, it doesn't simply *leave us* somewhere, it actually *brings us* somewhere! Where might that be? If we are going to believe in *destiny*, regardless of how one defines it, the implication is that of necessity there has to be a *"Destiner"* if you will. For those of us who share in a worldview that has been shaped by a Judeo-Christian heritage, there is as Ray Charles indeed *saw*, an intelligent design to the universe, a Supreme Being. For the atheist, we offer no apology for recognizing that it doesn't all begin and end with being human. It all begins and ends with a renewed appreciation for what real humanity was intended, and even *destined* to both be and become, because in fact, *destiny* is all about *being* and *becoming*.

For the adventurer who embraces the mystery of the yet-to-be-fulfilled and wants to experience life on what someone called "the living edge", they can all too often ignore the *being* aspect of their journey, and focus only on the *becoming* component of it. On the other side of the argument lives the individual committed to the *being* side of existence in life because you can only live life one moment at a time, so NOW becomes vitally important and practical, and NOT YET simply is nothing to focus on because it isn't NOW.

Truth is often held in the tension of opposites. If there is darkness, there also has to be light. If there is sorrow, there also exists joy. If there is adversity, there is also blessing. If indeed we were created, then there is a Creator. If there is a Creator there is an intention in the mind of the Creator. If there is an intention in the Mind of the Creator for their creation, there has to exist a means of communication between the Creator and the created, so that the created can fulfill the intention of the Creator.

Isaiah the prophet of Israel, lived in the 8th century B.C.. He uttered these words as a message from the Creator to us: *"I will lead the blind by a way they do not know, in paths they do not know I will guide them"*. Again, Ray Charles had it right, and *saw* what many people who have physical sight fail to see: there is a Director who governs the paths we take, and deep trust is required if the *blind* is to get to their *destination* (can't get away from that word *destiny* can we?). So for the person who thrives on going after the mysterious side of *destiny* the truth is that even in pursuing it, you have to deeply trust that where you are going is where you are being led, and that you are not the master of your fate.

At the same time, this same Isaiah says these words: "Who is so blind as My servant, or so deaf as My messenger whom I send? Who is so blind as he that is at peace with Me, or so blind as the servant of the Lord?" Wow, for those more intent on the practical "being" and doing side of destiny there is the same reality, that regardless of what you do see, there is a certain kind of blindness that is required if we are to accomplish all that is intended. That blindness involves admitting that even in the present moment, and in the practical daily hands-on issues of walking out the journey apart from wanting to peer into the future, even the present moment is filled with a certain amount of reality that cannot be seen by mere mortals.

So regardless of whether you are on the *becoming* side of your expectations of *destiny*, or the *being* side of how you believe *destiny* is influenced and manifested, a power greater than ourselves is at the helm and in charge. As a human being, your journey in and to *destiny* is not an either/or issue. *Destiny* is all about *being* AND *becoming*. It is as significant for the neurosurgeon as it is for the sanitation worker. It is as promising for the philosopher of logic, as it is for the theological mystic. It is both practical and powerful. It involves a very skillful dance between the known and the unknown, the familiar and the unfamiliar, the seen and the unseen, the tangible and the intangible, the temporal and the eternal.

Having said all that, I ask you the proverbial question: How do you eat an elephant? And as you may have heard, the wisest answer is "one bite at a time". *Destiny* evokes so many different feelings and beliefs because it indeed is as huge as an elephant. Remember the proverb about the five blind men and the elephant all standing and touching different parts of the elephant. Each could only *see* that part of the elephant that they were touching and describing. However, you don't have to let the thought of *destiny* overwhelm you. I have coached people in mid-career transition who have felt as though *destiny* had passed them by. I have also coached alpha-male leaders who believed that *destiny* was theirs to control, when all the while their family and personal life was falling apart.

Destiny is much bigger than we can fully comprehend and yet not beyond our grasp. Destiny is both mysterious and practical, especially when you begin to understand it and apply certain life principles and life truths based on the intention(s) of the One who destined you. The God who made the world and everything in it transcends the boundaries of human comprehension, and yet makes Himself known in the simplicity of faith to any who will humble themselves to acknowledge Him in all their ways. And though God is not far from any one of us, He determined your appointed times and seasons in life, and the boundaries of your existence, and His purpose in that was that you might seek

Him, and even feel about blindly and uncertainly for Him. How come? It's your *destiny* to know Him. It's in Him that you live, move, and have your being. So wherever life finds you, *destiny* is both calling to you and seeking you out. Yours is to answer the call and pursue it. So how do you do that?

LaVerne has provided you a "bird's eye view", perhaps more accurately, a heavenly and divine view of what destiny is all about. It is much easier to appropriate life processes in destiny when we see things from God's perspective. The blind men each only saw one part of the elephant. God made the elephant and can give you the big picture, and then help you break it down into bite-sized pieces.

LaVerne has done most of the difficult work for you. She has taken time to explain the rich heavenly meaning of destiny and brought it down to earth in practical and powerful soul-searching questions that will unlock things inside you that have been held back for a long time. She understands how to lead you and guide you, one-step-at-a-time, and one-bite-at-a-time, to digest and assimilate some powerful and transforming truths tied to your destiny. She will invite you to face your greatest strengths as well as your greatest fears, and with compelling questions show you the way to freedom and fulfillment. It is important in life to remember that when you are seized by a powerful question, you then are compelled on a glorious quest. Quest is all about destiny.

LaVerne is going to be your coach as you enter this quest, and I am persuaded that if you will do what she invites you to do, face what she invites you to face, own what she invites you to own, and all the rest, you will be and become all you are invited to be and become by the One who intends for you to fulfill your destiny. Embark on the journey, destiny awaits!

Mark J. Chironna, B.A., M.A., PhD,
Pastor, Master's Touch International Ministries, Orlando, Florida
Author of *Live Your Dream*

Preface

For the over ten years, I have been writing and speaking to audiences all over the world about how to live more fulfilling lives and to create their own destiny. I have taught people how to visualize what they desire in order to make this their current reality. I have shown people how to attain all of their goals. I have helped people discover the way to build wealth, prosperity and freedom though business ownership as well as how they can transform their current adversities into their own university.

I believe that people can discover powerful solutions for overcoming fear, failures and other obstacles. All they need to do is take action and turn any current distress into success. The fact of the matter is that destiny is what each of us as unique individuals is put on earth to become. Our destinies reside within us. Destiny is our freedom, the great potential we have, the "supposed force" waiting only for our minds to unleash it through dreaming, planning executing and soaring.

I also believe that everyone has a higher calling. Something that they are to do that is above and beyond their destiny that includes giving back to the world. And this is exactly what Dr. LaVerne Adams does with her book *Driven by Destiny*. She masterfully helps us to understand that we all have a divine destiny and that our ultimate destiny is in the hands of an awesome God. She helps us to see that without God at the helm, life does not make much sense and we will be on a never-ending quest for meaning. LaVerne challenges us to live our lives in a way that we do the important work that comes with fulfilling our destiny .She makes it clear that destiny is work but it is well worth it.

It is clear that her work is not only scholarly but profoundly transformational. She becomes a personal life coach to every reader to guide them into a richer, fuller life, filled with discovery, revelation and transformation. LaVerne inspires us to fulfill our purpose and turn every obstacle into an opportunity. She shows us how to raise our expectations and prepare to see miracles. LaVerne is vigilant about getting us to achieve a dynamic future by helping us to put to rest our past by preparing in our present. She is obviously passionate about seeing others succeed.

Finally, although LaVerne is well educated and trained her desire to help transform lives is clear as she transparently uses her own personal life's lessons to help us see hope for our own. She is intentional about helping us all to "get it". She does not speak down to us but respects the knowledge that we all bring and builds on that. It has been a pleasure to work with her as a publishing coach as LaVerne is highly motivated to succeed. And she is destined for further success. It is for this reason that I call her the "Diva of Destiny". She has rightfully earned this title. Read this book and apply its principles to your life and soon you will find yourself being driven by destiny and living the life of your dreams.

Patrick Snow, International Best-Selling Author of
Creating Your Own Destiny and *The Affluent Entrepreneur*

Introduction

If you have ever wondered about your purpose and your reason for being on the planet, then this book is for you. It was designed with you in mind to help you on your journey of self-discovery and the fulfillment of your unique and marvelous destiny. My desire is to help you gain a sense of clarity, value, and self-worth and to help you live a better quality of life. You can discover the keys to a dynamic future and gain the understanding that you were created with a great purpose. This is your opportunity to open up a long awaited and often neglected dialog about where your life will ultimately end up in life. Regardless of where you are now or where your life seems to have taken you, I want you to know that you have a phenomenal future that is divinely designed by God. All you have to do is look at the tips of your fingers to confirm that you have been imprinted with a unique and marvelous destiny.

Understanding that fulfilling your destiny is your divine right will help you advance more easily through this process. Sometimes our lives can spin far out of control and end up in the strangest places, and we are oblivious to how we got there. We lose sight when what we find does not resemble what we hoped for, imagined, or dreamed. What our life has become is certainly not what we envisioned. To make matters worse, we stay in that unfamiliar place longer than is helpful. One day we turn around and our lives look unrecognizable. It is then that we begin our indelible quest for meaning.

Then there are times when we simply stand in the doorway to our destiny peering in and hoping to go through but fail. For some reason, we can't because we just cannot seem to keep ourselves out of the emotional danger zones that deny us our true destiny. We continue to be drawn into these places with a hypnotic pull that we feel powerless to resist. We try to convince and delude ourselves that things are not quite as bad as we think. Then we make threats to leave because it is more than we can stand … but we never do.

This is when we begin to recognize that we need a power greater than ourselves to deliver us from where we are to where we should be because our own attempts have become futile. Other times we are held captive by our own thoughts that tell us we are better off leaving things the way they are rather than exert the energy that demands change. Then we try to make our dysfunctional circumstances work for us and for as long as possible. Sometimes it seems like it is less trouble to remain in our painful circumstances rather than to fight the forces that are ruining our lives. For years I told myself lies because I did not have the courage or the skills to make the dramatic changes necessary to align my life with my destiny. I was told early in my life that I should be careful about the decisions that I make because, "I know what I have, but I don't know what I am going to get." I governed my life, thoughts, and actions by this unfounded but familiar adage. Then, I came to the realization that although I was unsure about my future, I was completely convinced that anything was better than what I was experiencing in my present! This awakening was the first step toward realizing my true destiny and wholeness in my life.

Driven by Destiny is a destiny roadmap designed to help you discover your divinely inspired purpose. Here, destiny is presented as a metaphorical journey through the many divine dimensions that are critical to the fulfillment of your ultimate purpose in life. As you take this journey, you will transcend your past, present and future and become completely realigned with God's timing for your purpose in life. It is only as you navigate through the progressive process of revelation, realization, and realignment that your destiny will be achieved. These revealing truths will inform you. Your realization will position you but the realignment is up to you. This book is specifically designed to help coach you through this transformational process. With the abundance of information found within it, you will be empowered to make destiny decisions that advance you toward your purpose in life. It is like having your own personal life coach in a book.

Although you may be feeling a sense of desperation in your life right now please resist the urge to dash into destiny. Do not feel pressured to rush through this wonderful destiny process. Simply see these destiny keys as stepping stones to a dynamic future. As you move through each of these twelve inspiring keys, your destiny will become remarkably clear. It is what you see that will become the driving force in your life and allow you to proceed easily and with increasing confidence through each dimension. You will see immediate results as you continually submit to this process. You will be energized as your destiny delightfully unfolds before you. Your destiny vision will drive you to each destiny location. Soon you will become completely unstoppable.

You can look at these twelve keys like numbers on the face of a clock and as you pass though these "hours", you can anticipate seeing a brand new day in your life. If you feel that you are at the point that you can take twelve consecutive days to begin this dynamic process of transformation, fantastic. But if you cannot, please feel free to make your process last as long as you deem necessary and turn these twelve keys into twelve weeks or even twelve months. Use this book as a guide and move effortlessly at your own pace. Customize your own transformation journey that leads you to the life that you only dared to imagine.

In order to facilitate your destiny fulfillment process, included is this book are a series of activities that will cause you to generate a new "Divine Mental Diet" designed to help you visualize the infinite possibilities resident in your future. You will be able to develop your critical thinking skills which will allow you to think on a deeper level about your future. You will also be given the opportunity to go to a deeper *Divine Destiny Dimension*. This will impact you to proactively make quality decisions about your own life rather than depend upon others to make them for you. You will make *Divine Destiny Declarations* designed to shift the course of your life and even be able to create some of your own. These steps are critical to help you realize your ever expanding destiny because you have what you say as well as what you see!

This book is designed help you think more carefully about where you are and where you want to be. It will also help you to take a deeper look at your inner thoughts and habitual patterns to determine the real culprits of an unfulfilled life and defeat. You must make some important destiny decisions in order to progress through the many dimensions of the Master Architect's design for your life. It is also critical to understand that destiny is multidimensional. You will also explore the three facets of your destiny found in your past, present, and future. As you align yourself with God's dream for your life, please remember that destiny is about being in the right place, at the right time, doing the right thing with the right people, with the right agenda and the right attitude! Once you embrace this revelation, you are well equipped for your journey toward realizing your dreams and fulfilling your destiny.

To assist you in opening a destiny dialogue, each chapter is equipped with a *Divine Destiny Diary* to help you chart your own destiny progress. Writing down your discoveries will increase your likelihood of you accomplishing your goals. You can also record your internal destiny discussions and the life-changing decisions that you make to move you closer to your destiny. You also want to obtain the *Driven by Destiny Discovery Manual* to help you chart your course as you define and set goals that move you towards your destiny. In it, you can completely assess every area of your life to determine how well aligned you are to your destiny path. You are also going to want to get the *Driven by Destiny 30 Day Devotional* to keep your life on track and aligned with your destiny. You can get you're a copy of these valuable resources free with your Driven by Destiny book purchase. For more information please go to: www.DrivenByDestiny.info. In the back of the book, you will also find a certificate of completion congratulating you on all of the hard work that you done to get you positioned to be driven by destiny.

Over the past 20 years, I have helped countless individuals all over the world to realize and lay hold of their destiny. Many have gone back to school, gotten better jobs, opened businesses, stepped into leadership roles, and even developed a deeper relationship with God. I specialize in coaching celebrities and high powered professionals in need of spiritual guidance and support. If you feel you need additional assistance feel free to contact me.

I present this material for your personal advancement, not as one who has arrived at destiny but as one who is being God-driven as I watch my destiny remarkably unfolds. I share with you the joys and the challenges of my journey as well as some insights that I have learned, in hopes that you may be inspired and strengthened in your resolve to press forward, to be driven by your destiny. As you will see, my life will serve as a model of one who has realigned to destiny and has gained a sense of satisfaction and harmonious fulfillment in life. I will also use stories of others that you may find helpful.

Because of God's grace, I now have a passion for helping people to improve their performance levels and achieve their goals quickly. I have a desire to see others success by providing motivation and support. After applying the information set forth in this book, you will find that it is like having your own personal life coach and a doctor! You can think of me as one who, like a chiropractor, is here to help realign you. Or who, like an ophthalmologist, is here to help you see your future more clearly. Or maybe even like a cardiologist, I am here to help you realize the dreams that lie deep within your heart.

However you want to see me, my ultimate objective is to serve as your journey ambassador, helping you to define your destiny and maximize your potential so that you can naturally and effortlessly live the life you dream about. Should you need further assistance, insight and inspiration, you may contact me to let me know how I may serve you. Also contact me to let me know how this book has helped you advance in your destiny success story. I am delighted to let you know that you are eligible to receive a destiny discount on all of the services that I provide by virtue of the fact that you have purchased this book. Make a destiny decision today to make your dreams a reality, and your life will never be the same.

Seizing my destiny,

Dr. LaVerne Adams, DMin.
The Doctor of Destiny® ..."*Your prescription for a dynamic future!*"
Personal Pastor®
www.TheDoctorOfDestiny.com
www.DrivenByDestinyNOW.com

This Driven By Destiny Dream Book is designed to help you keep your dreams alive. Use the space provided to record your destiny dreams that come to you in your moments of reflection. As you progress through the pages of this book, you will discover destiny altering strategies that you can use to help make your dreams a dynamic reality.

The Lord has given me the tongue of the learned, that I should know how to speak a word in season to him who is weary. (Isaiah 50:4)

"(Ladies and) Gentlemen, Start Your Engines!"
"Rrrrrr……Rrrrrr……Rrrrrr…"

Contents

PART I
REDESIGN

"People grow through experience if they meet life honestly and courageously. This is how character is built." —Eleanor Roosevelt

As you prepare to navigate through the dimension of life, think about the sum total of your life experiences. What do you see as its themes, purposes, hopes, and dreams? Think about where you are now and where you want to be. What might be inhibiting your progress? What do you believe is the underlying reason for being stuck in a rut of dissatisfaction, confusion, and frustration? Now think about the changes that you would like to see in your life and where you would like to see them. Imagine that you can develop a strategy to help you attain the victory to overcome every obstacle in your life . . . and prepare to move forward toward your destiny! Write your thoughts in your *Divine Destiny Diary* at the end of this chapter.

"Engineered to move the human spirit" Mercedes-Benz.

1. The Secret Key to Review Your Life
"Start With the Frame"

WHERE IT ALL BEGINS

When I was in the hospital giving birth to my first child, there was a woman in a room nearby in so much pain that she yelled uncontrollably for a very long time. That is not to say that I was absolutely calm, but her screaming certainly took my mind off my own pain. Then she said something that I will never forget. As she

3

was preparing to give life, she wanted to die and asked the nurses to kill her. This woman saw death as an alternative to stop her pain while she was in the midst of giving life. Although I was inexperienced and did not know what to expect, I was stunned by her response toward this life-giving event. Although it was just moments before I would deliver, I couldn't help but wonder what else was going on in her life that would cause her to say such things. Whatever the reason, the framework of her life was obviously not designed to carry the weight of where her life had taken her. How we handle life has everything to do with the framework of our lives when and where we were born, how we were raised and our ability to cope with circumstances early in life. It is what we put on this framework that determines how well we do on our own personal journeys.

For almost twenty years I have had the privilege of being a confidant to many. For some reason, when people find out that I am a minister they feel the need to talk and even confide in me. During these times I frequently hear people say, "I am not sure what I should be doing with my life." Because these people feel a great deal of uncertainty about life, they feel uncomfortable with the direction their lives are taking. Because of a sense of ambiguity, they find themselves doing some strange and senseless things.

Uncertainty can be quite dangerous. It's the stuff that discontentment, addictions, and rages are made of. Sometimes it drives people over the edge. Too often people do not have healthy boundaries to govern their lives and attempt to reach out for help in unhelpful ways. This is why I believe that it is important and even urgent that everyone have someone in which they can confide to check the validity of their thoughts and behaviors. People need someone to whom they can be accountable in helping to advance their lives as well as to help keep them from doing some really dangerous things. I also believe that the person and the place that they go to for help should be somewhere that they can be safe enough to reveal their souls. Unfortunately far too few places and too few people like this exist, and many people are left floundering. This is the reason why I was prompted to write this book to reach the millions of people who are packed with potential but have no one to guide them toward the fulfillment of their destiny.

That is what makes my work so rewarding. I have the joy of helping people to define their destiny and maximize their potential to live the life of their dreams. I enjoy creating a place for people to feel safe enough to open up to be their truest, most authentic self. It is important to me to make a space for people to be accountable and to accomplish their goals. The tragedy is that it is difficult to find these kinds of opportunities in life. This is why the life coaching profession is in such demand. People crave supportive relationships with people who are committed to their success. I believe that everyone has the potential to be successful. They just need people who can help them along. One of the reasons that I wrote this book is to support you as you journey toward your success. I sincerely believe that you have what it takes to accomplish your goals.

When we have so many expectations put on our lives too often we feel as if we cannot be our true selves, even with those people we believe love us. This dearth is what leaves us feeling alone in a room full of people. It is why we tend to feel like no one really understands us. This is what makes going through life unbearable at times. Sometimes we just need a little help, a clue, or even just a brief orientation of what life is really all about. Too often, we never get it. I certainly do not claim to know all of what life is about, but I have had a variety of experiences that have helped me to put the pieces together in the puzzle of life —and even back together when life has fallen completely apart.

It is this wisdom, gathered from years of education, experience and training, that I want to share with you—in hopes that it will help give you a sense of orientation about the direction of your life. Sharing my experiences has been helpful to many. Like street signs, they point the way as well as give direction. But it is solely your decision whether or not you want to follow the direction given to you. The choice is yours how you should proceed as you determine the outcomes for your life. The only person who is responsible for where you end up is you.

THE EFFECTS OF LOSS IN LIFE

Eleanor Roosevelt knew this concept about life all too well. As a shy child born in New York as the niece of President Theodore Roosevelt, she experienced a tremendous amount of loss at an early age when her mother died when she was only eight years old. Then at ten years old her father died. She was sent away to school in England when she became a teenager. Everything that she had known to be her foundation in life disappeared. Yet she persevered. When she turned twenty one, she married a distant cousin, Franklin D. Roosevelt and had six children, one of which died. But she did not let this loss prevent her from actively serving others in the community and through the American Red Cross. When her husband suffered from polio she assisted him in his political career dramatically changing the role of the first lady of the United States of America to one of prominence. Rather than be relegated to domesticated duties, she became extremely outspoken in the fight for human rights, the well-being of the poor, and women and children. She was a champion in the fight against racial discrimination and said "No one can make you feel inferior without your consent".

Her life shows us that you can overcome any and every tragedy but you must be willing to take personal responsibility for your reactions to the vicissitudes of life. This idea of taking responsibility is directly related to our decision making power. It becomes even more apparent when we find that a recent study in the Archives of Internal Medicine showed that by maintaining only four healthy habits, we can reduce the risk of developing common chronic diseases such as heart disease, diabetes, or cancer by a remarkable 80%[1]. These healthy habits include: not smoking, maintaining a healthy weight, exercising regularly, and following a healthy diet. This information is so vitally important to people who want to live healthy lives but are struggling. But even though most people understand this information they may have difficulty in making the choice to actually incorporate these concepts into their lives.

I propose that the reason why people have no trouble starting a healthy habit but are unsuccessful at maintaining them is because they are only dealing with one layer of the self. For example, they may want to stop smoking but have not dealt with the underlying issue as to why they smoke in the first place. This first layer of the self is physical. Smoking is a physical behavior that negatively affects the body. Yet the body can't stop doing this on its own. This is because smoking, like all other addictions, is also is a mental addiction. This involves the second layer of the self or the mind, will, and emotions. The person thinks in their mind

---

[1] http://www.physorg.com/news169140891.html

that they need to smoke and therefore does it repeatedly. Their will is overruled and their emotions are taken captive.

Lastly, there is the third layer of the self is the subconscious or the human spirit. This layer is the most true and authentic self and wants to do and be what is best. Too often, this part of the self is so overruled by the other parts of the self that it is not free to direct the whole life. This is partly due to a myriad of dysfunctions that plague the human condition. This tri-level existence is proven when we talk ourselves in and out of healthy habits. Exactly who do you think we are talking to? The answer is: the other parts of you. In addition, we must consider the other outside influences and forces that must also be addressed. I believe that if a person strengthens this third layer of the self, the human spirit, there is no goal that they cannot accomplish. When we address all of who we are, we are in harmony with ourselves. We can accomplish and achieve anything being our highest and truest self.

But different people have different ideas about what this means. This is where the confusion comes in as it relates to religious practices. I believe that everyone has a path that they will choose to follow that will eventually bring them to stand before God. The Bible teaches in Matthew 25 that everyone from all nations will one day stand before God with people being judged and separated according to their works. This leads me to believe that one day you will meet your maker and therefore any road will get you there. But before that time comes, you need to determine how you want to arrive at your final destination and take that path. Although I am a Christian, I believe that it is important to allow people the freedom to make their own choices. I can present Christ as the way, but it is entirely up to you to choose. But regardless of the path you choose, be sure that you are strengthened in your resolve to live your best life and make a contribution to the common good. I believe that this choice will ultimately lead you in the right direction.

But please know that you do not have to make this journey alone. There are many who have treaded a similar path in life and can help make your journey a bit smoother. This is very important if you have ever felt that you have detoured from your destiny. One sign of a destiny detour is dissatisfaction. Another sign is frustration. When you feel these things, your life is telling you that you are in conflict with yourself. The good news is that it is easier than you may think to get back on track to move in the direction of your destiny. You must make a destiny decision to wholeheartedly realign your life to the destiny dream that God designed for you when you were created. The signposts are all around you that point you directly to your destiny but you must choose to follow them. And then, there are people along the way who willingly cheer you on -- even if it is only from the sidelines.

ENTRYWAYS TO LIFE

I have discovered eight entryways of life and will explore their characteristics as a way to determine where you are on your journey through life. Everyone will inevitably pass these thresholds sooner or later, voluntarily or involuntarily. But not everyone crosses them successfully. Some will pass through these thresholds more triumphantly than others. Some have discovered, developed or been coached with lifestyle strategies to help them to succeed in life. Others have a more disappointing and even tragic story of discontentment. But in order to truly fulfill our destiny, we must be aware of and prepared for the passageways through which we travel and navigate. Although these entryways are natural to life, they also have spiritual implications. Because the spirit world is important to the foundation of fulfilling our destiny, it is with this spiritual

The good news is that it is easier than you may think to get back on track to move in the direction of your destiny. You must make a destiny decision to wholeheartedly realign your life to the destiny dream that God designed for you when you were created.

aspect with which we must also reckon.

Too often we try to make it through life one dimensionally. But because you were created as a three-dimensional being—body, soul, and spirit—you will never truly succeed in life until every part of you is addressed and aligned toward your destiny. For example, you may be a financial success but spiritually bankrupt. Or you may be physically fit but have no peace of mind. This is why I use the term *divine destiny*. Your divine destiny is that which I believe is God-inspired. This is what is destined to be God-driven and not self driven and encompasses your total being and the complete purpose for which you were created. When you were created, it was God's Desire that you be a success in every way. God expects for you to be a success in life.

There are several thresholds you must cross in order to realize your dreams, goals and ultimately your destiny. It is important to determine where you are in life and what you need to do to move closer to your destiny path. It is only when you understand where you are, can you chart the course for where you are going. These thresholds include:

Infancy

Infancy is considered to be the state of complete innocence. During this time a baby is completely dependent and needs continual and constant care. In most cases, regardless of what a baby does, this bundle is a constant joy to his parents!

Childhood

Children believe that everything they see completes their world because their perception is limited. They have not yet seen anything different and therefore they think this is all there is. They become familiar with others but have no real understanding about them except in relationship to themselves. Children are somewhat selfish because of their limited need for only those things that make them happy and comfortable.

Adolescence

As the child grows into older childhood she begins to gain an awareness of other people and worlds. She begins to ask the question "why?" about life because she can now see the differences in people, places, and things. This is also where the rebellious stage begins to emerge as a result of unmet emotional, social, physical, and spiritual needs. Her mission becomes limited to self-fulfillment that is often demonstrated acting out and defiance. Adolescents are often self-centered.

Older Teenhood

Teenhood is the stage that begins independence. This is where we see higher levels of rebellion, dangerous risk-taking and experimentation. This is because teens want to prove that they can do life on their own. They get angry when anyone tries to help or baby them. At this stage in life they are mentally self-absorbed with their own desires. Because of their inexperience, they sometimes set peculiar goals and don't know how they will accomplish them leaving them vulnerable to potentially dangerous options.

Young Adulthood

This can be a season of uncertainty especially if the young adult has not been properly nurtured earlier in life. This is when insecurities begin to manifest from the effects of dysfunctions previously experienced. During this stage, self-esteem also becomes an issue because the expectation to be able to competently handle the affairs of life can become overwhelming. There is a tension between youthful irresponsibility and full adult responsibility. This can be a difficult time because of the myriad of uncertainties regarding important decisions that will determine the quality of a future lifestyle.

Adulthood

During adulthood, one should be able to handle responsibility. By this time an adult should have a fair resolution of the issues that affected one earlier in life. They should be able to take responsibility for their actions physically, mentally, and spiritually as well as being able to manage their personal affairs and responsi-bilities with a level of confidence. During this stage, there is a sense of selflessness because there is a general understanding that responsible adults do things that they don't necessarily enjoy for the sake of the common good. This mature awareness recognizes that it is important to do what is in the best interest of others.

For example, adults get up and go to work even though they may not feel like it because they know that their family is depending on them. This can be a complex stage as well because too often there are those of adult age whose behaviors resemble that of younger stages of development. It can be particularly frustrating when a forty-year-old acts irresponsibly like a teenager. This is an unfortunate state because when the emotional age ceases to mature, there is no possibility to advance it without intervention.

Older Adulthood

The caregiver as adult now needs care. This is a time for inner reflection. This phase of self re-actualization begins when the older adult asks, "Who am I really?" They can no longer identify themselves with what they do or what they have because all of these things have changed. They must now engage in the arduous task of getting to know and present the most real and deepest essence of who they truly are without any material connections. This can become very difficult for those who once based their identity on outside factors—such as employment, possessions, or people. This is where we begin to see a reversal of life from maturity to childlike behaviors because the sense of insecurity can be overwhelming.

Eternal Life

This is the time to cycle out of this life and into eternal life. This should be a time of GLORY! But it is critical for us to understand that in order for this to happen, we need to spiritually prepare to successfully transition into the glorious presence of God. In order to do this, we must accept God's Plan to get us there. This is not automatic. Some very important decisions and actions must take place to ensure that this encounter is joyful and fruitful. The Bible teaches that if we are to receive eternal life, we should believe in God's Son, Jesus.[2] Therefore, it is

---

[2] John 3:16

crucial to spend the former part of life getting ready for the most significant portion of life: eternity.

SPIRITUAL LIFE ENTRYWAYS

It does not take rocket science to see that there are issues of morality that plague our world that cannot be solved with governmental policies. If we live long enough, we realize that regardless of how hard we try, we cannot be perfect in and of our own selves. We need a power greater than ourselves to help us. The Bible teaches us that when we accept Jesus Christ's work done on the cross to save humanity from its sins, we can receive his power to transform our lives. Therefore, as we are born in the natural world, we are also born into the spiritual world. In order to attain the truest and highest destiny that God has designed, we must accept the plan that God has presented with our best interest in mind. When we do this, we become born again into a new realm of life everlasting.

When we make a comparison between the spiritual and the natural life, we can recognize that there are similarities to our natural and spiritual existence. Being a spiritual infant is very similar to being a natural infant. The scriptures teach that the moment you believe that Jesus Christ is the Son of God and Savior of the world you are reborn and possess the power to overcome every obstacle and receive the benefit of eternal life. But when you are at the stage of spiritual infancy, you are totally dependent, needy, and completely self-centered. At this stage of your new spiritual birth, you experience and sense the fruit of the spirit of love, joy, and peace—although it is at a very immature level.

Our younger spiritual life abilities are limited like those of a natural toddler. We learn to walk but toddle to keep life balanced. We have a natural propensity to be low to the ground, crawling in our faith, keeping to only what feels comfortable. During this stage, there are tendencies to be easily depressed, down spiritually, and frequently moved emotionally. At this level you may crawl, barely making it, with little or no spiritual strength. We spiritually fall down and often depend on others to help us get back up. We are spiritually needy and need to be supported to walk and given a sense of direction. Our spiritual mothers and fathers help us to continue moving toward maturity to walk in the things of God. This is why it is important that we make room for spiritual parents in our lives.

During spiritual childhood, we do childish things. We have a limited understanding of our spiritual reality. When we are spiritually immature, all we basically understand is that we are loved unconditionally by God and do not have a maturity to understand why we need to modify our behavior to the extent that we change our childish disposition. Without spiritual leadership, you have no real sense of direction. Here is where longsuffering, kindness, and goodness are activated through those spiritual leaders who watch for your soul on your behalf. The apostle Paul said that when he was a child, he spoke like a child and did childish things[3]. This is primarily because children naturally have limited knowledge and experience and not much more is expected. Similarly, spiritual children who have limited knowledge do childish things. Children do not always know what is best and therefore need the valuable guidance of their spiritual parents and those given the responsibility of watching for their soul.

Spiritual adolescence is the beginning of a greater spiritual awareness. Yet, similar to natural adolescence, it is here that authority is questioned and we begin to see signs of rebellion. Fortunately, this is only a phase. We must grow to a level of understanding that we are not the center of the world as we are challenged to exemplify the characteristics of longsuffering, goodness and gentleness toward others. We need to gain a deep sense that the spiritual world does not revolve around just us as we develop a concern for others. What is unfortunate is when Christians seem to get stuck in this stage of constant rebellion to authority due to the lack of maturity and misunderstanding of their place and purpose in the Kingdom of God.

It is during spiritual teenhood that we sense the beginning of independence but we also see defiance. This is because we want to feel independent but soon realize that we must remain completely dependent upon God and accountable to those who are responsible for us. Our spiritual life abilities resemble that of a natural teenager. We have physical stamina and agility but we still need to develop the deeper spiritual knowledge facing the reality that there are no alternate routes to seeking the will of God for our lives.

---

[3] I Cor. 13:11 KJV

The spiritually young adult can be frustrated, filled with uncertainty, and struggle with faith as well as have difficulties taming the body and the emotions. Sometimes the overwhelming weight and expectations of spiritual maturity brings about spiritual frustration and sometimes even an abandonment of the faith. This is the stage where most backsliding can occur, under the duress of temptation. This is where one can surrender to the deception that a truly disciplined lifestyle cannot be realized. It seems easier to go back to the familiar old ways—and many do. But the objective of the struggle is to press in and persevere to gain a new level of faith, not to turn away from it. Here one is stretched to acquire a greater aspect of strength and realize their personal power.

Equally as frustrating can be that of older adulthood. It has been said that when we are older, we will need to be led around rather than lead. Here we see a reversal of the spiritual life cycle. It is what we have done in the former spiritual life stages that will prove how we weather the storm of old age. As we prepare for transition towards eternal life, our works should precede us so we can prepare to hear God say, "Well done!"[4] This is where the spiritual fruit of our faith, meekness, and temperance is really put to the test.

It is important that we have been wise enough to create a spiritual legacy, because at this stage the spiritual caregiver needs care. This means that all the spiritual sons and daughters that you have reared should now pour their love and energy back into you. Old age is when you will be led around rather than lead and you must assure that whoever is leading is headed in the right direction. There is a need now for an official surrender of responsibilities to those that have been prepared through succession planning, embracing the spiritual legacy that has should have been created.

The ultimate objective of the Kingdom of God is to bring people into the fulfillment of purpose. This happens when people develop spiritual maturity. This is the time to do what Paul recommends and "put away childish things."[5] It is in this state that we embrace responsibility while gaining a sense of purpose. The pinnacle of the Christian walk is to enter a state of spiritual stability that resembles what the Bible calls "the measure of the stature of Christ."[6] Jesus is the

---

[4] Matthew 25:21
[5] I Corinthian 13:11 KJV
[6] Ephesians 4:13 KJV

ultimate model of spiritual maturity. The fullness of Christ is displayed when Christians are able to manage personal affairs with excellence as well as handle corporate responsibility with distinction in every area of their lives. These are the people who make a positive impact in the world and advance it to its highest level of morality. This includes possessing the ability to resolve issues in a way that exudes integrity as well as exemplary ethical behavior. I am sure that you will agree that this is something that the world needs more of.

DIABOLICAL FORCES

In order to successfully attain your destiny, you must be aware of the diabolical forces that are designed to keep you from successfully moving toward your destiny. The plan is to keep you trapped and helpless in the realm of a physical, mental, and emotional abyss of the world. Anytime you feel oppressed and emotionally unable to move forward is an indication that this plan is activated in your life. In addition, your enemy's goal is to thwart your growth by disorienting you using tactics of guilt, dysfunction, and fear in efforts to cause you to walk directionless and in constant confusion. I am sure that you, like I have experienced life in this state at one time or another in life.

Be steps ahead of your enemy and determine to mature to adulthood in your faith. Ask yourself, "Where am I stuck in life and why?" "How did I get here and where do I want to be?" The answer to these questions will produce the groundwork for change. Ask God to give you the wisdom about how to cancel your enemy's assignment against you. Do not cooperate with the covert operation that ensnares you with the words of your own mouth. Ask God for the power to overcome these deadly obstacles and give you the power to see the fulfillment of your divine destiny.

MY PERSONAL JOURNEY

When I became aware that this diabolical assignment was actively affecting my life that is when I learned that I had to take responsibility for my own actions, decisions, and choices. As I matured in my walk with the Lord, I began to understand why I experienced frustration in my relationships. Most of the problems was as a result of the poor choices that I was making. Then I noticed a recurring theme of betrayal, abandonment, and rejection in my life. As I began to trace back to the early part of my life, I realized that this theme had followed me for as long as I can remember and apparently was now becoming a vicious cycle. Then I realized that the root of this cycle began from a very early age.

When I was in parochial grade school, I asked my best friend, to join me on a project in the science fair. We built the popular volcano experiment with baking soda and vinegar. I did most of the work because I was naturally creative and loved working with my hands, I just did not want to enter the contest on my own. To my amazement, we won the contest. But there was only one medal given to share between us. I gave her the option to take them home for her parents to see and then I would have the opportunity to show it to my mother later. I am not sure what happened, but I never got the medal back nor did I see or hear from my precious friend again. Perhaps I moved away or changed schools but you can imagine how crushed I felt as a child when I realized that my reward and my friend had disappeared. I felt abandoned, betrayed and rejected. I later forgot about it because I cared for her. But as I got older I noticed that people to whom I gave my trust abandoned, betrayed, and rejected me. It wasn't until later that I realized that this recurring theme was beginning to bring a cycle of discouragement, discontentment, and destruction into my life. And it was effectively working against me.

I asked God to give me a revelation about how I handled my relationships. Then, I saw that my need to give others things including my total and absolute trust was rooted in issues of abandonment by my father, whom I have never met. I realized that I wanted so desperately to be accepted and loved by him that I gave people things and trust to get them to love and accept me. Because these people did not realize that I was attempting to subconsciously meet unmet needs by proxy, they unconsciously crushed my intentions through betrayal and rejection because they ultimately could not keep up their end of my bargain.

But it was around that time that I recognized that there was something happening that was consistent but beyond my control. It was a diabolical assignment in place designed to destroy my hopes and dreams and ultimately my destiny. I noticed that I began experiencing one disappointment after the other, and I realized that there was a plot set up against me that would eventually destroy my life. Unfortunately, I was actively participating with the plan. I needed to take control of my thoughts and words in order for me to see the different outcomes that I desired from my relationships. As I did, I became free from the grip that the enemy had on my mind to improperly satisfy my emotionally unmet needs. As I matured into adulthood, I had to come to grips with the fact that this cycle was not only a result of the choices I was making but also an assignment to get me to give up hope for a good future. But I had to first cooperate with God and take full responsibility for my actions and determine that I would intentionally make better choices for my future. In addition, because I strategically resisted the enemy in this area, the vicious cycle of abandonment, betrayal, and rejection was broken and rendered powerless and ineffective in my life.

An interesting twist to the story about my best friend from grade school; we recently were reunited after forty years. Although she did not remember the science projector or the medal, we were able to renew our friendship which was even more valuable and has brought a sense of restoration and healing back into my life. It is amazing what happens when we open ourselves to be positioned to be driven by our destiny.

FAMILIAR SPIRITS

Based upon my spiritual experiences, I have found that there are familiar spirits that also act as gatekeepers to the doorway of the soul. These familiar spirits were lurking there when you were born. They know everything about you and your entire bloodline because they are demonically assigned to your family. Their assignment is to keep you in bondage to the particular dysfunction in your bloodline and keep you to continue in its stronghold. This includes negative personality behaviors as well as addictions, illness, and even chronic diseases.

The fact that you continue in these patterns is not a coincidence. Rest assured that all of these negative influences do not emanate from you. This is a tactic that the enemy uses to thwart your destiny. This diabolical assignment is designed to negatively affect your mind, will, and emotions and seeks to rule you with deception and to get you to believe that you are doomed. This force wants you to believe that the negativity that you are experiencing characterizes your entire life and must continue because this is the way that it is and the way that it must always be. The strategy at work is to get you to believe the lie that you are obligated to continue this legacy of dysfunction and sustain this generational curse for another lifetime. But you can make a destiny decision not to participate with this outrageous plan, break the generational curse and take control of your life and destiny.

You can make the choice not to believe these lies. Intentionally choose to be liberated from each destructive grip in every area of your life. For example, even though depression may run in your family, you have a choice how you will allow this dysfunction to affect your life. In other words, the level of your depression is a choice. Despondency is a choice. Disease is a choice. You may say that there are many people who are sick and it was not their choice. But I submit to you that even though that may be true, we are given a choice of how sick we are going to be. We can either give in to the infirmity or fight with every ounce of strength and take advantage of every available treatment known to humankind.

I will never forget the time that I experienced this truth in my own life. I was devastated by the betrayal of trust by someone very close to me. I found myself weeping uncontrollably almost every night for well over a month. I felt myself going down into a deep pit of depression and despondency. I pleaded with God to please make the pain stop and to help the person understand how much they were hurting me. God clearly spoke back to me that only I had the power to allow someone to hurt me and only I had the power to stop crying and come out of my depression. It wasn't long afterward that I made a decision to stop crying and end my depressive behaviors. Every time I felt the urge, I thought about God's Words to me that day. Needless to say I have experienced a complete turnaround and I intentionally bring joy into my life every day.

The objective of the enemy of your soul is to stunt your growth and to stop your spiritual development so that you will not be a threat to Satan's kingdom. The enemy wants to keep you in darkness, stuck in a spiritual and a natural entryway so that you will be frustrated and have no desire to move into the maturity that will access your powerful destiny. For example, if you are stuck in spiritual infancy you will be continuously helpless. If the enemy can keep you in the state of spiritual childhood, he knows that you will perpetually lack understanding.

If he can keep you in spiritual adolescence you will be extremely effective in his plans to disrupt the mission of the church to transform lives, he can use you as an arsenal to operate in rebellion and division. If you stay in spiritual teenhood and are constantly defiant, then the enemy can use you to effectively dismantle the order in a church. And if you continue in the state of young spiritual adulthood you will be insecure about your spiritual status and be ineffective in spiritual warfare and battle. In other words, the enemy wants to render you useless in advancing the Kingdom of God and lacking the ability to make a difference in the world.

The enemy also tries to frustrate us when we get to older adulthood with the assignment of confusion. This assignment is particularly brutal because it is difficult to muster up the strength to fight against the enemy in old age. This is when it becomes very important to stay connected with spiritual children and the body of Christ who can fight on your behalf and undergird you in difficult times.

KINGDOM OBJECTIVE

Our overall objective should be to persevere into a level of spiritual maturity using supernatural strategies of divine discernment that advances our destiny as well as the Kingdom of God. When you are strong spiritually, you discontinue allowing your emotions to rule you. Instead you have the mind of Christ and use your spiritual intelligence to defeat your adversary. You ask yourself the question: WWJD?" (What would Jesus do?), in addition to "WWJT?" (What would Jesus think?). To gain absolute victory it is important to operate in all of our God-given abilities and exhibit spiritual maturity.

Rather than crawling around or toddling in your mind, you should gain enough power to successfully pass through life with strength and a sense of purpose and direction. In doing so, you will run through the troops of opposition and leap over the walls of every obstacle. Just as adults have confidence in their natural capabilities, we can have spiritual confidence. But our confidence is in the capabilities and power of God. When you operate in full spiritual maturity, you become agile in your faith. You fully understand that the joy of the Lord is your strength. Your spirit controls your destructive desires and your emotions are intact.

Your spiritual legs are strengthened and you can literally leap for joy! You can leap with a double-edged strategy of faith and obedience. With this strategy you leap double the distance, twice the height. God gives you double for what you have lost and gives you double the time you need to get the job done. God gives you double strength and honor and causes you to receive a double reward. Because you have a full understanding of who you are in Christ, you will be assured to receive double portion[7], double honor[8], double restoration[9], and the double destruction of your enemies[10]

As you strive to move into your destiny, it will be the leap of a lifetime through the dimension of life into your destiny. Always remember that regardless of how difficult things become, life is meant to be lived to the fullest. You can avoid a destiny disaster as you make your strides to review your life and overcome every obstacle by doubling your efforts in prayer, praise, and worship. Determine to persevere and move from spiritual infancy to true spiritual maturity. Allow your destiny dream to be the driving force that directs you as you take the leap of faith toward your future, into your promises and determine to live the life you dream about... now!

> *Our overall objective should be to persevere into a level of spiritual maturity using super-natural strategies of divine discernment that advances our destiny as well as the Kingdom of God.*

[7] Isaiah 40:2 KJV
[8] 1 Timothy 5:17 KJV
[9] Zechariah 9:12 KJV
[10] Jeremiah 17:18 KJV

DECODE
YOUR DESTINY
REVIEW YOUR LIFE

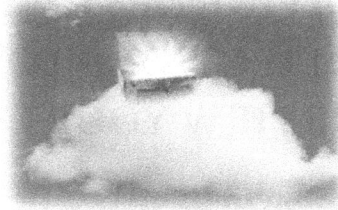

Developing Your New Divine Mental Diet is the key to fulfilling your destiny. Your life will be literally transformed as you begin to get a better understanding about where you are right now. Then you can determine the direction that you need to take.

THINK ON THESE THINGS - Open your destiny dialog by honestly answering the following questions about where you are on your life's journey:

Are you an infant, child, teen, young adult, or adult in your faith?

1. Can you give examples about how you are making this determination?

2. What are your spiritual capabilities? What is it that you feel you do well spiritually?

3. What are some positive behaviors that you can implement into your life to move toward greater spiritual maturity? List them here.

4. What evidence will you see when you are spiritually mature?

5. How long will it take for you to implement these behaviors? Be specific.

DIVINE DESTINY DIRECTIONS TO REVIEW YOUR LIFE

Now it's your turn to chart the course on your destiny roadmap as you take the information that you have learned to plot out your life location. Where do you think that your life is right now? Where do you think you are headed? How are you going to get there? This is the place to ignite your destiny dream and give it the attention it deserves.

GOING TO THE NEXT DIMENSION AND REVIEW YOUR LIFE

As you go through this dimension of life you must be fully developed emotionally, socially, physically, and spiritually. Make the decision to take full responsibility for where you are and advance to a new level of spiritual maturity. Use this divine destiny declaration as an affirmation of what you want to see in your life.

DIVINE DESTINY DECLARATION

"I thank God that I am fearfully and wonderfully made. I am created in the image and likeness of God. I was created to bring God glory therefore I honor God with my life, my thoughts, and actions. I honestly assess where I am in life and take full responsibility for where I am going. I press toward the mark of the high calling of God in Christ Jesus. As I review my life I realize that although I may have experienced painful things in my past, I endeavor to forget those things that do not serve me in my present or future. As I mature in my faith, I know that I am completely responsible for my actions and thoughts regardless of the motives of others. I take responsibility for the direction my life is heading from this point forward. I will put my trust and hope in the One who created me so that I can receive direction for my life. Because God's will is my priority, I know that God will order my steps. God is the Author and Finisher of my faith, I feel confident with God as the ultimate source in my life. Therefore I am destined to succeed. It's my time to have the best life ever."

WRITE YOUR OWN DESTINY DECLARATION REVIEW YOUR LIFE

Personalize your Divine Destiny Declaration to accommodate your unique situation by writing your own below. Be sure to include the vision you receive from the destiny dreams that you see in your heart. As you nurture them by reviewing and saying them daily, you give your dreams the power to materialize. This is a living document so feel free to update it regularly.

DIVINE DESTINY DIARY:
USE THE SPACE BELOW TO WRITE
YOUR THOUGHTS ABOUT YOUR
DESTINY LIFE

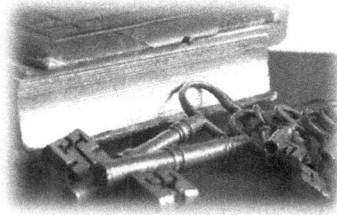

Only a life lived for others is a life worthwhile. —Albert Einstein

You cannot teach a man anything; you can only help him discover it in himself.
—Galileo Galilei

As you enter this dimension, think about your levels of adventure. Think about whether or not your current experiences broaden or limit you. Think about what areas in your life are open for the fresh wind of God to blow and what areas are not. Now think about all of the adverse circumstances in your life. Expand your thinking to the possibility that these situations arise to help you discover something wonderful about yourself that you never imagined before. Write your thoughts in your *Divine Destiny Diary* at the end of this chapter.

"The power to surprise - Kia"

2. The Secret Key to Your Rediscovery
"What's Under the Hood?"

I read a story about a mother who came home from work tired only to be greeted by her small child who was begging for a story to be read to him. The mother, in her exhaustion, came up with an idea to occupy the child to give her time to settle down and rest. The mother tore a page out of a magazine and began to tear up the paper into small but manageable pieces but she knew that the intricate graphic on the page was sure to be a challenge for the little boy. She asked her son

27

to put the puzzle back together and when he was done, she would read him the story.

Amazingly, the boy finished in record time. When she went to see what the boy had done, she found that the boy discovered a photo of a person on the reverse side of the intricate design that she had given him. He discovered that if he could put the person together, he could solve the puzzle. This puzzle is a lot like life. If we can discover the secrets that lie "under the hood" of our lives, then we can put all the pieces together... and find lasting peace.

To some of us this may come as a surprise but one of the most vital experiences that we can have in life is that of wonder. From the time that we are born, we go through a series of discovery moments that help shape and bring interest into our lives. Then one day the unimaginable happens and somehow life takes a turn and we lose our sense of wonder. Circumstances beyond our control cause us discontinue our journey of discovery, and we get stuck in dysfunctional zones. Life becomes dissatisfying, dull, and dreary. When we wonder if there is any way out, the answer can only be found in yet another discovery. In order to fulfill our destiny, we must once again enter this realm of discovery.

Like the puzzle, if we can discover the secrets that underlie our lives, then we can put all the pieces together... and find lasting success. I believe that you are about to discover some tremendous things about yourself as you continue to read this book. As you complete all of the exercises you will begin to discover more about where your personal power lies. Sometimes it is the difficulties of life that force us out of our comfort zone and into a rediscovery mode. This is the reason that regardless of the level of education I have attained, I have made the decision to be a life-time learner. I posture myself to learn from my experiences, people, and the world daily. I am an avid reader and love to study as much as I can about people, their behaviors, and how to help them improve in their interactions with their Creator. I have found that your attitude is one of the most important commodities that you can have in life.

PRESSING YOUR WAY

Oprah Winfrey once said that *"The greatest discovery of all time is that a person can change his future by merely changing his attitude."* She should know because her attitude about life could have been quite "sour" based upon her humble yet difficult beginnings. She was born to a housekeeper and a soldier and struggled through a severely dysfunctional home life. For this reason, she lived with her grandmother until the age of six. She did not allow the fact that people constantly mispronounced her biblical name, Orpah, to discourage her. She merely changed her name! And because she maintained a positive attitude about her circumstances, she advanced herself by learning to read during the time that she spent with her grandmother. She lived once again with her mother in poverty she endured physical abuse. Although her mother was unsupportive of her educational advancement, because of her own desire to discover more about life, she was able to skip grades and even received a scholarship by the time she was 13. And as if she did not suffer enough confusion in her life, she was shipped off to her father. Fortunately, he made education a priority and as a result she won a full scholarship to Tennessee State University and by the age of 18. In addition, she was crowned Miss Black Tennessee. Had she not persevered past her circumstances she would have never gone on to be the successful media giant that she is today as a producer, book critic, actress and international celebrity. She is just as down to earth as she is philanthropic. But she has truly shown us how important it is to have a great attitude about life and about ourselves regardless of what life brings in order that we might discover our way on the road to destiny.

THE LADDER OF DISCOVERY

The Bible tells of the story of a man named Jacob who left his hometown, Beersheba, and set out for Haran. Beersheba is located on the southern edge of Israel, symbolizing the bottom of civilization, society, or life. As we will see, Beersheba also represents the state of Jacob's life, who has yet to discover his destiny.

Beersheba is also Jacob's comfort zone. It is the place Jacob knows and is most familiar with. Oftentimes we find ourselves in a comfortable place that is difficult to leave, even though we know that it is not in our best interest to stay. There are many factors that cause us to feel connected to people, places, and things. When life is well organized around the familiar, regardless of how dysfunctional it may be, we sense the illusion of stability. This is sometimes rooted in the unhealthy need to maintain an imbalanced psyche because it is all we know. We feel compelled to maintain the status quo because it gives us a sense and feeling of security. This is the reason why we can go to great lengths to protect and maintain even toxic environments and relationships. We may refuse to challenge what makes us uncomfortable. Sometimes we do this without understanding why.

But it is crisis that often makes us aware that we have played the fool and built a house of cards, which ultimately comes tumbling down. In order to move forward and advance into our destiny, we must recognize that transformation must manifest in every area of our lives, both on a conscious and subconscious level. Sometimes it takes crisis to cause us to realize how desperate our lives have become. Only God knows we need drastic change in our lives. Therefore God often allows crisis to become our opportunity to shift into the greatest moments of our lives. This shift is designed to more closely align us with our destiny.

In the case of Jacob, his change came in the form of a dramatic series of events that led to his twin brother Esau threatening his life. The familiar Beersheba now became Jacob's impending place of demise. It was not until his life was in jeopardy that Jacob was forced to make the decision to move from the familiar out into the unknown…or risk death.

We too must arrive at the intrinsic understanding that if our current environment remains dysfunctional, it has the potential to kill the destiny dream within us. We would be much further along toward realizing our destiny if we could embrace this revelation. We must be aware that when our dysfunctional lifestyles become the norm, all abnormalities blend into the woodwork. In this state, we become disoriented and blinded to the fact that these conditions are committing the crime of slowly robbing the life out of us! The underlying cause of this blindness is not evident. We chronically complain about our circumstances and yet make no real advances for change. This cycle repeats and reveals the trap that our lives are in. Although we are completely dissatisfied, we see no real way out.

MY NEW SHOW

I have come to the place of refusing to rehearse any drama that has haunted my life. The problem with rehearsing the past is that its intended purpose is to perfect the performance! By using the wisdom of the ancient texts of the Bible, I have been able to be transformed by the renewing of my mind and reinventing my thought patterns. I make intentional mental notes to tell myself that through God, I have the power to rewrite the script of my life and put on a brand new show. This new show has a happy ending. This new one is where I am the heroine and overcome instead of remaining a victim in the horror movie called "My Life." This then means that I must do more than change the channel but take the action steps necessary for my lifestyle to change to match the new drama or the new channel to which I have switched. When I do this, I can anticipate a brilliant outcome.

I dislike re-watching films because the real entertainment for me comes with the element of surprise, not fully knowing which direction the script is going. This intrigue keeps me inspired to continue watching. When I became aware of the dysfunction that was plaguing my life, I had to come to grips with the fact that I have already seen the movie a thousand times! A repeat show was neither desirable nor healthy. I was ready for a new storyline in my life—one of suspense and excitement; one where the hero dramatically wins and justice is fully executed.

And I am convinced that the new drama of my life should include comedy and joy! I love to laugh because it brings healing into my life. But what brings me the greatest joy is when I can envision my life the way that God desires and intends it to be. I make it a habit to find scriptures and affirmations that help me change my outlook on life and tell the truth about who I really am in Christ, regardless of my circumstances. I can do this because my situation may be true, but it is not always the truth found in God's Word which is God's will for my life. This way, the new story for my life is intrinsically connected to God's eternal vision and destiny design. I find joy when I am reminded that I can overcome every obstacle because the script has already been written and my victory is found in the Word of God. As I align my life with this design, it is inevitably realized.

This new orientation extends to how I relate to others and their problems. Although I am more than happy to listen to people tell me their story; I have also made a decision not to continuously listen to the same person complain about the same problems over and over. Although I am willing to let them have the chance to vent, I am unwilling to sit for the rehearsal of the tragedy of their lives over and over again. This can be quite exasperating because this energy could be better used to develop a new destiny-oriented dialogue. The time would be better spent in the development of a new, creative, and meaningful drama of their future.

THE DISCOVERY DIALOGUE

As a parochial school student, I learned about God, the angels, and that I could pray. I will never forget my first prayer experience sitting on the closet floor as a child, crying out to God not understanding why I had got a spanking. In that moment, I had an awareness that God was real enough to talk to and kind enough to listen. I needed someone to talk to about my little life, and God was there.

This is when I first discovered the possibility of having an internal dialog with God. As the youngest of six girls in my single-parent home, life was never easy, to say the least. I know what it feels like to be hungry. I understand what it means to live with a sense of rejection, neglect, and abandonment. I know what it feels like not to be understood and to be lonely in a room full of people. The result of these experiences ultimately found their way into my adult life. Developing the habit of internally communicating with God gave me a sense of comfort and helped me to feel connected to my purpose and value.

From my humble beginnings of coming from a family that received public assistance, having a sense of purpose was critical. Since then, I had the awesome privilege of watching my mother work her way off welfare to become a homeowner. Later, I watched her build her own house and then retire and live comfortably. Her model helped me to see first-hand that if you are dissatisfied with your life, you don't have to stay where you are. You can change it. I learned that no one is doomed to a life of poverty and pain and that life is filled with potential and possibilities. I believe this experience gave me the foundation to believe that I could do and be anything. It was then I began to have dreams about doing more with my life and even going to college.

I came to the realization that it is pointless to blame others for the condition of my life. I discovered that I possess the power to choose and change many of the things I dislike in my life. We all have the power to make choices about what we will do and with whom we will share our lives. By the same token, there are times when we have to make even harder choices about what we will not do and with whom we will not share our lives; but we must be willing to exercise that power. In the end, I believe that destiny has the greatest potential to be fulfilled when we have made the most important decision to have a personal relationship with God and allow God's Wisdom to guide us in our choices.

I have discovered that communicating with God is the one most important act that I could ever do to be aligned with my destiny. I believe that God's purpose for my life is the only pathway to true greatness. Regardless of what success one has attained or material possessions that one has acquired, only what is God–breathed can truly be worthwhile and have eternal value. Making it a priority to spend time listening and talking to God daily has made all the difference in my life.

I remember as a teen wanting to make a decision to give my life to God. Somehow I knew that I needed God in my life, but I did not know where to turn. Life was becoming too confusing, I was desperate and I needed answers, so I went to a church that I was invited to by my boyfriend. But instead of being encouraged to have a relationship with Christ, I was directed to have membership with a church. Sadly, not much changed in my life after I joined the church. I was basically going through the motions of the church culture. Later, I came to understand that although I was in the right location, I was not in the right place with God. I had not truly surrendered my life to God had no real relationship with God, I was therefore void of the source of power to change my life.

We must mature to the place in the Body of Christ to recognize that there is a difference between *going* to church and *being the church.* We must also realize that there is a tremendous difference between living in the world and living in the Kingdom of God. Too often, we keep the good news, with which we have been entrusted, inside of the walls of the church building, focusing on the members. This is precisely opposite of what I believe Jesus anticipated would happen with his message of the Kingdom of God. I believe that Jesus expected that we would lead by example and reach out worldwide to impact the destiny of multitudes by strategically encouraging them into the Kingdom of God.

MY TURNING POINT OF DESTINY

The beginning of the awareness of the unfolding of my destiny happened while I was in high school. Because I was always moving my mother's furniture around as a youngster in the house, I was particularly interested in how spaces functioned. As a result, I chose an elective course in architectural drafting. Because I was particularly good at it, my teacher took a special interest in me and my work. It made such an indelible impact on my life; I still have those drawings in my possession, over thirty years later.

One day, my teacher said something that shocked me: "LaVerne, if you do not go to college, your life will never amount to much." I never knew why he said those words, but they struck me deeply. It was something I never forgot. That was when I became more serious about attending college and began actively preparing. That was the first time I remember anyone caring enough about me to speak into my life that way.

Later, I became fond of drafting and felt confident with my abilities and decided that, although it was unconventional for a female, I would study architecture in college. I went to my guidance counselor and told him of my dreams. He told me that it was not a good idea because I would never get accepted into a college for that major and that I should consider something else. I was surprised that the counselor, who was supposed to guide me in the direction of my interests, steered me away from them rather than giving me the tools that I needed to move toward them.

I do not know how I was able to persevere as a young teenager, but I ignored his advice and applied to colleges to study architecture anyway. I don't know where my life would be had I allowed him to rob me of my dreams. Although I was turned down by a few, I did get accepted to one and it was there that my destiny would continue to unfold.

CHANGING THE SCRIPT

Sometimes we need to discover the underlying storyline of our lives to determine the reason why the scenes are not changing. I am reminded of the movie *Groundhog Day* where Bill Murray's character kept waking up and repeating the same day. This is because the script of his life had not changed. His habits, values, and belief system forced him to rehearse the same lines over and over locking him into a vicious cycle. But one day out of frustration, he allowed himself to awaken to the reality of what really mattered in life. It was in this "new day" that virtually rewrote the script so that he was able to move on with his life. Like this character, we too must wake up and rewrite the script in order to dramatically change the scenes in our life that help move us closer to our destiny.

We need to make a shift in our thinking that incorporates the understanding that if we want to see something different happening in our lives, we need to do something different. You may need to discover how to do something drastically different—or risk the death of your dreams.

Jacob could not stay in Beersheba! Jacob had to relocate and change the course for his life. In other words, Jacob had to shift and it was a matter of life and death! Sometimes it takes life-threatening situations to get us to see the need to change the direction in our lives even though we see we are getting nowhere.

If you were anything like me, rather than go around the mountain, you would be determined to tunnel through! Now get this: I was determined to work out my own circumstances and then believe that I did it with the Lord's help. Because of my incredible drive to over-achieve and accomplish my goals, it was difficult for me to see beyond my own determination. I was actually working harder to maintain my circumstances, not to change it. I was so blinded by my own

I have heard it said that we never really know how strong we are until we are tested. And this is absolutely true. You will never know how much a plastic bag can hold until you fill it, even stuff it, to the brim. Sometimes that is what it takes with us. Often we feel similarly stretched.

ambitions to solve my problems that I was oblivious to other methods available to attaining what I truly desired in life! In other words, I may have been doing all that I knew to do, but that does not mean that that is all that there is to do. This revelation was the turning point of my life as I discovered and learned new skills.

I eventually came to the realization that the most successful method to aligning with my destiny was surrendering my circumstances to God. This does not mean that I would not just sit around and do nothing. Rather, my philosophy is to do all I possibly can and leave the outcome to God. I have a strong suspicion that my tendency to overachieve was rooted in the condition of my low self-esteem. Oftentimes we work against ourselves by overcompensating for our own shortcomings. It is then that we become our own obstacle and our own worst enemy. This is where divine intervention becomes necessary.

I became engrossed with the delusional idea that I possessed the power to make my life better by working harder. But this methodology simply did not work. It merely exhausted me. I believe that I was also unsuccessful because I became quite comfortable in my familiar patterns and ways of solving my problems. My solution was: if things don't work out, try harder! I was determined to make problems work out with my own stubborn tenacity. And that is what they did! They worked me over, wore me down, and wore me out!

I have since come to a more healthy level of understanding that there could be another more productive strategy for solving my problems. I have learned to say, "If this doesn't work, I must abandon my fruitless techniques and develop a new strategy or learn a new skill." Although this seems like it is no great revelation, I cannot tell you how long it took me to figure this out. Then, I also discovered that I was not getting the results that I was after because I was taking the wrong course of action. I had to submit to the fact that there was so much I did not know.

Many times we give up in frustration saying, "I've done all I know to do, and nothing is working!" Well, that statement is true, and I empathize with you because I have said it myself a thousand times. But have you ever considered that you must extend your thinking to include the fact that there may be something that you don't know that could dramatically change your situation? In other words, although you have done everything that you know to do, your solution could very well be beyond your repertoire of understanding. This liberating fact will open your eyes to see new levels of possibilities that could dramatically change your life and open the door that allows you to learn new and much needed skills.

Typically, when we find ourselves in circumstances that cause us grief and pain, we often shift into automatic pilot and allow our emotions to rule the show. In other words, we go into survival mode. Unfortunately, we forget to reset the controls to emotionally adjust to any new circumstance or different situation. When we do this, we continue to move in the same, sometimes undesirable, direction as we go through life. Then at some point in our lives, we crash and burn. It is then that we must leave our old dysfunctional methods behind and, like Jacob, desperately set out to discover a new course.

The Bible says that, "Jacob left Beersheba and set out for Haran"[11]. In Easton's Bible dictionary, Haran means mountaineer or road caravan route. It is located north of Israel in northern Mesopotamia and the most northern extension of the Fertile Crescent near the Euphrates. As Jacob moved north geographically, he becomes a mountaineer in his upward route to destiny. He was on his way up in the world in more ways than one.

HARAN: THE DIMENSION OF OPTIONS

Haran is a very interesting place because it represents a doorway to Jacob's new options as a fugitive. Jacob's father, Isaac, recommended that he go to Haran. Isaac had journeyed to Haran and maintained his connections there. Perhaps

---

[11] Gen. 28:10

Isaac remembered his own journey and discoveries toward manhood in Haran. And Jacob's mother's brother, Laban lived in Haran. Isaac's grandfather Abraham was from Haran. Haran was obviously a place that connected this family to their destiny. To Jacob's relatives, Haran was a familiar and reachable location, but Jacob had never been there himself. He had only heard about it. Haran became the place where Jacob would discover a new way of life. This was his opportunity for him to move from his comfort zone, which had ultimately become the danger zone, to a place of destiny.

How many times have we stayed in a place that we knew was dangerous physically, mentally, and emotionally? Jacob knew it was time to move, and Haran was the open door for him to find a new course in life and ultimately to find his true identity. We too must find the place that connects us to our destiny. May God open the many doors to us that show us who we truly are and discover the course that leads us to our destiny. We must also be prepared to be given the direction from those who have gone there before us.

As a large commercial city, the industry in Haran would give Jacob the option to find countless opportunities. When we are open, there is a place where we can find limitless possibilities. Although Haran represented the possibility of options for Jacob, the only problem was that Jacob had to get there. The route to Haran would require him to travel north the entire length of Palestine, to the vicinity of Damascus. Then he would have to cross the desert to the Euphrates. This trip was typically traveled by foot. A day's journey would only take you about 20 miles. Haran was 500 miles from Beersheba and would take about twenty-five days if he traveled continuously.

I've heard it said that it takes about twenty-one days to develop a new habit. Perhaps the length of his journey was just the right amount of time to bring about lasting change in Jacob's life. Because this journey was such a distance, it would be arduous. Jacob had to take the risk and leave his comfort zone and all that he had ever known and go out into the unknown. But this decision would be crucial to aligning him on the path to his destiny. Moving from one location to another can be difficult for even the most adventurous. But the results could be life changing.

Jacob's trip to Haran proved to be quite productive. Haran, a familiar place to his parents, became a fruitful place for him. In fact, beyond a vocation and good fortune, Jacob also found the love of his life, Rachel, in Haran. Jacob prospered because he was willing to take the risk and leave the familiar. This should encourage us to take a deep breath, close our eyes, take the risk, and go to our Haran—the place to discover new possibilities. We, too, must muster the courage to take the journey regardless of how daunting it may seem.

MY DISCOVERY OF OPTIONS

I will never forget the time I was faced with feeling that I had no options. Getting pregnant out of wedlock and living with a man whom I would eventually marry, I was sitting at home with my newborn son. I had to drop out of college because I had gotten pregnant unexpectedly. Although motherhood was a new and exciting experience, because I was so young, I began to feel trapped and confined to this new routine of being a constant caregiver. I was no longer able to continue my carefree lifestyle of a young woman of twenty-one years old. But I was not getting any younger. I needed to make a decision about the direction that my life was headed.

During the months of being at home, I sat and reviewed my life whenever the baby was napping. I was disenchanted because my life looked differently than what I had planned it would be. Although I wasn't sure if I should get married because I already had a son, I did it anyway. On my wedding day, filled with uncertainty, while sitting on my bed preparing for my "big day", I asked myself if I understood exactly what I was doing so I did it anyway. I did not have the understanding to know what to do or how I could change the course of my life. I felt powerless. Suddenly the words of my high school drafting teacher came back to me, "If you don't go to college, your life won't amount to much." At that moment I realized just how prophetic his words were. Those words guided my life to put me back on track to my destiny. I felt compelled to do something that would bring clarity and order to my life.

It was at that point that I was inspired to continue to pursue my dreams of going to college. I began seeking opportunities so that I could continue to study and keep my mind active. Because I was not working and had no income, I could not afford to go back to college. I decided to take real estate classes, which were inexpensive at the time but were filled with the promise of prosperity. The classes were being offered in the evening, so I could go when the baby's father came home from work. It was a great outlet and an opportunity not only to keep my brain active, but also to be around and communicate intelligently with other professional adults, which was something I really missed.

I eventually finished the real estate course, passed the exam, and received my real estate license. I was equipped with knowledge that enhanced my earlier undergraduate courses in architecture. Although I learned a lot about real estate, it did not work out as I planned. I had not taken into consideration the personal resources necessary to be a real estate agent. It meant I had to get leads and take people around to find houses and not recoup the benefits for months or even years. On our limited budget at the time, this was not possible, so I discontinued this endeavor. From this experience, I also would come to realize that nothing I learned was wasted but merely added to the skills and knowledge that I would eventually need to fulfill my destiny. This is when I discovered how important it is to understand the layers of destiny and to continue moving toward my destiny despite the obstacles. This real estate experience laid an important foundation and was a destiny connection. But I was still restless to do more with my life. But I knew that I knew that I had to keep a positive attitude.

ON HIS WAY

When Jacob reached a certain place, he stopped for the night probably because the sun had set and it was dangerous to travel in the dark. Taking one of the stones he found, he put it under his head and lay down to sleep. After walking for perhaps 20 miles, Jacob was now weary. The energy that it takes to move out of your place of familiarity is tremendous. There are so many areas that are affected physically, emotionally, socially when you make a move. I once heard that moving ranks with the top fears such as death and public speaking because it contains all the elements of fear of the unknown. This is why many people give up, give out, or just quit, convincing themselves that it is not worth the effort.

I am often amazed at the number of immigrants who leave their families and come to America seeking a better life. I can't imagine what circumstances force them to make such a drastic decision to leave all that they hold near and dear. Perhaps it is the lack of opportunities and jobs in their home countries. But whatever the reason, they have my utmost respect for taking the risks that so many would never dare.

It goes without saying that Jacob found himself at a difficult time in his life. His journey was neither a casual vacation nor a weekend excursion. It meant that he must disconnect from everything that he loved. This had to be difficult. Perhaps the decision was so hard that he didn't notice the hardness of the rock where he had laid his head. Maybe the rock was a metaphor for where he had arrived in his life—in between a rock and a hard place.

When life seems to be at the point of crisis, this is an incredible opportunity to hear from God. It is what you hear that will drive you toward your destiny.

Although it takes enormous courage to leave everything you know to take the risk and go out into the unknown, this is exactly what is required to see your destiny fulfilled. If you are unwilling to move, you will be stuck in the rut between dissatisfaction and frustration. Sometimes when we make the hard decision to move from where we are to get to where we want to be, we are struck with the fear of the unknown and become immobilized. We know we should move, change, and alter our lives in some way. But once we get up the courage and take action, sometimes reality sets in and we become gripped with fear. We become paralyzed midstream and overcome with thoughts of turning back. Once the familiar fades, fear has the opportunity to set in. We force ourselves to believe that at least we have something concrete we can hold on to. The future is unknown and becomes scary because we have nothing with which to compare it.

It is times like these that we need to internally gain insight, direction, and encouragement. But this is also a good place to stop and rest. Jacob was probably stressed out, tired, and perplexed as he had traveled for as long as possible in the daylight. His journey could have naturally led him to the place he stopped, but that doesn't mean he would have taken the time to rest. He could very well have worried through the night about the trip ahead, the next day, as well as his future. Instead, Jacob rested. It is in the place of rest and stillness, away from all the distractions of his tragic life, where God speaks to Jacob. It was there he received a dynamic revelation that was instrumental in catapulting him into his future and the discovery of his destiny.

It just may be the same for you. When life seems to be at the point of crisis, this is an incredible opportunity to hear from God and rediscover the potential that is already within you. It is what you hear that will drive you closer toward your destiny.

DECODE
YOUR DESTINY
REDISCOVERY

Developing Your New Divine Mental Diet is the key to fulfilling your destiny. Your life will be literally transformed as you begin to get a better understanding about where you are right now. Then you can determine the direction that you need to take.

THINK ON THESE THINGS - Open your destiny dialog by honestly answering the following questions about where you are with your self-discovery:

1.   Have you discovered anything new or different about yourself lately?

2.   What situation or experience brought about this newness?

3.   Are you struggling with something in your life that you know needs to be changed because it keeps you from fulfilling your destiny? What?

4.   How can you develop a plan to organize your life to create change that you would like to see?

5.   What would happen if your dreams and goals were actually realized today?

6.   What do you feel God is saying about what you should do concerning your dreams?

DIVINE DESTINY DIRECTIONS TO YOUR REDISCOVERY

Now it's your turn to chart the course on your destiny roadmap as you take the information that you have gained to plot out your destiny location. As you look at Jacob's life, do you see any similarities? Can you build a bridge between where his life started and where it ended up? Now do this for yourself? Chart your beginning. Now imagine your ending and write it here.

GOING TO THE NEXT DIMENSION TO YOUR REDISCOVERY

As you go through the dimension of discovery there are many things that will be revealed about who you really are. We often find out who we are when faced with a crisis. You must embrace this knowledge as destiny clues that can take you to your next level. Determine to make every improvement necessary to advance toward your destiny. Below is a powerful affirmation to say to keep you focused on your goals to make new discoveries about your destiny.

DIVINE DESTINY DECLARATION

"Because my heart is toward God, I discover something new and wonderful about myself every day. As I remain in the center of God's will, I am open to the knowledge God wants to reveal to me about my attitude, behaviors, and actions. I acknowledge that I am ever evolving and transforming. I understand that the circumstances that arise in my life are messages that aid me in the discovery of my unique level of strength, wisdom, and integrity. The pain that I experience in my life is a sign that I am moving in the wrong direction and that I should move toward what brings me peace and joy. I now realize that it is a matter of life and death and I must move forward without delay. I love the truth and I desire the truth to operate in my life to bring about new levels of awareness. It's my time for my divine discovery!"

WRITE YOUR OWN DESTINY DECLARATION FOR REDISCOVERY

Personalize your Divine Destiny Declaration to accommodate your unique situation by writing your own below. Be sure to include the vision you receive from the destiny dreams that you see in your heart. As you nurture them by reviewing and saying them daily, you give your dreams the power to materialize. This is a living document so feel free to update it regularly.

DIVINE DESTINY DIARY:
USE THE SPACE BELOW TO WRITE YOUR THOUGHTS ABOUT YOUR DESTINY REDISCOVERY

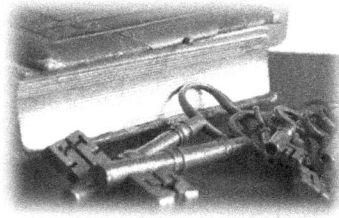

The greatest discovery of all time is that a person can change his future by merely changing his attitude. —Oprah Winfrey

God's revelation has nothing to do with an ideology which glorifies the status quo. —Karl Barth

As you go through the dimension of revelation, think about the last time God revealed something to you. Think about the way in which God may have spoken. Was it in a still small voice or through another person? Or maybe God speaks to you by making an impression on your heart? Or maybe you feel that God has never spoken directly to you. Now, think about ways that you could position yourself to hear a word from God about your life. Determine in this season to get a revelation from God so that you can move toward you destiny with clarity. Write your thoughts in your *Divine Destiny Diary* at the end of this chapter.

"Inspiration comes standard - Chrysler"

3. The Secret Key
to Your Revelation
"Available Options"

There is a fable about a man who falls in love with a blind woman. After years of dating, he finally popped the question and asked her to marry him. Feeling completely unsure, the woman blamed the problem on her sight, wishing with all of her heart that she could see. Suddenly, to her surprise, a pair of eyes was donated to her, fulfilling her deepest desire. Now she could see everything all around her, including her proposer. When she saw that he was blind, she respectfully declined the marriage proposal stating that was not the life that she wanted as a now seeing person. Departing in pain, the man wished the woman well and asked her to take care of his eyes.

Sometimes it takes very revealing circumstances to show us who people really are. And sometimes we learn from some very costly mistakes. If we don't learn from our experiences, we will find ourselves repeating the same mistakes over and over again without understanding how to break free. Many times we get stuck or hit a wall in life unable to move forward feeling that there are no other options. This is signified by the frustrations that we feel when things in our life don't go quite the way that we planned and then they remain that way for a very long time. It is during these times that we should seek assistance but don't because we think that we should be able to figure it out ourselves. I want to assure you that you do have options and that you have what it takes to give and receive inspiration. You just have to make yourself available to receive the revelation when it is presented to you.

Another reason we don't know what to do is that there is a shortage of people who can give us the wise counsel that we need. The people with whom we are closely associated are often suffering from similar experiences, or worse, and they themselves don't know what to do. I am not sure where my life would be right now had it not been for the people who helped to reveal some very valuable information that enabled me to move forward with my life.

UNLIKELY GENIUS

I am always inspired by the story of Dr. Benjamin Carson, who was born in Detroit, Michigan in 1951. Although his mother dropped out of school in the third grade, she was determined that her sons would achieve. When she saw that they were falling behind in the fifth grade and Ben at the bottom of his class, she swiftly moved into action by limiting her son's television time and play time outside until their school work was done. She also required them to read at least two library books per week and provide her with two written reports on what they read. With her poor education, she was challenged but checked their homework daily.

It did not take long for the boys to turn around and one day in class Ben was able to identify a rock from his readings that his teacher brought in. It was at that moment that he realized that he was not a "dummie" as called by his classmates and within one year, he continued to amaze them by climbing to the top of his class. His hunger for knowledge caused him to be an avid reader as he decided to become a doctor. After graduating from high school with honors, he attended Yale University earning a degree in Psychology. After Yale, he went to medical school at the University of Michigan and became interested in neurosurgery. His skillful hand-eye coordination and reasoning made him a superior surgeon and at 32 years of age, he became the Director of Pediatric Neurosurgery. Ben Carson says that he started reading the book of Proverbs and three hours later, he had a different view of the world. In it he found a plethora of wisdom, but had it not been for the ingenuity of his mother, there is no telling where his life would have ended up.

This is why it is critical to maintain inspiring connections with people who are spiritually mature and well adjusted to help reveal life's deep secrets about our destiny. These types of people easily recognize our present condition and sometimes intimidate us. They make us uncomfortable because we do not want to face the truth about ourselves. We get the sense that we will never arrive to their level and therefore see no need to maintain the relationship. But this is an unfortunate assumption. Most people gradually come into spiritual maturity. There are well meaning spiritual persons who have the ability to give wise counsel because they know full well from whence they have come and therefore can empathize with where you are right now.

On the other hand it is much easier to see the truth about others than it is to see it in ourselves. I once counseled a gentleman in my office that proceeded to tell me how humble he was because of how often he fasted and prayed. Although these are excellent qualities and disciplines, the man failed to see that his participation in them were for the wrong reasons and therefore defeated the purpose. In addition, the man used a prideful tone when describing himself and his practices. I wanted to tell him to go ahead and eat because his outcomes were completely contradictory to his objectives to be more humble. Although I gently tried to help this man see this sense of false humility, he refused to see this about himself.

The Johari window[12] can better help us understand this concept and is a tool used to help in self-awareness. This diagram is a window divided into four panes. The upper left quadrant of the window represents both what we know about ourselves and what everybody else knows. For example, we might be tall or have a jovial personality. This is common knowledge. The lower left quadrant represents what we know about ourselves but perhaps no one else knows. For example, as a child you may have stolen something from the corner store. Although you may still feel guilty about it into adulthood, it is something that you are unwilling to share because you are afraid of what people may think of you.

God is always willing to interact and speak to us. When we receive revelation from God, it is imperative that we respond in appreciation for what we have received.

The upper right pane represents what everybody knows and can see about us, but it is unknown to us. An example could be likened to when we go to the bathroom and come out with toilet paper on our shoe trailing behind us. Although everyone we pass sees it if they do not inform us it remains unknown to us. This can also be played out in a myriad of relationships. For example, you may be involved with someone who withholds some very important health information that could drastically affect your life but they do not have the courage to tell you. This dynamic of secret keeping affects our relationships in a variety of ways.

The lower right pane represents information that is completely unknown to us and others but is only known to God. This is why revelation is most important. We should always seek to know more about ourselves than others know about us. The most important and greatest revelation that we can receive is that which gives us more information about ourselves—especially the things of which we are unaware. We get disenchanted when others don't have the answers for our lives. Sometimes they offer suggestions but sometimes we are so disconnected from ourselves due to past trauma and dysfunction that it is difficult to hear what

---

[12] http://en.wikipedia.org/wiki/Johari_window

others are trying to tell us about our behaviors. Our life is skewed and it is difficult to see who we truly are. This is where it may be helpful to look at the lives and stories of others for answers and perhaps we can find ourselves. That is why so many movies are so impactful—and helpful to the viewer.

YOUR DOORWAY TO HEAVEN

We become actors who put on the performance of a lifetime when we force ourselves to believe that we are doomed to our present circumstances. We behave as if we enjoy the way things are, and sometimes even convince ourselves that this suffering is for a good cause. The truth of the matter is that sometimes we are too afraid to enter into a place of revelation because we may hear what we really know to be true: that a change has got to come! When we feel obligated to maintain the status quo to make others happy, we are falsely keeping the peace. But when God breaks newness on the scene of our lives, it always leaves us in a state of awe. Traces of this newness will affect every area of our lives. When you truly hear from God, it has an awakening effect upon your life.

When Jacob awoke from his dream, he said to himself, "Surely the Lord is in this place, and I was not aware of it".[13] He was filled with reverential fear and said, "How awesome is this place! This is none other than the house of God; this is the gate of heaven."[14] After his dream, Jacob is not just awake but also alert. The revelation that Jacob receives is so overwhelming that it causes Jacob to be afraid, but not in the way that paralyzes him. This fear brings him to a new awareness about God. God speaks to Jacob and says, "…I am the Lord, the God of your father Abraham and the God of Isaac. I will give you and your descendants the land on which you are lying. Your descendants will be like the dust of the earth, and you will spread out to the west and to the east, to the north and to the south. All peoples on earth will be blessed through you and your offspring. I am with you and will watch over you wherever you go, and I will bring you back to

---

[13] Gen. 28:16
[14] Genesis 28:17 KJV

this land. I will not leave you until I have done what I have promised you."[15] These words bring revelation to Jacob about his future.

For possibly the first time in his life, Jacob has a personal encounter with God. This encounter brings Jacob to the doorway of his destiny, and it is here he intrinsically understands the power and the greatness of this pivotal moment. He does something at this point that will set the course for the rest of his life. The next morning Jacob got up very early. He took the stone he had rested his head against, and he set it upright as a memorial pillar. Then he poured olive oil over it. He then named the place Bethel, which means "house of God." At the dimension of Jacob's revelation, Jacob does something significant! Too often when revelation comes into our lives we become immobilized in indecision, inactivity, and insurrection. But when God reveals something to us, it is not the time to be still. It is the time to act. This act establishes several things for Jacob. First, the act acknowledges that God has acted favorably toward him. Second, it would serve as a constant reminder of the revelation of the goodness of God. When God takes the initiative to reveal meaning into our lives, we need to respond with acts of appreciation. This is because the times that we hear directly from God are rare and should therefore be cherished.

God is always willing to interact and speak to us. When we receive revelation from God, it is imperative that we respond in appreciation for what we have received. How would you feel if you did a kind act for someone you loved and it was simply ignored? In other words, when God intervenes in our lives in any way, we should respond with significant acts of gratitude. The fact that God is mindful of us or grants special graces is remarkable. Likewise, the psalmist declares, "What is man that you are mindful of him or the son of man that you visit him?"[16]

Jacob had the wherewithal to understand that what God had done for him was marvelously wonderful. He responded by doing four things:

1) <u>The next morning Jacob got up very early</u>. It is a powerful discipline to rise early and make a holy exchange with God at the breaking of a new

---

[15]Genesis 28:13-16 NIV
[16] in Psalm 8:5

day. There is something about the freshness of the day when one is free from all distractions. It is a time when one is capable of being focused on communicating with the Almighty without any interference.

2) <u>He took the same stone he had laid his head against, and he set it upright as a memorial pillar as a place of worship.</u> Jacob so appreciated this experience with God that he wanted it to be remembered long after he lived. So he marked the place of his encounter with what supported him when he was confused and weary. His pillow became his pillar commemorating his life-altering revelation. Sometimes we need to use the things that supported us in our difficulties as a reminder of how God has shifted us into a new place. After Jacob's experience with God, he received a new perspective about God. Sometimes we need physical reminders of what God has done, and this rock signified an experience with God that literally transformed his life.

3) <u>Then he poured olive oil over it.</u> This was a sign that Jacob was intentional about consecrating and making this space sacred. Jacob was not just moving stones around. He was intentional about memorializing his encounter with the Holy One and sanctified that place as a memorial using anointing oil.

4) <u>He named that place Bethel.</u> Of all the things that Jacob did, this is probably the most telling. Naming the place Bethel, or "the house of God" proves his awareness of the change in his circumstances and that everything in his life was transformed. He went from being "in between a rock and a hard place" to being at home in the presence of a God who promises to be his sustaining life force. This was a new revelation for Jacob therefore every area of his life would change to rise to the level of this new vision for his future.

Too often we have pivotal moments, and we fail to celebrate and commemorate them. When we delude ourselves into believing that this crystallizing moment is just like any other moment, we miss a golden opportunity. When we fail to recognize these moments for what they are, we will miss the chance to advance toward our destiny. May God help us to recognize these transforming moments before they fade away and disappear, untapped and unavailable. For the first time in Jacob's life, he had an encounter with God, so he relished the moment that would change the course of his life forever.

JACOB'S VOW AT BETHEL

Then Jacob made this vow, "If God will indeed be with me and protect me on this journey, and if he will provide me with food and clothing, and if I return safely to my father's home, then the Lord will certainly be my God. And this memorial pillar I have set up will become a place for worshiping God, and I will present to God a tenth of everything he gives me"[17]. Jacob is very clear that he has experienced a life-changing shift in his understanding about God. He gets up early, takes a stone and stands it up, pours olive oil over it, and renames the place of his encounter "the house of God." Likewise when we commemorate the house of God with our presence, it is the place where we can receive numerous messages and blessings from God.

Then Jacob makes a vow to the Lord that involves his possessions. To make a vow means to declare a desire solemnly or earnestly. In today's technological culture with its identity theft and scams, it is difficult to find truly sincere people. We find ourselves drowning in the disappointment from those whom we thought we could depend. This sometimes makes us suspect of those who are true and also causes us to be suspect of every motive. But when we understand the times in which Jacob lived, we must recognize that someone's word was their bond. To make a solemn vow meant that you staked your life on your word. Though it might be hard to imagine

> *Isn't it amazing how difficulties in life can be transformed into the stuff that worship is made of?*

the level of Jacob's commitment, even in today's society it is a bona fide and sure promise.

---

[17] Genesis 28:20-22 NLT

Jacob defines his new understanding in relation to his material possessions by telling God he would give God a tithe or ten percent of all God gave him. He knows that everything he receives from this point forward will be directly from the Hand of God, making it easy for him to pay tribute to God for such great generosity. This is where we see one of the first accounts of tithing. It shows us that the true heart of one who tithes is one filled with heartfelt appreciation and gratitude.

Some people make a similar promise to God to tithe when they are blessed by God. Then when they get in a tight place financially, they bargain with God and talk themselves out of their own commitments. When we make a vow or commitment to give or to tithe, nothing should get in the way, because we have made a solemn promise. This type of commitment is with the understanding that the principle of tithing a portion of our possessions causes a blessing to come upon the remainder as well as additional benefits. When we put God first, we embrace the reality that God is obligated to care for us and meet our every need. We must embrace the fact that we should be grateful for all that God gives. Tithing is a God-inspired, God-ordained way to say thank you for the gifts that God gives in life regardless of the forms they take.

We can learn from Jacob as he makes this absolute commitment to God and then keeps his promises. All of the other things that Jacob did were relatively temporary acts. But this commitment to tithe would follow him throughout his lifetime and serve as a reminder of God as his Source. His act of tithing would always connect him to the moment when he had this pivotal encounter with God. More importantly, Jacob's tithing kept open the door for continual blessings from God.

And this is how it should be for us. When we make a conscious decision to bring the full tithe into God's house for the purpose of sustaining the work of the Church and expanding God's kingdom, we connect with a faithful God who promises to sustain us.[18] As God has provided for us in the past, we depend upon God to be our ultimate source in the present and in the future.

---

[18] Malachi 3:10

THE REVELATION OF DESTINY

As my son got older, I felt compelled to continue my education. The opportunity came for me to go back to college but this time I switched my major from Architecture to Construction Management. I remembered how difficult it was in the days when I studied architecture and how biased the industry was as it relates to gender and race. When presenting my architectural designs, if the professor asked for three drawings, I would bring in six. I always had to do more to prove that I was as good as, if not better than any of my white male counterparts. I had a difficult time convincing them of my worth. I understood that my difficulties had everything to do with the fact that I was often the only African American female in the class, yet I persevered.

As I struggled through racial and gender discrimination, I was more determined to reach my goals. Once I had a professor in architecture that had no choice but to grade my work on the merits, giving me "A's" and "B's", because of my obvious additional efforts. When he gave me a C as a final grade, I was bewildered. Petrified, I was left with no option but to approach my professor. Realizing that he was quite intelligent, I asked him how he arrived at the final grade given the average of my "A's" and "B"s. He seemed surprised that I would question his ability to do a mathematical equation or that I would even care. He immediately changed my grade and was faced with his own blatant act of racial discrimination. This situation helped me to see that destiny does not always come easy. Many times I had to fight for what I knew was rightfully mine.

After I received my degree in Construction Management from Pratt Institute in Brooklyn, New York, I became a field contract supervisor managing construction companies that were contracted to replace the concrete streets throughout the city. I have never forgotten how this job taught me about enormous challenges that come with gender differences in the field of construction. But what was even more significant was the revelation I received about tithing.

As a new Christian, I had learned to be faithful in tithing even before I was gainfully employed. I was consistent regardless of the circumstance. If all I had was five dollars, fifty cents was sure to go to the church. But when I finally got some real money, this suddenly became a problem. I had to get a new car to get to work, and this additional expense dramatically changed my budget. So I made a deal with God that I would stop tithing and, when I got it together, I would return to this discipline. It was unfortunate at the time that I did not recognize that it was God who allowed me to finish school with honors, receive awards and scholarships, and then get a great paying job. The first chance I got, I turned my back on my commitment to God. Needless to say, my life began going downhill. I vowed to God that if he would help me get my life back on track, I would never stop tithing again. Over twenty-five years later, I have kept my vow and have watched God miraculously provide and keep me through the years with enormous favor and grace.

THE JOY OF DREAMING

As we can see from an earlier chapter, Jacob had to make a dramatic shift in his life. In his case it was a matter of life and death. Sometimes although it is difficult for us to see, we are faced with the same dilemma. We allow others to rob the life out of us, and before we realize what is happening, it's too late and we give up on and bury our dreams. We sense that something is wrong but cannot identify the root cause. But the truth of the matter is that some of those closest to us should be convicted of murder because they have successfully killed many of our hopes and have ultimately robbed us of the joy of dreaming.

Jacob's outlook had to change, and he knew if it didn't, it would be the death of him. Not only did Jacob move from everything that was familiar to him but he also had to make a tremendous shift in his life and change his behaviors. We can learn from Jacob about how to receive revelation to move to the next level of destiny in our lives. And when the message comes, we should acknowledge the moment in our lives with wonder, excitement, and awe. Sometimes we can be so casual when God reveals to us our future but we should take a few cues from Jacob and be awestruck by an awesome God who desires to interact with us in an awesome way.

More importantly, we should commemorate our experiences with God with material action! In a world filled with constant crisis that has a tendency to rob our faith, we need a place that we can go to be reminded of the absolute power of God, even if it is only in our minds. We should go back to the places and stations in our lives where we saw God move mightily on our behalf. We must commemorate those places so that we can remember where they are located in our psyche and draw from them in difficult times. We need to commemorate those times in a tangible way as a constant reminder that God has done a great work in our lives and just how far God has brought us.

These prophetic acts are crucial to the consummation of our faith for the promise of our future. As God's creation, we must move out of the realm of indifference and do something that proves, not just suggests our devotion. Sometimes our personal fear of displeasing God often keeps us in the realm of inactivity. We want to wait until we feel sure. We must break the spirit of skepticism when it relates to God. We never have to worry if what we are doing for God is right. God will surely let us know and bless us for our efforts done with a pure heart.

The Bible teaches us that the just shall live by their faith. We must operate by faith in all things and remember that without faith it is impossible to please God.[19] When we move prophetically, we are moving in faith, believing that what God has promised, God is well able to perform. Sometimes a prophetic act is writing a check even though we know there is no money in our bank account. We write the check in faith and then ask God to provide the way for us to give as much as we desire to build the Kingdom of God. When the money comes, we don't hesitate to fulfill our vow.

DON'T MISS THE DOOR

There are times when we can miss a dimension of revelation that would bring about peace, completeness, and soundness into our lives. God wants to get us to the doorway of heaven but instead we miss some very important messages because we get distracted by the following:

Bait – sometimes we get distracted with the bait of Satan when we are easily offended and taken off track to our promised destiny.

---

[19] Hebrews 11:6 KJV

<u>Date</u> – other times we may be waiting for a particular date. When we do this we could get out of the divine timing of God. We should always be in alignment with God's timetable and agenda. God can move whenever, wherever and however God wants.

<u>Hate</u> – We will miss our blessing by keeping our eyes on others, by being envious or jealous of the status of others.

<u>Late</u> – This is the most tragic of all traits. When God's people are tired, tardy and even lazy, it is impossible to be prepared to receive a true revelation in the timing of God.

<u>Mate</u> – We miss God because we are depending upon someone else to go with us to receive a revelation. God's revelations are uniquely personalized. What God has for you is specifically personalized just for YOU!

<u>Rate</u> – Sometimes we rate ourselves with feelings of unworthiness. God has made us worthy by his Son to receive every blessing and promise intended for us.

<u>Wait</u> – Sometimes we make ourselves wait due to uncertainty or wavering.

When we allow these deterrents to keep us distracted from the door of revelation, we miss the door of heaven and find ourselves at the door of hell.

THE DOORWAY OF HELL

I don't know about you but there were times that I felt like I was living in hell! Much of the reason for this has everything to do with the choices that I made. When our intentions are ego-driven and self-centered, our actions lead us into a prison of our own hell and we pay a terrible price.

When fear of what others think rules the show, the need for attention and elevation becomes insatiable. No matter how much you feed the ego, it is never enough! These needs will never be satisfied because there is a constant hunt for more: more money, more fame, more men, more women, more clothes, and more things. This type of hunt can take you on a never-ending journey that leads to an unfulfilled life.

We often identify egotism as a male problem. When males are ruled by their ego they are blinded and lack insight and direction. If the mind of the male is not reformatted to understand this problem, he will eventually fall into self-destructive behaviors including sexual promiscuity, greed, and other addictions. Far from the door of revelation that would save his soul, his life spins out of control overtaken by pride, and insecurity. We see these conditions rampant in our society.

> *...we must not hesitate to give God permission to erase from our memories those things that do not serve us as we move toward our destiny.*

A solution to this dilemma is raising the awareness of the dangers of yielding to the ego. This recognition is an act of the will so that the male gets rewired to receive divine revelation. However the male must be fully ready to receive this revelation in order to gain real peace and satisfaction. Sometimes this does not occur until all other avenues have been exhausted. Just like Jacob, this is a matter of urgency and a matter of life and death.

Being egotistical is not just a male issue. The female counterpart to this hellish experience is women who are emotionally driven, believing that they are the center of the world with everything revolving around them. When a female is ruled by feelings such as insecurities, fear, and desperation, she will do anything to get her needs fulfilled. But this will also lead her to the doorway to hell. This is confusing because socially, females are expected to be emotionally driven. Although it is natural for females to express emotions, it is spiritually unwise to be ruled by them. Many women don't even realize this is a problem. The greatest problem is that feelings are temporary and subject to change. To depend upon emotions keeps one in a state of flux and filled with dissatisfaction. The solution is to reformat the female mind to allow it to receive new revelatory data that gives spiritual strengthen which is enough to overrule her emotions.

Before we had recent technological advancements, the way to store computerized information was on a 5-1/4 inch floppy disk. In order to use them, they had to be reformatted to receive new information. When you reformat a disk, it would completely erase anything that was previously on it. But before the process begins, it asked for permission to erase and reformat the disk.

In the case of both men and women, we must not hesitate to give God permission to erase from our memories those things that do not serve us as we move toward our destiny. Thoughts of unworthiness or haughtiness and other dangerous emotions that deter us from the fulfillment of our destiny need to be erased to make room for the valuable information necessary to get on course with the future. When we reformat our memories, we also reformat our thought processes. When our thinking is clearer; our thoughts are more refreshed ready to receive the revelation of new information that will set us on the course to fulfilling our destiny.

DECODE
YOUR DESTINY
FOR REVELATION

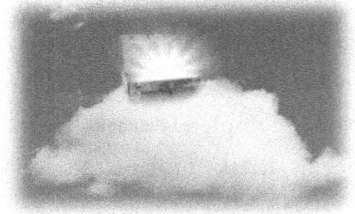

Developing Your New Divine Mental Diet is the key to fulfilling your destiny. Your life will be literally transformed as you begin to get a better understanding about where you are right now. Then you can determine the direction that you need to take.

THINK ON THESE THINGS - Open your destiny dialog by honestly answering the following questions about how revelation impacts your life. As part of your destiny dialog, think honestly about your journey to receiving divine revelation.

1.   Have you taken the bait of the enemy and gotten off track with your destiny?

2.   With who are you offended? Who or what is a stumbling block to you?

3.   Do you have a special date that you are waiting for to make changes in your life or have you yielded to God's timing? What is significant about your date if you have one? Does it coincide with God's timing?

4.   Be honest with yourself and ask if there is anyone you hate because of envy, jealousy, and guile. How can you quickly overcome this bondage and move forward?

5.   What are some of the things that you can do to break the tragic cycle of lateness and laziness if it is keeping you from your path of destiny?

6. Which mate, partner, or friend are you waiting for before you can pursue your destiny? How can you be sure they will be ready when God is ready for you?

7. Do you suffer from feelings of unworthiness? How can you change your thinking to understand that you are worthy because you were created in the image of God?

8. What ways are you wavering or waiting before moving forward because of indecision or uncertainty?

9. In what ways can you move past your fears to move forward with a sense of urgency toward your destiny and receive the revelation for your future?

DIVINE DESTINY DIRECTIONS FOR YOUR REVELATION

Now it's your turn to chart the course on your destiny roadmap as you take the information that you have learned to plot out your location. Do you feel like there are some directions on the roadmap to destiny that are hidden to you? Take this opportunity to write those down. This week go on a scavenger hunt and find clues to this missing information that puts you back on the path to your destiny. It may mean that you interview an older family member to excavate your family history. Pay special attention to those people who were exceptional or gifted to see if you see a pattern for your own purpose and destiny.

GOING TO THE NEXT DIMENSION FOR YOUR REVELATION

As you go through the doorway of revelation, there are numerous realities that you must be prepared to see. Position yourself to receive those things that God desires to reveal to you. Use this declaration below to help position you where you want to be. By doing so, you will nurture your dreams and help them to become realities.

DIVINE DESTINY DECLARATION

"My ears are in tune with God so that I can hear God's revelation clearly regarding every area of my life. I tune my hearing through fervent prayer, study, meditation, praise, and worship. I seek to hear clearly from God every day through every encounter. Whenever I come into the presence of the Lord, I desire to hear a word from the Lord that speaks directly into my life. As I yield to the spiritual guidance of the Holy Spirit, I also submit myself to the sound teaching of the spiritual leader that God places in my life and joyfully embrace sound doctrine. I strive to gain the integrity, accountability, and maturity to discern the truth for my life. I thank God for sending a mentor who takes a special interest in me personally and speak prophetically into my life to help me fulfill my divine purpose. It's my time to receive supernatural revelation from God about my destiny!"

WRITE YOUR OWN DESTINY DECLARATION FOR YOUR REVELATION

Personalize your Divine Destiny Declaration to accommodate your unique situation by writing your own below. Be sure to include the vision you receive from the destiny dreams that you see in your heart. As you nurture them by reviewing and saying them daily, you give your dreams the power to materialize. This is a living document so feel free to update it regularly.

DIVINE DESTINY DIARY:
USE THE SPACE BELOW TO WRITE
YOUR THOUGHTS ABOUT YOUR
DESTINY REVELATION

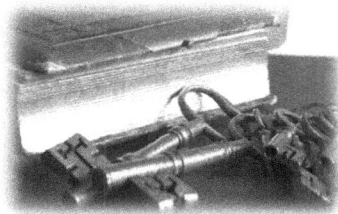

Minor things can become moments of revelation when encountered for the first time. —Margot Fonteyn

People, even more than things, have to be restored, renewed, revived, reclaimed and redeemed; never throw out anyone. —Sam Levenson (often attributed to Audrey Hepburn)

As you come to this dimension, think about your habits and how long you may have had them. Then think about the process by which these habits may have developed. Now, consider how you can develop new disciplines that can bring renewal into your life. Imagine a spring of refreshment bursting forth in your life to wash away the stagnant waters. Write your thoughts about what you think that would feel like in your *Divine Destiny Diary* at the end of this chapter.

"The relentless pursuit of perfection - Lexus"

4. The Secret Key to Your Renewal
"Remanufactured"

There is an interesting phenomenon that occurs with fleas. They are trainable because they surrender to their imposed limitations. When put in a box with a cover over it, they learn just how high they can fly—to the top of the cover and no higher. So when the cover is taken off, they never go any higher than they can when the box cover was intact because they instinctively remember the limit and do not attempt to go any further. This can also be true of caged animals.

Sometimes people are like this too. They restrict themselves to only what they are accustomed to and therefore never try to go higher than what has already been attempted. But with every passing day, we have the phenomenal opportunity to strive for a better day, relentlessly pursing perfection in life – even if that perfection means that we have found what we enjoy in life. But sometimes it's just not that simple, especially when we may have gotten off to a bad start or even worst, our lives have gone in the wrong direction. The good news is that it is not too late. We have the power to remanufacture our circumstances to begin anew.

Even nature contains within it the wisdom to know the time that it needs to replenish and renew itself. We have only to look around to appreciate this powerful ability of regeneration with every season. There are numerous plants and trees and animals that display this natural phenomenon. But not all of creation understands this marvelous concept. For whatever reason, humankind has a tendency to resist this natural process of renewal and somehow views this vital renewal process as a luxury rather than a necessity. I believe that as you tap into this awareness, you will find yourself being renewed and refreshed in a multitude of ways.

Wedged into habitual comfort zones, many people would rather fight than switch toward a new way of being, thinking, and living. But if we are to fulfill our destiny we must be willing to experience seasons of renewal. When we don't our life becomes dry and disorienting. When we do our lives are refreshing and energizing giving us the power that we need to move forward toward our destiny.

I am not sure what it is that makes us want to keep things as comfortable as possible for as long as possible. But when we are lulled into a sense of security, it often takes the crowbar of crisis to pry us out of our place of contentment. But crisis is often an opportunity to experience life on a deeper level. There is a quality of depth that is missed when we seek to maintain the status quo. In addition, when life becomes stale we become less effective in our daily dealings. Leaders, in particular need to be careful because we can transfer this staleness onto those we lead and infect others with our stinking thinking.

4. The Secret Key to Your Renewal   73   *Destiny Dreams*

RENEWING THE MIND

The famous Italian physicist, Galileo Galilei, born in 1564 understood the concept of renewing the mind to see things differently as he made the radical discoveries about how the earth revolved around the sun. Although he came from a financially troubled family, he was able to look past his circumstances and see the possibilities from a new and fresh perspective. He was extremely observant about the world around him and during a casual experiment watching a chandelier in a cathedral, he discovered the basis for the first pendulum clock. His inquisitive nature led him to go on to develop a renewed concept of the telescope that gave him a closer view of the moon and see "spots" on the sun. He was even able to see the four moons of Jupiter and thereby discovered that everything did not have to orbit the Earth. But more importantly he discovered some really great things about himself. He recognized that it was his persistence that led him to the findings were at that time was considered heresy. Nonetheless, it was his nature that allowed him to see things in new and exciting ways that allowed him to make amazing discoveries about himself and his world that we still utilize today.

If we can discover the secrets that underlie our lives, then we can put all the pieces together... and find lasting success.

Our discovery about who we are—who we truly are—sometimes only happens when we are pressured by circumstances and our backs are up against the wall. When we look through the lenses of others, we are privileged to enter their world and share their experiences. We can often relate to many of the experiences of others and then there are those that are new to us. It is this interchange between what is old and new that can bring us to the threshold of discovery. It is here that we get in touch with ourselves and perhaps even see ourselves in a whole new way. It is vitally important that when we discover information to improve our lives and our relationships, we use it to move us closer to our destiny. Too often this vital information goes untapped. In this book, I will present numerous real-life bible characters that you can research and follow them for yourself. I will also share some of my own experiences with you in hopes that you can learn from them as you set sail on your own journey of discovery.

MY MANDATE FOR RENEWAL

Self-renewal is critical if we are to continue to move forward to successfully fulfill our destiny. I recently decided that after twelve years of being full-time pastor and executive director of our community outreach and eleven years as a professor, it was time for me to take a much-needed sabbatical. I spent a good portion of my life working six and seven days a week to build a community of people that were strong spiritually and who would intentionally serve their community. I committed most of my waking hours to this mission as well as much of any vacation time for twelve solid years. In addition, I spent many occasions on the mission field visiting countries around the world.

This all-consuming work had now consumed me and much of my energies. Life was becoming stale, difficult and pointless. I knew that I was in a danger zone and needed to do something quickly. I felt signs of burnout after my eleventh year of service at the church and had the courage to express it to my congregation. I was tired and needed real rest.

My decision was wholeheartedly and empathetically received by our congregation. Although they supported my efforts, they watched me as I tirelessly worked to build our ministry. But the decision to take time off to refresh and renew could only come from me. It took a great deal of courage because this news was received with mixed emotions by others. Many were shocked to think that a pastor would have the audacity to leave one's congregation for an extended period of time for the purpose of renewal. Some even thought it was scandalous and held significant reservations.

But I had to have the wisdom to put things in perspective and make a firm decision to stop the madness. If I was to be able to serve this faith community in the future, I needed to take a break from the grueling day-to-day routine that was now killing me and do some serious self care. I had to come to grips with the fact that the God who kept watch over the church and the community work while I was there, was the same God that would keep the church while I was away. With all humility, I became keenly aware of my role as merely a caretaker entrusted with a work. I had to recognize that the church was not mine, but belonged to God. And these were God's people. As difficult as it was, I progressively began to pry myself away from an oppressive daily routine to find, once again, my passion for my work and my life.

I am not sure how it is that many continue for decades without a real break from their work to refresh themselves. For some it is not difficult because their objective is to maintain the status quo. But for others it is obvious that they have burned out and are no longer effective. Yet there are a small minority who are like the "energizer bunny" that keeps going and going and going. But we should also notice in this case that there are still tremendous limitations. When we are tired and worn, it is critical to recognize that our thinking becomes skewed and we do those in our care a disservice. We must be the captain of our own ships and make every effort to keep our-

> *But liberation comes when we allow ourselves to be renewed and restored. Then we can begin again with a new sense of hope and thereby regain the ability to bring hope to others.*

selves afloat and out of exhaustive danger zones. No one else can do this for us. We must give ourselves permission to overcome the overbearing expectations to be superhuman and give this gift of humanity to ourselves.

My bishop, Elder Milton Hobbs, retired after forty years of service. Shortly after his retirement he told me that if he had to do it all over again that he would not have worked so hard for so long. He encouraged me to take more time to enjoy life and not wait until you are too old to do it. I welcomed his advice. Too often, when we feel burnt out and discouraged, we have a tendency to just keep going feeling unable to do anything about it. Then we begin to feel trapped in drudgery. Whether we realize it or not, we project these feelings onto those whom we serve. Self-care is a very important part of people care. If we do not care for ourselves, we cannot adequately care for others in a healthy, logical way. But liberation comes when we allow ourselves to be renewed and restored. We can then begin again with a new sense of hope and thereby regain the ability to bring hope to others.

There is a story about a pastor who worked hard for many years. One day he keeled over and died from exhaustion. He died leaving a wife and children penniless with no pension or benefits. After all of his hard work he had nothing to show for it. The moral of the story is that it is more important to have a balanced life than a martyred life. It is not ungodly to think about one's health and family. Although the clergy is expected to give all of themselves to the ministry, this allegiance must be rewarded and reciprocated with proper care and concern from the membership. Although this is a biblical model, this is often not the case today. A pastor who seeks to secure a future for him or herself that includes their health benefits and insurance and pension for their family is often viewed as a mercenary. This is a dilemma for clergy because parishioners who seek the same benefits are viewed as wise. Here we see a hypocritical contradiction which seriously needs to be addressed. If the congregation is not willing to take care of their minister, the minister has the right to seek out the care needed.

Fortunately for me, there was an organization who proactively addresses the plight of ministers who are so captivated by their work that it has become detrimental to their health and the ministry. The Lily Endowment offers grants to hardworking, well deserving ministers to take time off to refresh and renew. After applying, this organization awarded me a grant based upon my years of service and accomplishments. I was able to fulfill a lifelong dream of learning Spanish and traveled to Latin America and Hispanic countries in the Caribbean. I had the opportunity to attend several Spanish language immersion schools and learned more about the culture, people, music, and even the dance. Needless to say, this experience really changed and reinvigorated my life.

As I returned back to work, I felt a sense of accomplishment and renewal. I felt strengthen to start again to build an even greater work. I became broadened in my worldview, as I see things quite differently now. I am more sympathetic to those persons who travel to the United States in hopes of finding a new life but are confronted by the language barrier. This often creates some dangerous scenarios and even exploitation. Many times during my travels I have been challenged by the same barriers and it was extremely discomforting. Fortunately for me, I was surrounded by people whose main objective was to support me in my endeavors—but this is not always the case.

I am ecstatic that I can now speak a new language, have met new people, ate different foods, danced a new dance, and even sang a new song. I have discovered the many people who are doing some really significant work all over the world. This feeling is exhilarating. As I reentered my work, I gained a new energy level to tackle the work ahead. I even feel more confident to reach out to new people groups to show them the love of God. Our congregation is the recipient of this new vigor and vitality and is inspired in many new ways.

More importantly, during this time I had the opportunity to get in touch with myself and my humanity. I was reminded that God is the great Shepherd. I remembered what it feels like to be one of God's sheep. This rekindling experience has helped me to care for the sheep on a deeper level as I returned to the flock that God has entrusted to my care. I was able to experience the love and care of the Father's Hand who provided for and protected me as I traveled alone to Barbados, Trinidad, Costa Rica, Mexico, the Dominican Republic, Puerto Rico and Venezuela. I was reminded of the omnipresent nature of God who was with me protecting, providing, and intervening for me as well as for the people in our church community. Because of the support of my Bishop, David Evans, Overseer Michael Anthony and a host of caring preachers, my church and congregation was better when I returned than when I left!

> *As we venture to get a fresh start, we prepare for the fresh anointing, new connections, and new manifestations of God's presence and power that are part and parcel with our destiny.*

On so many occasions, I saw the hand of God making a way for me. I have experienced angels working on my behalf to overturn circumstances of impossibilities. And I also was able to explore the dreams in my heart and even revive some of them! I became a student of life, rather than the experienced teacher I was when I left. I learned some really valuable life lessons all over again. Our members will reap the benefits in their lives for many years to come. As I have a sense of fulfillment, the members are filled with a sense of excitement and anticipation as I share my experiences about my travels abroad with them. You can only imagine what all of this means for my church, my students, and those whom I coach. They will experience renewal because I have been renewed. They will be able to see things differently because I see things differently and am sharing my newfound knowledge with them. They too, will be able to understand the importance of renewing themselves because I have modeled this before them and showed them how and why it is important work to do. Many have said how much they have appreciated the fact that I did not just leave but I took them with me as I shared my experiences with them on Facebook and YouTube. Though they never left the city, they felt that they went on a journey as well. I will share more of these experiences in my new book, *A Woman's Right of Passage* available in late 2010.

Whenever we think about being aligned with our destiny we must also think about the many new opportunities available to us to change and renew our lives. As we venture to get a fresh start, we prepare for the fresh anointing, new connections, and new manifestations of God's presence and power that are part and parcel with our destiny. This also means that we should be prepared for a new abundant harvest of blessings. With this new season, we gain strength to defeat and conquer the enemies that keep us from realizing our destiny. But we must realize that some of these enemies find their way into our lives through our own self-defeating behaviors. This is where we must be cognizant of the times when we become our own greatest obstacle.

ALL THINGS WORK TOGETHER

After working for just a short time in the construction management field, I purchased a new car when I began working. After diligently researching, I found a dealership with the best deal where I would purchase my car. After my selection, the dealer said that he needed to prepare the paperwork and I could come back the next day to pick up my car. When I went to the dealer to pick up the car, the salesman had changed everything on the contract. He said that the rates and terms had changed, which of course would cost me more money. Some things were added to the contract that I had not approved but being inexperienced, I signed the contract anyway. It seemed too complicated to undo at the time.

Then, I became pregnant with my daughter. I was a gestational diabetic and was considered a health risk. I was so ill that I could no longer remain employed. I went back and forth to the doctors and spent the last month of my pregnancy in the hospital. It was a difficult time for me in many ways, but I was encouraged because God had spoken to me about my pregnancy and even revealed that, "she would be the fairest in the land." Needless to say, God was right! My baby girl was born and was the most beautiful thing I had ever laid eyes on, and she is just as gorgeous today. What is even more wonderful is that she is equally as beautiful on the inside and is a caring and loving person.

Experiencing difficulties in my pregnancy, and unable to work, I became concerned about how I would pay for my new car. As I reviewed the documents to see what I could do, I noticed that the car dealer added a clause for disability insurance. Since I was physically unable to work and under a doctor's care, I was eligible for this disability coverage, and the dealer paid for my car for the next two years! God really turned that situation around to work in my favor. But this also helped me to renew my mind to see how God works all things together for me to be blessed in the long run. God had transformed the mess into a miracle!

At that time, I found myself at home taking care of my children. I was more mature now, and I recognized the need for me to remain home and prepare my children for the life ahead of them. This decision was particularly important to me because of the challenges I experienced early in life. Knowing what it was like not having my mother available to me because she had to work all the time because she was our sole provider; I was more intentional about being there for my children.

After being a housewife for ten years, I felt I was ready to get back into the workforce and was considering preparing myself by going to graduate school for a Master of Business Administration degree. I was getting back in touch with my dream of owning my own architectural construction firm. I had always been creative and had a mind for business, and I felt as though it was time for me to get out of the house and start pursuing my own dreams. I began investigating what it would take to pursue this degree and began researching institutions.

As I began filling out applications, I heard the Lord speak to me and ask, "What are you doing?" My response was, "God, you know the plan. I have dreamed about it for so long." But God's response was, "But this is not what I planned for you." I was in shock, because after putting my life on hold to raise my children, I was ready to move forward to being a more productive citizen. But little did I realize that God was calling me to a higher purpose and vocation. At this point, even though I had maintained my dreams for many years, I was transformed by renewing my mind and yielded to God's higher plan for my life.

It was around the same time God revealed to my pastor that I was called to minister to God's People and inspired me to enroll in the study for a Master of Divinity degree. I am grateful that Rev. Charles Quann, who had the courage and foresight in facilitating my calling by licensing me as the first women in the 108 year history of the Bethlehem Baptist Church, in Penllyn, Pennsylvania in 1991. This was no small task. I must admit the decision was not an easy one. I was quite resistant at first because I did not believe that God had called me to preach. I was perfectly fine visiting people in hospitals, nursing homes, and orphanages. I was quite comfortable doing Bible Studies in my home without being a preacher. But it was not until God spoke to me personally that I submitted to God's plans. I had to completely renew my thoughts and reorder the orientation for my life. Although I was an active Bible study teacher and visited the sick, afflicted, and needy, my calling into the ministry took me completely by surprise. There were so many things in my life that had to change in order to fulfill my call. The first would be to complete what would be a five-year course of study at seminary. But it was a decision that I have never regretted.

I had not taken into consideration how much would have to be sacrificed for me to embrace this dimension of my destiny. A lot of these changes were painful. But as I look back, I would not change a thing. I renewed my mind to align with God's purposes in order to get on track to where God was taking my life. But there was still more work to be done with my will. We never know which experiences God will use as our teacher.

A RENEWED MIND

There are opportunities for renewal anytime and anywhere in our everyday lives. We just need to recognize them when they come. On one occasion when we were selling our home and I needed to clear out items from my basement before we could show the house. I rented a U-Haul truck and hired some men to help move these unwanted items. I expected this to be a quick job because I had used this company before. Since I had a walk-out basement, the moving man suggested I drive the truck around back on the lawn to make packing it easier. I mentioned that the lawn was a little wet and maybe it was not a good idea. I noticed a bit of a sour attitude in the man that was different from the first time that I had used his services, but I ignored it because it was a small job that would be over soon. I drove the van to the door as he recommended.

Just as he said, it was faster. It was easier to get the truck loaded because the men didn't have to walk as far to reach the truck. They packed the truck fairly quickly as planned. But when they were done, the moving man took the keys and drove the truck out further than before but this time because it was a little heavier, the truck got stuck in the mud. No matter how hard he tried to drive it out, the wheels kept going deeper and deeper. Needless to say, I was horrified.

After numerous attempts, he came up with the idea that he could pull the truck out from the back with his van. That didn't work. The wheels just kept going deeper and deeper. This experience gave new meaning to the saying "stuck in the mud." While this episode was unfolding, the man got angrier and angrier. His helper started cursing and getting upset. I told them both to calm down and think clearly about what to do. I suggested they take the load off the truck to lighten the truck to perhaps be able to push it out of the mud.

Unfortunately, this still did not help because the wheels were stuck so deep. The moving men still kept trying with everything that they could think of to get the truck out. Their last attempt was to try by pulling it out from the front! Finally, the moving man realized that he had to call AAA. This small job was quickly turning into a huge disaster! By this point, with my possessions spread out all over the lawn, I felt exhausted, embarrassed and humiliated.

I began thinking how dumb it was on the moving man's part to pull the van out so far into the soft part of the lawn. I knew he should have just taken the original path, but I assumed he understood this. I was quite surprised to see him turn out the wheels of the truck. Meanwhile, he kept telling himself, "I should have known better because this is not the first time this has happened to me!"

This situation was a juicy opportunity for me to get angry, out of control, and out of character. I felt my emotions escalate as I went over the episode in my mind. But during this ordeal, I continued to pray: "Lord, please manifest Yourself in this situation. I need you now!" Exhausted, I sat down on the steps in surrender and told the Lord, "I yield." Although I felt upset that things did not go as smoothly as planned I had an unusual sense of calmness. I knew I was completely at God's Mercy for the outcome. This was when I became aware that a miracle was taking place.

Little did I realize that during this whole ordeal, the Lord was working on me! Earlier in the week, during my prayer time, the Lord revealed to me that I was going to experience yet another adversity in my life, but that the situation was going to be the final blow that would reveal the "diamond" of my character to prepare me for my future. I was not sure what that meant nor was I necessarily happy about what I heard from the Lord. I thought "Haven't I already been through enough. How much more work do I need?" Instead of falling into pieces, knowing that God had prepared me for this moment is what held me together in peace. I can't say enough about spending regular time in prayer

Once the AAA truck had arrived, the young moving man, covered in tattoos, came over to me and said: "I wish I could learn to be as calm as you!" Little did he realize the work that was happening on the inside of me. Without thinking I replied, "You can, when you have God as the foundation in your life!" My calm behavior became a witnessing tool for them to see the power and demonstration of God's at work in my life. This moment of mind renewal was the catalyst for me to witness to the man about how he needed Jesus in his life. But more importantly, it was my behavior that brought glory and honor to God and therefore opened the door for his salvation.

The first moving man thanked me for remaining in character. He recognized the many times that I could have easily gotten angry, upset and wildly out of control. I shared with him that it was because of Christ at work in my life that I was able to have peace and maintain my composure. As small as this may appear the fact that I was able to remain calm was nothing short of a miracle. My typical modus operandi before this point was to get upset and out of control and then deal with the casualties later. Through prayer, I had matured to the place where I realized that this expenditure of energy was a fruitless and an ineffective way to solve my problems. As a result of being tested, I recognized that I needed to stop feeling and start thinking! My thinking helped me to exhibit behaviors that were more honorable.

My participation with God in this moment was crucial if I was going to receive the promise of my destiny. I could have easily forfeited my blessing had I lost control. During this entire ordeal, I sensed that God was at work. I never imagined that hauling away unwanted items would bring about such cleansing. But it is only when we are willing to haul away the refuse of our lives that we can recognize the truth. This is the time that we can see that renewal comes in many forms but it is crucial that we discern these moments.

A PRESCRIPTION FOR RENEWAL

Sometimes we wait until we burnout before we realize that we need to rest and be renewed. This feeling of burnout is one of the first major signs to reveal that it is time to begin a renewal process. It is our announcement that things need to change in our lives. It is during this crisis that your body, your mind, and your circumstances are all making an announcement to you that it is time to shift. These warning signs manifest as physical ailments like chest pains or headaches. All too often we ignore these important messages, which can eventually turn to disaster.

I remember an incident regarding stress early in my church ministry. I began to develop chest pains. They became stronger and stronger. One evening when I was taking my long commute home, the pain became unbearable, and I drove myself to the emergency room. They took every test imaginable, and the attending physician could not find anything that would cause such symptoms. He carefully looked at me and asked me my occupation. I sheepishly told him that I was a full time pastor. Suddenly, he looked at me in a very strange way and said, "Physician, heal thyself!"

At that point, I was dumbfounded. That was the last thing that I expected this doctor to say, and yet it was everything that I expected to hear. I needed permission to shift and live a healthier lifestyle. Immediately, I changed my workload and began delegating more duties to others in the congregation. This was a real turning point for our ministry as well as my leadership style as I learned the importance of team building.

Next, I had to re-educate myself on more healthy ways for me to live out my new leadership style so I attended a leadership conference and got more than I bargained for. The information was so radically transformational for me that it changed the way I led the church which would be radically different.

I knew I could not let it stop there. I took the opportunity to re-educate and re-train our church leaders as well. I set up a Leadership Meeting and showed the videos from the leadership conference. After the first video, there was not a dry eye in the room. For the first time, I became vulnerable, and I poured my heart out to them about the enormous stress that I had been under. I could no longer keep up the charade that all was well. I was in trouble and the stress was beginning to take a physical toll. Many of the leaders apologized for their negligence and for allowing me to carry so much of the weight of the ministry alone for so long. I can truly say after that day, we were no longer the same. It was shortly thereafter that we began our Leadership Academy in order to properly prepare and equip our leaders for effective congregational leadership.

RENEWING RELATIONSHIPS

Finally, we need to assess the value of every relationship in our lives. We must determine if people are an asset or a liability. This is probably the most difficult thing to for us to do. When we feel uncomfortable with someone, things are not as out of our control as we would like to believe. We simply need to take the time to reflect on what each person brings into our lives as well as what they take away. If they take away more than they bring, then they can be labeled as joy robbers and handled in the appropriate manner—at a distance. We should gather close around us those who inspire and encourage us because those are the people who bless and refresh us.

It was critical that I developed a new relationship with the many other people that I had in my life. It was a good time for me to reflect on which relationships were healthy and which others were not. I discovered that many of them were dysfunctional and some were even toxic. Deep in my heart I knew that some of the people whom I had closely associated myself did not have my best interest in mind. I had to make some important decisions as to whether I was going to continue the drama or end it. As I honestly assessed everyone, I discovered those that were salvageable and those that were not. I have had to muster the courage to let some go, even though some of those relationships were long term. We must understand that we are truly only as good as the company we keep. If we are not comfortable with our relationships, then they are doing us no real good.

> *We should gather close around us those who inspire and encourage us because those are the people who bless and refresh us.*

Going through the dimension of renewal will affect us on at least three levels. The first is revelation and relates to our attitude, our willingness and ability to see things in a new way. The second is educational and relates to the ability to retrain our thoughts and behaviors. The third is relational in how we actually deal with others as we incorporate our newfound information.

We must be willing to release every unhealthy thing in our lives that keeps us from realizing the dream of our destiny. This is because only a God-inspired dream has the power to breathe real depth into your life. Let God renew your mind and you will be able to radically change your world. You will overcome every obstacle as you renew your thoughts to get delivered into your destiny! Your dreams will become a reality. It is only with God's help that we can take off the brakes in life. It is only by God's power that we can accelerate through the dimension of renewal and be positioned to be enthusiastically driven by destiny.

DECODE
YOUR DESTINY
RENEWAL

Developing Your New Divine Mental Diet is the key to fulfilling your destiny. Your life will be literally transformed as you begin to get a better understanding about where you are right now. Then you can determine the direction that you need to take.

THINK ON THESE THINGS – Open your destiny dialog by honestly answering the following questions about the renewal of your life. As you engage in your destiny dialog, be honest with yourself and answer the following questions relating to your future.

1. How might your thinking be outdated being unable to get you to your future?

2. What do you think is the cause for this way of thinking?

3. What is your style or way of doing things now? Are these behaviors able to sustain your dreams for tomorrow?

4. Do you ever find yourself saying, "What's wrong, I would like for things to stay the way things are?"

5. Is your life telling you that it is time for you to try something new, what is your plan to implement that new thing?

6. How soon could you start? How will you measure your progress?

DIVINE DESTINY DIRECTIONS FOR YOUR RENEWAL

Now it's your turn to chart the course on your destiny roadmap as you take the information that you have learned to plot out your location. In life there are turns that we do not necessarily want to take but know that we should because we know in our heart that it is our only hope to reaching a new course in our destiny. Develop a strategy for yourself that is revelational, educational and relational to move you forward. What is it that God is revealing to you now? What is it that you need to learn? What is it that is relational as you consider who it is that you can take on this journey that will support where you are going? Now accelerate and move forward in your destiny direction.

GOING TO THE NEXT DIMENSION FOR YOUR RENEWAL

As you go through the dimension of renewal you must be willing to shed your old ways of thinking, believing, and behaving. Use this Divine Destiny Declaration to help affirm the renewal that you want to see in your life.

DIVINE DESTINY DECLARATION

"I am thankful because I am learning what it means when God says in His Word that He will make all things new. I am releasing every old way of thinking, doing, and being that does not serve me. I shed every bad memory and make room for good, new, and exciting ones. I operate in forgiveness and release every old hurt and fear caused by others. I prepare myself for God to bring a total renewal in my life that includes new people, places, and things. I walk out of my past and step into my new future. My future is bold and bright—filled with new opportunities and possibilities. I am set on a new course for a phenomenal destiny. I let go of the old and embrace all things that I need to move into a new season. It's my time for the supernatural renewal I need to fulfill my destiny!"

WRITE YOUR OWN DESTINY DECLARATION FOR YOUR RENEWAL

Personalize your Divine Destiny Declaration to accommodate your unique situation by writing your own below. Be sure to include the vision you receive from the destiny dreams that you see in your heart. As you nurture them by reviewing and saying them daily, you give your dreams the power to materialize. This is a living document so feel free to update it regularly.

DIVINE DESTINY DIARY:
USE THE SPACE BELOW TO WRITE YOUR THOUGHTS ABOUT YOUR DESTINY RENEWAL

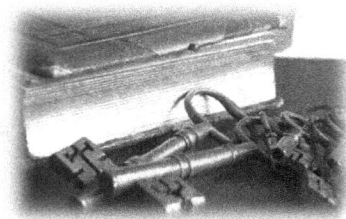

Nature often holds up a mirror so we can see more clearly the ongoing processes of growth, renewal, and transformation in our lives. —Anonymous

PART II
REALIGNMENT

Today's patience can transform yesterday's discouragements into tomorrow's discoveries. Today's purposes can turn yesterday's defeats into tomorrow's determination. —William Arthur Ward

Think about your life. Think about the last time you allowed something to be dramatically changed in your life and moved in a completely new direction. Think about what brought on the change, what the change felt like and the process involved. Think about what it could have looked like if you did not change. Now imagine changes in your character, outlook or appearance that will make your life soar into another dimension. Now, get ready to be transformed. Write your thoughts about this in your *Divine Destiny Diary* at the end of this chapter.

"Moving forward - Toyota"

5. The Secret Key
to Your Reinvention
"It Had to Be Totalled!"

In the late 1800's, the long standing Proctor and Gamble almost went out of business when Thomas Edison invented the light bulb. At the time Proctor and Gamble was the major candle sellers and the need for candles became obsolete. As sales plummeted, the company needed to move swiftly to save the business. As destiny would have it, a forgetful employee left his candle making machine on too

93

long and created a product from the residue that is what we now called "Ivory, the soap that floats." You can now find it in every household around the globe. The identity of the company was transformed and the rest is history. When we allow difficult circumstances to become the opportunity to transform us, the outcomes have profitable potential. There is real merit in scrapping previously made plans and starting all over again. This fresh start may be just the jumpstart that we need to get us moving from where we are to where we need to be.

We have already established that there are times when you need renewal. And then there are times when that renewal needs to go extreme and we need to completely reinvent ourselves. In other words, renewal works well when you know that your circumstances are relatively acceptable, and you simply need a fresh approach. You know that you merely need to step back and look at things from another perspective. But there comes a time when you need a total overhaul because you know that everything in your life just isn't working. After you have received revelation about your divine destiny and you take advantage of the time to reflect and renew, you realize that the old paradigms just don't work anymore. This is the time that you need to do something radically different and reinvent yourself. You are about to be remarkably transformed.

TRANSFORMATIONAL PROFITS

Jean Nidetch knew she had to do something radically different to transform her life and lose weight. She went from being an overweight homemaker to the co-founder of Weight Watchers International all because she knew she desperately needed to develop a new way of life for herself. She says that "Weight Watchers does not simply give you a method of losing weight. What it is, is a new way of life." And millions of people have benefited from the program that she developed through her own personal struggle as she became a successful business person. She was born in Brooklyn to a cab driver and a manicurist who did not have enough money to support the partial scholarship that Jean was awarded to go to Long Island University. But that did not stop her. Instead she took a course in business administration at the City College of New York and the rest is history.

A WOMAN'S RIGHT OF PASSAGE

During my travels for renewal in Latin America, I found a beautiful Blue Morpho female butterfly whose wingspan was about six inches in length. I did some research and found that this species of butterfly only lives in the tropical forests of Latin America from Mexico to Columbia. This butterfly is mostly brown with a patch of the most beautiful iridescent turquoise blue. Underneath is an intricate paisley design that would rival that of any clothing designer's best pattern. What is interesting is that their beautiful wings serve as a special defense mechanism. When an enemy approaches, the butterfly uses its wings to flash bright light in their eyes. This temporary blindness confuses the enemy causing them to flee.

This butterfly reminds me of my own metamorphic process. I had come to grips with the fact that I needed to do more than just renew. It was imperative for me to totally reinvent my behaviors, patterns and basically get a life! For the first time in my fifteen year ministerial career, I took the much needed opportunity to go on a five month sabbatical to take the time I needed to refresh, renew, and rethink the direction of my life. You can't imagine the numerous lessons that I learned during this time of reflection. The memoirs from this blessed experience can be found in my new book, *A Woman's Right of Passage: A Revealing Account of One Woman's Journey to Herself.*

> *As difficult as this may seem to hear, our lives may be telling us that we need to shift into a completely new dimension.*

What is more important is that during this time it was critical for me to overcome the obstacles and distractions that were trying to keep me from appropriately and wisely using this time. So like the Blue Morpho butterfly, I needed to develop a strategy to ward off every distraction and remain focused on my purpose by walking in the light through prayer, meditation, and affirmations. Soon, I was well on my way to achieving my goal of reinventing myself by getting an extreme life makeover.

As difficult as this may seem to hear, our lives may be telling us that we need to shift into a completely new state. To help me better illustrate, I will use the analogy of the metamorphosis of the butterfly. There comes a time in the caterpillar's life that it must change or it will die. The butterfly's life goes through four stages: the egg; the larva or caterpillar stage; the pupa or chrysalis stage; and the adult or butterfly stage. The first stage of the butterfly is very similar to our own human formation and can be likened to being conceived from an egg in our mother's womb. The female lays tiny eggs on a leaf and about five days later, tiny wormlike creatures hatch. In the second caterpillar stage, the caterpillar primarily eats and grows. This stage also resembles our life here on earth and sometimes all life amounts to is eating, drinking, sleeping. Life becomes merely a routine existence. Sometimes we feel like the caterpillar crawling around, blindly trying to find our way. If we stay here, life will never amount to much.

But thankfully the third chrysalis stage evolves and the butterfly emerges. In this stage chrysalides or inactive butterflies enclosed in a firm case or cocoon are formed in the open and are attached to a surface. The pupa splits and the butterfly crawls out. Its eyes are closed and it only has a proboscis to eat. It has six legs and when its wings are expanded, its blood pumps into them. It is warmed by the sun, and once it matures, it is ready to fly off to feed. Eventually it matures and lays eggs of its own. Just like humans, the different species of butterflies have a variety of life spans.

This chrysalis stage represents a time for us to slow down and reflect on how life is going. It means that we have to prepare to say goodbye to life as we know it and get ready for a metamorphosis. During this time it may appear that we are inactive but we become more reflective and introspective to take a closer look at our lives. This is also the time to activate our dreams of spreading our wings to move into a different dimension. This transformational time is often experienced in the open but there is something dynamic going on in private. When we are too attached to the familiar, this inhibits our progress. When it is time we too, like the butterfly, fly off into a totally new realm and as we mature we go through a similar process many times during our lifetime.

There are times when we must slow down and reflect on where we are and where we want to be. This is especially true when life becomes too difficult to handle and we have too little time to do the thinking necessary to change. Because we have taken on too many activities, this keeps us from the reflection necessary for living life to the fullest. During this chrysalis stage, the pupa covering is designed so there is little movement but its function is to keep the butterfly stabilized so secret growth can occur. We need to be like the butterfly and find our special place where we can slow down and develop new strategies. We need to become stabilized so our lives can look more like the destiny dream we see in our heart. It is from this place that we emerge after we have completed the process of metamorphosis and after a series of changes has occurred that a whole new life begins.

We will undergo several changes before we arrive at our destiny. Our true destiny also comes with a new identity. Just as the adult butterfly hardly resembles its earlier stages in its appearance and behavior, we too will take on a different form and we will think and act differently than before. The ultimate purpose of this metamorphic process is for us to reach the final stage, and like the butterfly, emerge in full maturity. As we complete this process, we soar into our best life ever!

> *It is from this place that we emerge after we have completed the process of metamorphosis and after a series of changes has occurred that a whole new life begins.*

RENEWAL GOES EXTREME

Perhaps you have seen the television show where people are given the opportunity to receive an extreme makeover. In most cases, the person's family members or friends recommend them for the makeover process and it takes them by surprise. But these caring people do this because they feel that what is on the inside of the person nominated does not match what is on the outside. They also believe that the person is valuable enough to invest time, energy and resources into. They feel so strongly about it that they are compelled to do something about it.

I believe this is the way that God works with us. God wants to give us an extreme life makeover and improve every level of our existence, not simply our physical appearance. The Bible teaches that the moment we accept Jesus Christ into our lives we position ourselves for a total life makeover.[20] But the makeover opportunity is pointless unless the candidate is willing to cooperate with the process. It is critical that the candidate cooperates and wants to see the change that they will receive at the end of the process.

In addition, it would be in the candidate's best interest to accept the proposition for a makeover when it is offered and take advantage of the opportunity because there is a lot invested and it may not come around again. Therefore, it is absolutely necessary to prepare and get a thorough understanding about what the upcoming process involves to advance through it successfully. God believes that we are worth the effort and that we possess the raw material that it takes to make the investment of an extreme life makeover worthwhile. The glorious finished product is realized when we are fully transformed into His image.

Reaping the full benefits of our efforts may mean that we need to make some really radical changes in every area of our lives. It is like when we need to get a makeover in our clothing, hairstyles, and even our attitudes. The reasons they are considered outdated is because they are no longer useful and no longer appropriately serve us. We become stagnant and unproductive because the behaviors that we have developed can no longer take us to the place we desire to go. If we don't make a destiny decision to change, our destiny is halted. This is apparent by our feelings of frustration.

If you are being hindered from moving into your destiny you must ask yourself, "Do I need an extreme life makeover?" You may need to begin by radically changing the way you are thinking and the approach by which you accomplish your goals. A good place to start is by changing your mental diet and developing a new way of thinking that advances you toward the fulfillment of your destiny. Paul recommends a great formula to help shift our thinking that can be easily incorporated into our daily routine when he says, "Finally, brethren, whatever things are true, whatever things [are] noble, whatever things [are] just, whatever things [are] pure, whatever things [are] lovely, whatever things [are] of good report, if [there is] any virtue and if [there is] anything praiseworthy--meditate on

---

[20] 2 Corinthians 5:17

these things." [21] This kind of thinking powerfully shifts your life in a positive direction.

Your life may be telling you that it is time for an extreme makeover but there are several stages that you will go through to get one. But when you have completed the process, you will be astounded with the results.

Extreme Life Makeover Stage 1

To begin our journey to an extreme life makeover, the first thing that you need to do is take inventory to check to see where you are by asking the following questions:

- How am I really doing? How are things really going?
- How am I keeping up with the timing of God for my life?
- Am I in God's timing to fulfill my destiny?
- What do I understand about the times that I am living in?
- How am I keeping up with these times I am living in?

If we are honest we would all admit that there is always room for improvement and that we need help in one area or another. Too often we think that we can handle difficult situations using old methods. But we have to realize new seasons require new strategies. We may want to take a closer look at what we are doing and get the help we need to get where we want to go. We need guidance to help shift us from an existence that is not a good fit for our future. This much needed transformation is critical in obtaining the new attitude necessary to achieve our destiny.

The first step of this total makeover process is that you must first get over you! Getting beyond how you exist right now is crucial to advancing toward your destiny. This new awareness is what prepares you to move forward. An extreme life makeover will help you change the way you see yourself, change the way you talk about yourself, and even change the way people talk about you! But this will only happen as you put forth a maximum effort to shift out of one dimension and into another.

---

[21] Philippians 4:8 NKJV

When I think of a character that needed a total makeover in his life, I think of the Apostle Paul, whose original name was Saul. Saul was one of the leaders of the Jews who fervently persecuted the early church with imprisonment and execution. He was so intentional about extinguishing these new believers that he went to the high priests in Jerusalem to ask them for authorization for his mission.[22]

But one day all that changed when he was confronted by Jesus while he was on the road to Damascus to hunt down and persecute more Christians. During this experience, Saul sees bright light flashes around him causing him to fall to the ground at which time he is struck blind. He then hears the voice of God asking him why he is persecuting Jesus or more explicitly Jesus' people. He is then instructed by Jesus to continue his journey into Damascus and to wait there for further instructions. It is a good thing that there were witnesses to this life-changing event or no one would have believed him or he would have been thought to be a lunatic. It is also interesting how Saul needs to get help from the very people that he has been persecuting. It takes Saul three days to figure out what hit him before he is met by Ananias, who laid hands on him and prays for him to receive his sight back. Saul, the persecutor of Christians is now converted to Christianity and is then filled with the Holy Spirit and baptized and becomes Paul. He was so different that he had to change his name. Now that is what I call transformation!

After this experience, Paul was faced with the task of reevaluating his personal beliefs about God and Jesus Christ in addition to his skewed understanding of the scriptures that he so adamantly defended. His thinking was so deeply transformed that he now believes the exact opposite of what he once believed. How is that for a turnaround? But now Paul is faced with reconciling his past life as a murderer and bounty hunter of Christians but he perseveres because he has now discovered his ultimate purpose and meaning in life.

How many times have circumstances in our lives caused our center to be altered and knocked us off our feet? If we are honest we may even admit that we needed this level of awakening in our lives. But when life strikes at us, be it through a death of a loved one, a divorce or the loss of a job, we have a tendency

---

[22] Acts 9:1-20

to be struck down by the shock of it all; we have fallen and we can't get back up. Sometimes it takes days, weeks, months and even years before we can figure out what has happened to us. But it is not what makes us fall down that matters; it's what causes us to get back up that is important. God's grace is what brings this transformation conversion in our lives and when He does, nothing will ever be the same because our whole world is turned upside down. We truly become new creatures.

Extreme Life Makeover Stage 2

The second step in the extreme life makeover process is that after we acknowledge where we are, we submit to the mission of God to get us onto a new course for our lives. This may mean that we are made a little uncomfortable as we determine to change old habits, old ways and old things, and whatever stands in the way of our progression towards destiny. Here is where we must make an honest assessment of how attached we are to our old life.

We can easily get distracted by the agenda of others and the world. When we do, we have a tendency to give a mediocre effort to the mandates of God and say, "this is all that I can do right now" because so many other things take precedence. When our intention is to please people and not God, our life becomes hinged in confusion. We are concerned about making other people happy even at the expense of our own spiritual well-being and we become overly concerned about what other people think. We become involved in things for all the wrong reasons as other people's preferences jerk us around. When we operate in mediocrity we are likely to suffer from poor experiences in our relationships because we are not committed to do the real work that good relationships require. At the dimension of transformation, we must force ourselves to press pass all levels of mediocrity in all areas of our life especially if we want to see the fulfillment of our destiny.

Extreme Life Makeover Stage 3

The next step to an extreme life makeover is to recognize that there is a particular mindset that you need to overcome. If you say, "How long can I stay where I am comfortable?", then you may need to update your thinking to fit the new and improved you! You may need to upgrade your mind and release the behaviors that hold you in place if you are to see your destiny fulfilled. It will require the development of new disciplines that will sustain the new you in a new dimension and this will take nothing less than your maximum effort!

When we possess this maximum mindset we might ask, "How far can I go in God?" and "What more can I do for God?" When it comes to pleasing God there should be no boundaries to how far we are willing to go. Only our maximum efforts get us to the place of our destiny in the least amount of time. We must push past all limitations in our minds and fulfill the destiny plan that God has already designed. For some of us it will be an uncomfortable stretch. Only a maximized effort will break us free. But in order to achieve this, our efforts must be hinged in faithfulness. We must be willing to do whatever it takes to be released from our prisons of mediocrity! We must be willing to die to our old ways and live to the possibilities for a new life. Rather than selfishness, we must move toward being transformed into selflessness.

A DREAM OF TRANSFORMATION

Allow me to illustrate the power of transformation by using one of my all-time favorite heroes, Dr. Martin Luther King, Jr. Because he was absolutely opposed to a system that oppressed humanity, he saw the solution to this problem in his mind. It is important to understand how he was transformed by renewing his mind to see the possibilities of what could exist in the future. In doing so he refused to participate in a system dominated by racism and fueled by hatred.

> *We must be willing to die to our old ways and live to the possibilities for a new life. Rather than selfishness, we must move toward being transformed into selflessness.*

Today we still experience the power of his dream because he dared to dream a dream that was bigger than himself and involved more than just him. He allowed himself to increasingly see how differently things could be and then sought out the strategies to dynamically change his world. He could have gone along with the system but because he saw something new he believed that something different was possible. What is so amazing is that Dr. King dedicated himself to the dream he saw in his heart until the dream became a reality, and he motivated others to do the same. There is no doubt that he was driven by his destiny because his relentless efforts produced global change.

CREATE A DREAM

In order to attain a dream, we must first create one. Creating a dream that will radically transform society is not possible if we continue to desire to maintain the status quo. We must use our God given ability to imagine life dramatically different and then ask for divine revelation to assure that our dream benefits the common good. Then, we must dedicate ourselves to the dream. We must be committed to seeing our dream come to pass no matter what obstacles may stand in our way. And finally, we must be willing to give the extra effort it takes to see our dream realized or else we risk it remaining unfulfilled.

DON'T DUPLICATE A DREAM

When you create a dream in your mind, don't try to duplicate someone else's dream or try to make someone else's dream as your own. Dream your own dream. Your dream must come from your heart in order for it to be fully energized by your passion. Just as God has given everyone a gift, God has also written a dream on your heart that fits within His greater purpose. Finally, we must be willing to allow our dream to not only benefit ourselves but the lives of others. Our deliverance will help to set other captives free. This is only possible as we resist the temptation to think selfishly and have the willingness to invest in our own dream.

DON'T HALLUCINATE A DREAM

When you begin to imagine a dream, don't hallucinate a dream that cannot be godly realized. An exaggerated sense of understanding causes us to be overwhelmed by self-delusion and leads us to surrender. We must avoid wasting our time with dreams and fantasies that merely advance us personally and do not benefit the world around us. When we do this we only perpetuate the problems of this world rather than eradicate them because we fuel self-centeredness which is the root of most of the world's problems.

Your transformation was planned from before the foundation of the world. God wants to miraculously transform your life. Jesus died to remove every obstacle that keeps you bound to the limitations of your flesh. In order for Jesus to be fully transformed and get a new and improved glorified body, he had to abandon his old life. In order for you to be transformed, you must be prepared to abandon everything in your life that ties you to your past and holds you captive. Jesus was driven by his destiny and powerfully resurrected for you to possess the same transformational power in every area of your life. And just like Ivory soap, you will find yourself rising above everything that could possibly keep you down.

DECODE
YOUR DESTINY
REINVENTION

Developing Your New Divine Mental Diet is the key to fulfilling your destiny. Your life will be literally transformed as you begin to get a better understanding about where you are right now. Then you can determine the direction that you need to take.

THINK ON THESE THINGS - Open your destiny dialog by honestly answering the following questions about the reinvention of your life. Think about your life now and continue your destiny dialog by discussing what may need to be transformed in your life by answering the following:

1. What radical changes do you believe that you need to see in your life?

2. What are some radical changes you could have made but resisted?

3. Why do you think you resisted those changes?

4. What is your strategy for handling the crises that arise in your life?

5. List some ways that you can be more intentional to see God at work, even in the most chaotic of circumstances, to bring about deep change in your life?

6. What would your dream life look like if you were completely transformed? Describe it here:

7. What are three action steps that could bring you closer to your dream life?

DIVINE DESTINY DIRECTIONS FOR YOUR REINVENTION

Now it's your turn to chart the course on your destiny roadmap as you take the information that you have learned to plot out your location. Look again at Paul's life and determine the level of difficulties that he had to face to accomplish God's purpose for his life. Now look at your life. What are the challenges that you face that could keep you from fulfilling God's Will. Chart the course that Paul took and follow those directions...

GOING TO THE NEXT DIMENSION FOR YOUR REINVENTION

In order to go through the dimension of transformation you must believe that you can experience dynamic change in every area of your life. You must desire it with all your heart. Saying this declaration daily will help affirm your desire to see transformation in your life and will move you closer to your divine destiny.

DIVINE DESTINY DECLARATION

"I thank God for this season of change that has come into my life. As I reinvent myself, I embrace the blessings God has prepared for me and receive the power of transformation. Through my transformation, I will reap from wherever I have sown because I know that God has an abundant harvest available for my life. I experience the transforming power of God because I have renewed my mind. I keep a careful watch over what I think and everything that I say. I intentionally participate with the change that God wants to bring into my life. I think about all the good that God is doing and embrace the purpose for which I was created. As I stay in the presence of God, God downloads pictures of my divine destiny into my spirit so that I may see my future with clarity and precision. I move into action so that my life looks more and more like the destiny dream God gave me. I see the changes in the people, places, and things in my life day by day. My transformation is proof positive that I am aligned with my destiny. It's my time for my supernatural transformation!"

WRITE YOUR OWN DESTINY DECLARATION FOR YOUR REINVENTION

Personalize your Divine Destiny Declaration to accommodate your unique situation by writing your own below. Be sure to include the vision you receive from the destiny dreams that you see in your heart. As you nurture them by reviewing and saying them daily, you give your dreams the power to materialize. This is a living document so feel free to update it regularly.

DIVINE DESTINY DIARY:

**USE THE SPACE BELOW TO WRITE
YOUR THOUGHTS ABOUT YOUR
DESTINY REINVENTION**

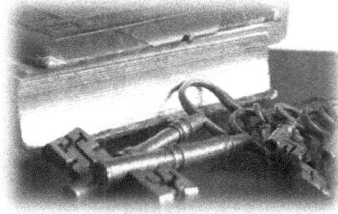

Today's patience can transform yesterday's discouragements into tomorrow's discoveries. Today's purposes can turn yesterday's defeats into tomorrow's determination. —William Arthur Ward

It is better to be prepared for an opportunity and not have one than to have an opportunity and not be prepared. —Whitney M. Young, Jr.

As you approach this dimension, begin to think about the level of opportunities available in your life. Think about how well positioned you are for advancement or success. Think about what obstacles might be in the way of your destiny opportunities. Now, imagine how far you could advance if all conditions were favorable for you to reach your goals. Get ready! You are about to embark upon the opportunity of a lifetime. Write your thoughts in your *Divine Destiny Diary* at the end of this chapter.

"Born to perform - Jaguar"

6. The Secret Key
to Your Responsibility
"Have Wheels, Will Travel"

A shoe manufacturing company wanted to expand its business globally to third world countries so it sent two of its top people out to explore the possibilities. One called in with the report that there is no opportunity for sales in the region because the people do not wear shoes. The other business representative sends an exciting email stating that there was a tremendous opportunity in the region because the people wore no shoes and that the company should begin marketing right away. Being successful when opportunity presents itself has everything to do with perspective. In other words, you were born with the power to drive your own opportunities with whatever resources you may have at your disposal. You can learn new skills to help you outperform any and every competitor using every skill, talent, ability and resource that you have available.

A LABOR OF LOVE

If anybody knows something about being pre-occupied with and loving their work, it's Denzel Washington. He clearly understands the importance of appreciating every opportunity that life has presented to him. With all of the accomplishments in life he says: *"The things that we have are not of my own doing. I am not the reason we have these things. God is."* He realizes that had he not attended the Boys & Girls Club in his youth, God knows he would have gotten in a lot of trouble. Then after the breakdown of the marriage of his parents, he and his sister were sent away to boarding school. He went on to Fordham University and studied journalism but had an inclination for acting and won a scholarship to the American Conservatory Theater in San Francisco afterwards working with the *Shakespeare in the Park Ensemble*. Needless to say, his ability to mesmerize audiences afforded him the opportunity to be awarded the Oscar on more than one occasion, direct his own films and star in countless films. Although he is an extremely talented individual, he has seized every opportunity presented to him in his life to achieve his destiny. If we are to accomplish our destiny, whenever opportunities arise we are required to take proactive responsibility.

THE PRESENTATION OF OPPORTUNITY

When we talk about opportunities the first thing that we should realize is that we are presented with many of them. You now have a tremendous opportunity before you as you read this book. I trust that you have the needed wisdom to use it wisely to bring you closer to your destiny. Jesus was an opportunist of sorts and used every opportunity to use his influence. He understood that influence is power, and Jesus often influenced others. Jesus always drew a crowd and he used every available moment to teach about the Kingdom of God. Subsequently, Jesus did what any person of influence would do when he had the attention of a crowd. He told them a story. But these were not just any stories. His stories were packed with eternal truths that allowed the people to better understand his message.

He once told a story involving the importance of appropriately seizing opportunities when they are presented. The story was about a man who went to a far country.[23] But this was not just an ordinary man. This was a man of great power and authority who had both wealth and servants. The average man at the time would not have the resources to travel, and so when Jesus told the story of this man who could, the people were all ears. It was like watching an episode of "Lifestyles of The Rich and Famous." The man of the story was a person of position and power, or what the people of Jesus' day would have called a nobleman. It was very probable that he was soon to obtain a position of even greater power and higher authority. In order to be appointed as such, he had to travel to a distant country.

Knowing that he would be absent for a time, the nobleman called some of his servants to him, to give them orders of what he wanted them to do while he was away. He gave them approximately 100 days' wages in the form of silver, each to invest for him while he was gone. For that day, that was a considerable amount of money. His command was specific and the servants were all to take advantage of the opportunity and do business with the money or "put the money to work," and make a profit for their master and ultimately themselves.

We cannot understand what the true value of the silver in today's market but some have placed the weight of a talent as ninety to one hundred pounds which would be valued at approximately $1,000.00. But what is most important to understand that it was considered an enormous amount of money. Any time that you think of 100 days' wages, you have to know that it is significant at any time in history. Today, if we looked at the salary of a household servant who worked a twelve hour day six days a week would earn about $7,200.00 in 100 days if they were paid $10.00 per hour. Needless to say, this is a substantial amount of money.

---

[23] Matthew 25:14-30

The story quickly moves to the return of this wealthy man from his trip. The moral of the story is not found in the fact that he went on a trip or that he had resources and access to wealth. Rather, the story is focused on those whom he had given the opportunity to produce something with what they were given. Although one version of the story says that he originally called ten servants, interestingly enough, the man only addresses three. Perhaps the other seven took the money and ran. Maybe they did not have the foresight to see the value in building a trusting relationship with this man of wealth and thereby proving their own worth. Maybe they were so shortsighted that they could not see that this was a chance to secure their future and make a better life for themselves.

When the nobleman returned, he called his servants to give an account. One of them did very well, getting a 10-fold return on his master's money. Another slave managed to invest his master's money to obtain a five-fold return. The third servant returned what he had been given and no more.

It goes without saying that the master was disappointed because he expected to get back more than he put into the hands of each of his servants. But this is the least that we should expect from a businessperson. Financial investors know that money should always increase over time, since it can always be loaned out at interest, or at least put in the bank where it can yield interest. This ruler understood that money has a time-value on it to reproduce and he did not want to waste any precious time, and therefore he left his servants to make a profit for him in his absence. He may have also wanted to know who he could trust to put in place for his new regime. People in leadership and authority need people that they can trust around them to help them carry out the business at hand. This was an excellent opportunity to reveal who those people were.

In today's world and economy, money is a sensitive subject. But it was sure to be just as sensitive when Jesus used it and yet he talked quite a bit about money. Jesus understood how important money was to people and the importance of being knowledgeable about how best to use it. That is why it has been said that Jesus did not carry cash because he always used his Master's Card!

The master, in the story, dealt with the first two servants in similar ways. The first servant, who seems to have been more diligent, received his master's commendation: "Well done!" The second servant was rewarded in the same manner.

Each received a position of authority directly proportionate to their faithfulness with regard to the master's money. Their faithfulness as servants and the profitable investment of their master's money resulted in them advancing to become rulers in this master's kingdom. The first observation I want to make about this story is that these two servants were given an opportunity in good stewardship, and they used this opportunity wisely and were rewarded for it.

The third servant was dealt with very differently. Notice that this servant becomes the focus of this parable because the most time, attention, and energy that is spent on describing him, although it is in a negative way. The third servant had no increase at all, for a very understandable reason: he had never put the money to any use. Instead, out of fear, he simply hid the money in the ground. In effect, he lost money for his master, since there had been no gain at all, not even interest from a bank.

This servant's response provides us with the key to understanding why he did not make an effort to do business with the master's money, even when he was commanded to do so. The servant feared the master. But I wonder if he was convinced that doing business was unnecessary because long-term investing of his master's money was foolish since his master would return and things would go back to business as usual? How short-sighted. Long-term investing is foolishness to those who have but a short-term mindset. The second observation I want to make is that when we are presented with an opportunity that affects our future, we should always watch our actions as well as our mouths! This man's deeds disappointed the rich ruler but his words insulted him.

This servant did not do business that profited. Instead, he hid the money, neatly wrapped in a piece of cloth. The master expected the servant to take his words literally and seriously but this servant did neither. But the master took the

> *The second observation I want to make is that when we are presented with an opportunity that affects our future, we should always watch our actions but more importantly watch our mouths!*

words of the servant seriously, judging him in accordance with what he said. The servant's description of his master was far from flattering because it was based in fear. The servant's description of his master is hypocritical because he says to his master, "I know that you are a hard man but you reap from where you have not sown."[24] If he truly understood this he would have taken every opportunity available to bring a return on the investment entrusted to him.

A very important lesson that this parable provides is that God wants us to be productive, prosper financially and advance the Kingdom of God. You do this when you take advantage of the opportunities presented to you and give them your best effort. This is because when you prosper, the Kingdom prospers. Many of us who have a job should give it our one hundred percent effort and do everything in our power to prosper in it with every effort to advance the purposes of God. But there are times when people are very dissatisfied with their work and it may feel like a joyless, occupational, burden (J.O.B.). I have heard Dr. Cindy Trimm say that you should, "quit your job and go to work!" This means that when you understand that your work is connected to your worth, it is your opportunity to prosper regardless of where it is or what you do. This does not always mean that you will work for someone else but that whatever you do, it should be with a sense of service, pride, and excellence.

When you think of an occupation is also connected to a residence. When you occupy a residence, you are the possessor of a particular habitation. Therefore, your work is where you live in your mind. Your work is where you live in your heart. Your work is where you live in your body. You should always be pre-occupied with your work and contemplate ways you can master it.

OPPOSITION TO OPPORTUNITY

Regardless of how good of an idea it is to move toward to your destiny and build your life, there always exists an opposing force that sometimes seems so innocent. For example, your friends can be jealous about your desire to find a better place to live and try to talk you out of it. Your family likes you just the way you are and therefore questions your desire to go to school and improve yourself. Your co-

---

[24] Matthew 25:24

workers are threatened when you try to get a promotion and therefore can't resist the urge to block you on the job. We must learn the skills to navigate through these aggressive behaviors if we are to overcome and accomplish our goals. Consider the following strategies when faced with opposition that comes from places you least expect it.

Don't participate – Often we give our enemies too much free press. Advertising is expensive and too often we give it away for free. We can give too much time and energy to negative commentary by grumbling and complaining about what is going wrong in our lives. That energy can be better spent strategically planning our goals and objectives. If there are those in our lives who are in direct opposition to our dreams and are determined to stand in our way, we are not obligated to advertise their displeasure. Even though there are plans that are formed to discourage us, it is imperative that we do not give power to them. These plots are only effective when you participate. You do have a choice, as difficult as it may appear. You can choose to remain focused and move forward with your plans of positive self-improvement. With a warlike resistance, we can choose not to get entangled with others' agendas for us. We must resist the temptation to defend ourselves. But of course this takes a certain level of discipline and intentionality. If you are serious about moving toward your destiny, you must strengthen yourself spiritually. The Bible says, "…resist the devil, and he will flee from you."[25]

There may be those we believe have our best interests in mind, but contrary to our beliefs but they are operating in deception. We want to believe that they want what is best for us, but their actions prove that this is not always the case. You are the only one who truly knows what is best for you. Furthermore, our wishful thinking about a person's agenda does not make it so. We must wake up to the reality that there are those with ulterior motives to control us for whatever the reason. Oftentimes people closest to us show a false sense of concern in order to keep us in the prison of their personal agendas.

People will go to great efforts to say one thing and do another and can cause a setback to our progress. When others do this, it can zap our enthusiasm and intensifies feelings of personal insecurities. In addition, when we are offended, a divisive spirit can set in and can become very distracting. This is just another

---

[25] James 4:7

tactic to rob you of valuable time, energy, and attention and throw you off course as you attempt to move forward toward greater things.

Don't be offensive – Be on the lookout for aggressive, attacking, and violent persons on assignment to detour your destiny. You must war for your future and your peace. Without your peace, you will be disoriented unable to make the wise choices needed to secure your future. This is another way that your enemy comes to steal, kill, and destroy you.26 War against division among believers and simply pray for those who intentionally come against you. The worst thing you can do is to fall into the trap and immediately react. Take a minute and think through what is happening and develop a plan of action to move forward in a positive manner. It is also important to stay out of the company of anyone who attempts to strategically steal your joy and kill your spirit through verbal confrontation. Choose not to wallow in the mire of mouth-to-mouth combat.

> *You must acknowledge and take action to explore all options and see every one of them as divine opportunities to move you in destiny your direction.*

Satanic bondage occurs when we allow others to oppress us mentally, physically, and emotionally. See this kind of relationship as nothing less than dangerous and intolerable! Evil and demonic personalities exist. Their ultimate plan is to disarm you and lure you into constant verbal battle. Too often we try to convince ourselves that this type of verbal violence is harmless. What we fail to realize is that life and death is in the power of the tongue[27], what does not bring you life and encouragement can kill your spirit. Aggressively war against this blatant diabolical assignment designed to break your spirit, discourage you and ultimately delay your progress.

Furthermore, there are those whose main objective in life is to not only to make you think you are crazy, but to make you crazy! Their tactics of confusion are rooted in their own insanity. They believe that if they can get you totally

---

[26] John 10:10
[27] Proverb 18:21

distracted with their agenda, then you will be derailed from your destiny and remain under their control. If you try to reason with them, you will be left feeling just as crazy as they are assisting them in their crazy-making agenda.

<u>Don't be self-opposed</u> – If opposition from others does not stop us, opposition from within will. It has been said that sometimes we can be our own worst enemy. This means that even when all conditions are favorable, we still cannot move forward with our own plans for an improved lifestyle because we have negative thoughts about our personal limitations. One way to overcome being self-opposed is to accept the fact that your life is filled with options and can be dramatically different from what it is right now. But simply realizing that you have options is not enough Then you must focus upon the opportunities that are before you and determine how you will turn every obstacle into an opportunity.

YOU ALWAYS HAVE OPTIONS

When wrestling with achieving your destiny, you must remember that you always have options. As a matter of fact if your dream is to fulfill God's plan for your life, regardless of the obstacles that may be in your way, there will always be many opportunities for you to reach your goals. Never let your dreams die. God can use a variety of alternatives to fulfill His plans and purposes for your life. Just know that you will have a myriad of possibilities to choose from. Let your imagination soar! When faced with opposition, don't allow yourself to be distracted by it. Stay focused on your goals. Don't come down to the level of your opponents by entering into verbal combat. One major strategy of your enemy is to rob you of the valuable energy you need to accomplish your dreams. Deny him access!

Instead, use your energy for more creative endeavors that build your life until it looks like your destiny dream. Proactively uncover all that God has made available to you. Once you embrace the fact that you already possess options, you no longer will feel trapped and can receive the revelation needed to successfully go through the dimension of opportunity. Know that God wants to exceed all of your expectations. When God gets ready to bless you, He will always goes above and beyond what you hoped for, dreamed, or imagined. At the door of opportunity, be prepared to go above and beyond anywhere that you have gone before by exploring all options.

ENEMIES TO OPPORTUNITY

I would never say that whenever we experience difficulties in life that God is trying to teach us something because that is not always the case. But what I will say is that the vicissitudes of life are excellent opportunities for us to learn a lot about ourselves. There is a story in the Bible about a man named Nehemiah. God put on his heart to start a building campaign to rebuild the wall of Jerusalem that had been torn down.[28] He had to get right to work because the city remained unprotected and vulnerable.

With all of his good intentions, Nehemiah faced an enormous amount of opposition from his enemies. There are times that we need to acknowledge that there are paranoid people who fight against you taking advantage of the opportunities that become available in your life. One of Nehemiah's enemies was named Sanballat, which means strength. Sometimes the enemy appears strong. But you must remember that no one is a match for God. There is no contest between God and your enemy. If you trust God, then rest assured that God promises to be an enemy to your enemies, to contend with anyone who contends with you, and to fight against anyone who fights against you.

Tobiah was another one of Nehemiah's contenders. His name means, Jehovah is good. Every now and then you need to be reminded just how good God is. The enemy often overplays his hand, using deception to try to make it look like it is the goodness of God when it is really a counterfeit blessing. This is where you need to use discernment. If it looks too good to be true, it probably is. It looks good from the outside, but on the inside lies a trap of discouragement. Just know that God would never send you anything that would harm you or send anyone that would take God's place in your life. Nor would God contradict God's words found in the Bible. When you embrace this reality then you will truly understand that all you need to do is put your trust in God and God will show you the truth.

---

[28] Nehemiah 2:17

Finally, Nehemiah's last enemy was Geshem, which means rain. He symbolizes the enemy who always tries to rain on your parade. It is this rain that discourages you and attempts to make you give up your dreams and abandon your promises through dark clouds of depression and despondency. We must be aware of these tactics and persevere.

In this story we see the strategies the enemy used to distract Nehemiah from the fulfillment of his destiny. The first thing the enemy said was, "Come." Satan would love for you to be tricked into doing battle on his turf. Never leave your position of safety to come down to the level of your enemy. Many people are lured out of churches, Christian fellowship, and the presence of God through a concocted offense. Then disaster strikes and they are left to deal with their problems alone. Too weak for the test, they are overtaken and overwhelmed. One strategy to avoid this is to build an impenetrable circle of support that can weather any storm.

The second tactic of the enemy is to try to convince you to see things his way. Nehemiah's enemies send him a message, "Let's meet together." The Bible teaches that light has no fellowship with darkness. This helps us to understand the impossibility of walking in unity with someone who wants to stay in the dark and keep us in the dark. Too often we get caught in this trap thinking that we can get someone, who refuses, to see the light. Most times this is a tragic waste of time. If you are absorbed in getting someone else to see your point of view then you are completely distraction from your own personal mission to fulfill your destiny. This ploy is designed to get your mind off of your goals onto someone else's dissatisfaction or disagreement with you. It is impossible to truly have a meeting of the minds with someone who already has a hidden agenda to detain you. These people will go to any lengths to accomplish their goals of sabotaging your success.

Nehemiah's enemies sent him a message, "Come and let us meet together in one of the villages in the plain of Ono."[29] This area was located in a valley, which is a symbol of the low places in life. But it is here that the enemy's low-down and dirty tactics and the truth are revealed. You would do well not to come down to your enemy's level. Instead, keep your head up as you dream your highest dream.

There is something about entering into a debate about your destiny and purpose that weakens your position. You immediately make your opponent aware of your insecurities. When you enter into a confrontation about your identity and destiny, you waste your power and energy on issues that are already settled in the mind of God. When you know and understand who you are and whose you are and what you are called to do, you have no need to defend it. It is a fact in the mind of God, and is undeniable and indisputable. When tempted to go to the valley of Ono, your response should be, "Oh, No!" and be like Nehemiah's and declare the following:

> *As I mature in my faith, I realize that when opportunities come, you cannot always expect to please everyone. But you can always seek to please God.*

"I am doing a great work!" – Whatever God has called you to do is a great work. No job or calling should be viewed as insignificant. All work that builds the Kingdom of God benefits humanity, is valuable and has a great reward. If your assignment were not important, the enemy would not be trying so hard to get you off course. Everything we do for the Kingdom of God matters and counts toward the greater vision God has for your life and the expansion of God's Kingdom on earth.

"I cannot come down!" – Your free will gives you the opportunity to make choices. You must choose not to come down to the enemy's level. Use your personal power and choose to fight from a higher level and vantage point where you assured the victory. Remember that because of Christ, you have the

---

[29] Nehemiah 6:2 NIV

privilege of being seated in heavenly places and, therefore, you are at a higher vantage point and this gives you the advantage over your enemy. Never abandon this post. Declare to the enemy that you will not come down from this God-given strategic position.

"Why should the work cease?" – This is a very important question. If you entangle yourself with the affairs of the enemy, you will not be focused on the work that you are called to do. This is the ultimate goal of your opponent to get you distracted and ultimately disabled and disarmed.

STANDING MY GROUND

After much sacrifice and overcoming many obstacles, I completed my course of study at the Eastern Baptist Theological Seminary, graduating with a Master of Divinity degree. I had to stay focused because there were many distractions that I had to overcome that included financial, familial, and even gender related issues about my calling. There were many difficulties that almost caused me to give up and quit – but nevertheless I persevered.

Although this was a huge accomplishment for me, now married with two teenage children, but I had no formal place of ministry in which to do my work. My pastor gave me an advertisement that he had found in the paper for an assistant pastor. I felt that after receiving my degree and working closely with him for over five years that I was qualified to lead my own ministry.

After much struggle, I applied for the position, although it was not what I had in mind. After two interviews, I received a call from a member of the search committee saying that although I was the most qualified, they could not offer me the position because they could not pay me. As an African-American female in ministry, it was difficult to get appointments in churches. I was so desperate to enter into formal service for God my immediate response was, "Please do not let money be a consideration." Please take note: I would never recommend this strategy to anyone because every person who works is worthy to be paid. My strategy was a way to get my foot in the door and get some pastoral experience.

The search committee agreed to appoint me and in September 1996, they called me as the co-pastor of the church. This was because not only was I more educated than the pastor, but because they felt that I was qualified to handle the enormous amount of responsibility of daily church ministry that I was being asked to perform. It was only a matter of weeks when an opportunity came to the church to run a homeless shelter. I was the only one qualified enough to write the proposal and direct the program. Miraculously, I was able to write my own salary into the grant. Later, the opportunity arose for me to become the senior pastor of the church. Had I not been able to discern to see that the first unpaid volunteer opportunity as a viable door, I would have never been able to advance to the other dimensions of my divine destiny.

Now, as a full-time pastor with over twelve years of experience, I have always seen the church as a work in progress. It took a lot of work to get the church to be the thriving ministry that it is today. But just like in the days of Nehemiah, the physical and spiritual walls of the church are always in need of rebuilding in some way. I can remember the early days when the building in which we worshipped needed a complete renovation. The windows, the walls, the floors, the pews, you name it; if it was on the church property, it needed work. It was then that my architecture and construction management background served me well, as I became project manager for all of the renovation projects in that the church became involved. This was the opportunity for which God had prepared me to use all the gifts and the training that God had invested in me. Because I stood my ground, even when thing got rough, I was able to advance toward my destiny. It became clear that regardless of the turns that we make in life, nothing is wasted, it all works together for our good.

Although it was a challenge early on, things went rather well until contention broke out among the leadership regarding a renovation project. What was meant to be a joyous time became a cesspool of emotions and flared tempers. Just as with Nehemiah, opposition arose from outside the camp. I refused to be distracted by personal agendas. Now that I look back, I honestly believe that this time was a proving ground to hone my leadership skills and abilities. Through it all, as a result of my formal training in architecture, construction management, and seminary, I was able to stay focused and keep the building projects on schedule. I set my face like flint and became determined to complete the work at hand as well as keep the leadership team focused spiritually.

Like Nehemiah, I was doing a great work, and I refused to come down, get distracted, and let the work cease. Eventually things began to take shape at the church, but not without casualties. As I mature in my faith, I realize that when opportunities come, you cannot always expect to please everyone. But you can always seek to please God.

THE ENEMY IS PERSISTENT

The Bible details how Nehemiah's enemies sent messages several times in order to entice him to meet them at their level and on their turf.[30] But Nehemiah was equally as persistent and gave them the same answer, "I can't come down." Be as persistent as Nehemiah and counter your enemy's demands. Do not allow his persistence to change your mind. This is another tactic of the enemy designed to wear you down. Let your "yea" be "yea" and your "nay" be "nay." Be consistent in your warfare and declare that you will lose no ground to his insidious attempts to take you away from your destiny and mission for God.

THE ENEMY TRIES TO INCITE FEAR

The story continues in detail like what appears to be a gossipy soap opera: "We're going to tell … that you have appointed prophets … to announce in Jerusalem, 'there's a king in Judah!' The king is going to be told all this … don't you think we should sit down and have a talk?"[31] All of these manipulative accusations were hurled at Nehemiah to try to frighten him into coming down to their level. Never let the fear of what people are saying be a motivation for you to operate in contradiction to what you believe. Never entertain the campaign of your enemy's lies. Just walk in faith and the truth will always come to light.

---

[30] Nehemiah 6:4
[31] Nehemiah 6:7

THE ENEMY TELLS LIES

The enemies start to get desperate. They send yet another deceptive message to Nehemiah saying, "Let's find safety behind locked doors because they're coming to kill you, yes, coming by night to kill you."[32] Always remember that greater is He that is in you than he that is in the world."[33] Do not believe the enemies' threats and lies that are designed to discourage and defeat you. Nehemiah gives his response to his unrelenting enemies: "There's nothing to what you're saying. You've made it all up".[34]

Make a liar out of your enemy. Let the truth make you free as you maintain your integrity. Your enemy's main objective is what Nehemiah finally figured out, "They were trying to intimidate us into quitting. They thought, 'They'll give up; they'll never finish it.'"[35]. Your response should always be prayerful when you are under the oppressive attack of the enemy. When all else fails, remember the words of Nehemiah as he was at the end of his rope, "Give me strength."[36]

It is absolutely critical that you deal with the enemies in your life. Most times we think that the easiest thing to do is to ignore them. But that is a very dangerous practice. If you don't confront and defeat your enemies, you allow them to have another opportunity to become more powerful to work against you. David declares, "You prepare a table before me in the presence of my enemies."[37] Be encouraged in knowing that God will allow your enemies who have sought to destroy you to see you take advantage of the abundant feast of opportunities prepared for you. God will bless you in spite of your enemies, but you must contend with the enemy and ascertain that your victory is assured as you stand against him with unwavering faith.

We can follow the example of Nehemiah, who deals his enemies a strategic final blow with a powerful prayer that can be easily incorporated into your own prayer life, "O my God, don't let [them] get by with all the mischief they've done.

---

[32] Nehemiah 6:10
[33] 1 John 4:4
[34] Nehemiah 6:8
[35] Nehemiah 6:9
[36] Nehemiah 6:9
[37] Psalm 23:5

And the same goes for the [ones] who have been trying to undermine my confidence"[38]. In other words, after you have stood your ground and not allowed the enemy to distract you from your mission, and after you have confronted your enemy, finish the job by putting them in the hands of an Awesome God!

Because of Nehemiah's persistence, "... the wall was finished on the twenty-fifth day of Elul. It had taken fifty-two days."[39] This lets me know that in 52 DAYS, anything can happen:

- You could get a new job ...
- You could find a new relationship ...
- You could obtain new finances ...
- You could get a new place to live ...

As a matter of fact, in 52 days your entire life could change in spite of your opposition. Nehemiah stayed focused on his goals and he was able to accomplish them in record time and so can you.

This tremendous victory took place in the Hebrew month of Elul, which in the western world's calendar is around August and September, which is time of harvest. After you have persevered past every obstacle, nothing is more satisfying than to reap the harvest and see the fruit of your labors. Nehemiah's dreams were realized because he dared to take a leap of faith and do the unthinkable: build a wall to an entire city that was devastated and broken down.

Sometimes all it takes is a leap of faith to overcome the obstacles put in your way. Accept the challenge. Take this opportunity to recognize your potential and fulfill God's Plan for your life. Nehemiah had to take a leap of faith and believe God to fulfill the purpose for his life to rebuild a broken wall. And based upon his example, we see that all it takes is a leap of faith to rebuild the broken places of your life. Based on this principle, any year can be a leap year. As you take your leap of faith, this could be your year to:

---

[38] Nehemiah 6:14
[39] Nehemiah 6:15 NKJV

LEAP INTO YOUR BLESSING!
LEAP INTO YOUR POTENTIAL! and
LEAP INTO YOUR PROMISE!

It all begins when you take advantage of even the smallest opportunity to make a difference in the world. Your ultimate reward will be the unfolding of your destiny. What a tremendous accomplishment indeed.

GET THROUGH THE DIMENSION OF OPPORTUNITY AND…

Pray with purpose – Make prayer plans to achieve your objective and goals. Decree those things that you desire to come to pass especially when you know it is the will of God.

Pray the promise – Find the place in the Word of God where God has made a provision for your promise thereby authorizing the way for you to receive your blessing.

Pray with power – Pray prayers that are potent with the power of faith to believe to see your dreams realized. If you can believe it, you can receive it! If you say it, it shall come to pass. If you see it you can have it! When you can believe it, say it, and see it, you will take the responsibility to seize every opportunity to be driven in your destiny direction.

DECODE
YOUR DESTINY
RESPONSIBILITY

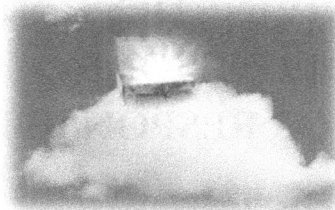

Developing Your New Divine Mental Diet is the key to fulfilling your destiny. Your life will be literally transformed as you begin to get a better understanding about where you are right now. Then you can determine the direction that you need to take.

THINK ON THESE THINGS – Open your destiny dialog by honestly answering the following questions about how you handle responsibility. Continue your destiny dialog and answer the following questions about how you handle the opportunities that are presented to you:

1. What are the S.M.A.R.T.[40] goals that you want to accomplish in the next 52 days?

> Specific –
>
> Measurable –
>
> Attainable –
>
> Realistic –
>
> Time-Based –

2. What is your action plan? Write it here.

3. When faced with opposition to fulfilling your goals, how do you tend to behave?

4. Now write how you will persevere and accomplish your goals even in the midst of opposition.

---

[40] Doran, George T. "There's a S.M.A.R.T. Way to write Managements' Goals and Objectives."Management Review 70.11 (Nov. 1981)

DIVINE DESTINY DIRECTIONS FOR RESPONSIBILITY

Now it's your turn to chart the course on your destiny roadmap as you take the information that you have learned to plot out your location. What is it about Nehemiah's life that strikes you as destined? What is it about your life that makes you feel the same? Now look at the roadblocks that Nehemiah had to overcome. Can you find any similar roadblocks in your life? What did Nehemiah do? Chart those directives on your destiny roadmap and follow those directions if you want to see something new build for your life.

GOING TO THE NEXT DIMENSION FOR RESPONSIBILITY

As you go through the dimension of opportunity, you must be willing to accept the opportunities that present themselves specifically designed for your advancement. Take advantage of every option without fears or trepidation. Here is a helpful declaration to say to help keep you focused and determined to overcome every obstacle and overtake your opposition to see and seize your destiny.

DIVINE DESTINY DECLARATION

"I am excited about the opportunities that come into my life. Opportunities abound because I take advantage of every option that comes my way. I approach every option with purpose, power, and promise. I commit to consistently persevere as more and more opportunities are released to me. I persist in every way because I build upon every new experience. I know that God is always presenting me with more and more opportunities for me to take advantage. I declare that I will go through every door that God opens for me. I receive the courage to move forward in faith. I press past my fears, doubt, and unbelief and make a conscious decision to operate in faith. I move past every obstacle and hindrance and believe that what God has promised, God is well able to perform. I will praise my way into my promise, recognize my potential, and take the responsibility to seize every opportunity. It's my time for every door of possibility to be opened to me...NOW!"

WRITE YOUR OWN DESTINY DECLARATION FOR RESPONSIBILITY

Personalize your Divine Destiny Declaration to accommodate your unique situation by writing your own below. Be sure to include the vision you receive from the destiny dreams that you see in your heart. As you nurture them by reviewing and saying them daily, you give your dreams the power to materialize. This is a living document so feel free to update it regularly.

DIVINE DESTINY DIARY:
**USE THE SPACE BELOW TO WRITE
YOUR THOUGHTS ABOUT YOUR
DESTINY RESPONSIBILITY**

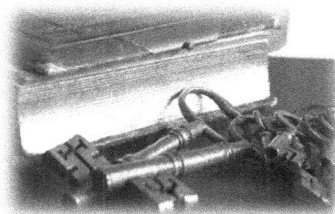

When one door closes another opens; but we often look so long and so regretfully upon the closed door that we do not see the one which has opened for us.— Alexander Graham Bell

Many people flounder about in life because they do not have a purpose, an objective toward which to work. —George Halas, American Football Coach

Think about your reason for being alive. Think about what could have been on God's Divine Mind when God created you. Now, think about your goals, dreams, and desires. Consider the possibility that there is a connection between the two. Determine that you will fulfill every purpose God intended and that you will stop at nothing until you arrive at your divine destiny! Write your thoughts in your *Divine Destiny Diary* at the end of this chapter.

""Find your own road - Saab"

7. The Secret Key
to Your Reason
"The Power of Dreams"

There was a man who liked to look at a person's purpose and reason for being in terms of volume capacity. He saw some people who were great and gifted global leaders as thousand-gallon containers which are rare and few in numbers. He saw others who did good national work as hundred gallon containers and still others who did the same type of work regionally as ten and five gallon containers. Finally he saw all of the local neighborhood people who did grass roots work as having the capacity of a one gallon container but there were a multitude of them. What is important though, is that in his mind, purpose was not being measured in quantity but in quality. We should never measure ourselves by worldly standards or be discouraged by thinking that those who have greater capacity receive all of the accolades and reward. The reality is that when we get right down to it an over-flowing half pint can outshine a half filled thousand gallon tanker any day. That is the power of a dream! It is our dreams that give us our reason for being and give shape to our purpose.

Many times people are confused about life because they are unsure of their capacity and purpose because they compare themselves to others. But it is critical that you find your own road in life and drive that to your destiny. More often than not I hear people who come to me say, "I don't know what *I* am supposed to do!" This becomes obvious after a brief discussion with them as they show how, over time, uncertainty has plagued every area of their lives leaving a very painful void. As you embrace the information in this book, your purpose for being on the earth will become more and more clear.

This constant ambiguity breeds a life of insecurity and a total lack of self-confidence. This is the reason why so many people fall prey to addictive and even abusive circumstances and they leave the outcomes of their lives up to chance. But leaving everything up to fate could be fatal. Even more dangerous is to put your destiny in the hands of another. If you are to achieve your destiny, it is urgent that you become empowered to move from the realm of indecision to make destiny decisions that help you to discover your purpose and your reason for being in life. Frustration is a sure sign that you are not fulfilling your purpose and you are out of alignment with your destiny. You must become aware of the power that lies within you to move your life towards your destiny direction. When you understand your reason for being here on this earth, then you feel more compelled to fulfill your purpose.

PURPOSE BORN OUT OF ADVERSITY

Alexander Graham Bell was born to a deaf mother who was a musician as well as an artist. His father, a teacher to deaf persons, invented "visible speech" as a coded language that showed deaf people how to use their tongue, lips, and throat to make speech sounds. Alexander had a similar passion to work with the deaf throughout his life. Although he only attended school from age ten to age fourteen but he never stopped learning. He used books from his grandfather's library to teach himself about many things. He faced tremendous hardship at the loss of his two brothers from tuberculosis. Although he too had the dreadful disease, the family move to Canada's better climate saved his life.

You alone are responsible for the outcomes of your life by the decisions and choices you make. And with God's guidance, you will be able to navigate towards the fulfillment of your purpose.

He went on to open a school for the deaf and then went on to become a professor at Boston University. It was his fascination with sound, or the lack thereof, that led him to the discovery of the telephone and the phonograph. He went on to start the National Geographic Society and served as president for several years. Needless to say his purpose was born out of his adversity. He allowed his adversity to be the process by which he would eventually overcome every obstacle to discover inventions crucial to the modern world.

THE REALITY OF PURPOSE

Discovering your purpose is a process. This process is pregnant with potential. Understanding your purpose is a lot like the developmental process of natural pregnancy. When you are pregnant with purpose, you are keenly aware of the changes that take place during this distinctive process. For example, when you first get pregnant, no one can really tell. You can even decide to keep it a secret for a while. Likewise it is the same with purpose. Once your purpose is initially revealed to you, you may not want to reveal it to anyone right away. Because you are just getting used to the idea of what your future holds you may want to incubate it and nurture it for a season. This is because there are many people who may not understand the things that God is doing in your life and seek to abort your vision with ridicule and questioning.

Regardless of how much you may want to keep it to yourself, eventually, just like any normal pregnancy, after you conceive and nurture it, your purpose starts to show. You will communicate your purpose through your words, your actions and your attitude. Those closest to you will notice that there is something different about you as you begin to move in your distinct destiny direction. They may not be able to put their finger on it but they can see a change nonetheless.

When the time comes when you have to share your vision, your dreams, and your purpose be assured to connect with the right people who understand the direction that your purpose is going. These people will help affirm the health of your vision by continuous love and support. They will act as experienced midwives that guide you every step of the way in the fulfillment of your purpose.

When you go through the birthing process, you will go through many phases, transitions, and changes. Too often there is a belief that your purpose will happen instantaneously but much like a natural birth as you will go through many transitions and changes. Similar to that of a natural birth, purpose has seasons in which to evolve and can even be seen to unfold in trimesters.

THE FIRST TRIMESTER

During the first trimester of birthing your purpose, you will begin to conceive the idea in your mind that your life has more meaning than just what is obvious. You begin to sense that God has a plan for your life and that it is your time to fulfill it. Because many people are plagued with ambiguity, they do not know how to help you to discover where their life is headed or see the direction that it is going. When you conceive purpose, this ambiguity begins to fade and your life takes on new meaning and identity. And when you are pregnant with purpose, you can never be half pregnant. Either you are or you are not. That is why it is important to make the destiny decision to nurture and develop your purpose by developing disciplines that move you toward and not away from your destiny. This is vitally important during the first several weeks of your destiny discovery so that you can be assured of a healthy destiny delivery.

During this first trimester, you must do all that you can to promote your destiny health spiritually, emotionally, and physically. Something powerful is growing inside of you and you want to make sure that it grows in the best possible environment. And just like a mother who would do anything to assure a healthy birth, you must make every effort to assure a healthy environment for purpose to develop. There may be some things that you need to stop doing or some places you need to stop going or even some people you need to stop seeing during this critical time of destiny development because they are a threat to the tiny destiny dream conceived inside you.

It is also important to be selective about what you eat during this delicate time. It has been said that you are what you eat because what you eat has a direct impact on your health and the development of your growing child. Likewise, what you ingest spiritually affects the health of the conceived purpose growing inside of you. During the first trimester in the development of your destiny purpose, taken in through your eye gate, ear gate and spirit, should be only those things that advance your spiritual health.

When you make the decision to communicate your purpose, your method is very important. As you wait until you are sure about what you are hearing in your heart, the communication of your purpose to others will be clear. It should be practical and it should include some very important details. You do not want people to question you and make you feel insecure about your own purpose. You may want to get some examples in your mind about what you have seen that are similar to what you will be and do. This is helpful because if you can see it you can attain it. You will never materialize anything that you cannot first conceive in your mind. Your body will never go where you mind has not been. Visualization of purpose is the outgrowth of the conception of your purpose.

This visualization will also include symbols that relate to how you see yourself successfully fulfilling your purpose. Can you get them in your mind? What will it look like when you have given birth to your destiny dream? Are you expecting a multiple birth? This visualization is important to a healthy delivery of your purpose. This is the place where you are beginning to show your purpose to the world, so you must be sure to use the symbols that bring clarity and that are closely aligned with your destiny dream. Then begin to nurture these visions daily with scriptures and spiritual affirmations.

You may want to also develop a slogan for yourself to keep you on track to the delivery of your purpose into the world. As the Destiny Doctor, my slogan is, "helping you to discover yours." This slogan is packed with purpose. I want you to know who I am and what I am purposed to do. I also want you to know that I am not trying to give you a destiny but help you on the wonderful journey to discover your own. This slogan also implies a process because I am *helping* you. I cannot do this process for you but I can support you before, during, and after your process of your destiny delivery.

It is also good to find a theme song! For the many stages of my destiny development and purpose, I have found numerous songs that speak to where my life is heading. I cannot tell you how the words to those songs made the difference in keeping me focused on what it was that God was speaking to me for that particular season. For my fiftieth birthday, my theme song was "Golden",[41] because it spoke to not only where my life was heading but also to how precious my time on earth had become. My latest theme song is "Just the Beginning"[42] because it gives me hope about my future in spite of all that I have been through in my life. I truly believe that there is so much more in store.

An excellent way to successfully deliver your purpose is to find success stories that are similar to the one you see in your destiny dreams. You can use these models to merely help to guide you but not necessarily to duplicate them. Allow these stories to encourage you over and over again. The fact that they are true is even more powerful because if it can happen for someone else, it can certainly happen for you. Real life stories also bring a sense of grounding and reality to your purpose process. Too often people confuse destiny with fantasy. There is a striking difference between what is irrational and what is impossible. You can easily determine the difference because most irrational fantasies are self-centered

---

[41] Written by Anthony Bell; Harold Lee Jr Robinson; James Darrell J Robinson; Jill Scott, recorded by Jill Scott, "*Golden*", "*Beautifully Human*", Copyright © 2004 Hidden Beach Recordings.

[42] Written by Kurt Carr, recorded by Kurt Carr and Vonnie Lopez, "*Just the Beginning*", "*Just the Beginning*", Copyright © 2008, Zomba Gospel.

and have no potential to benefit the common good. With God all things are possible particularly when it is in the center of God's will. God's plans are always about more than just individuals.

You should also seek to plan your life around your purpose. If you believe that your purpose is to teach, this is a pointless occupation if you yourself are not a learner. In addition, it is irrational to think that you can be a teacher of anything if you are unwilling to prepare yourself for such a position. Fantasies are dreams that do not have the potential of being sustained because there are no foundational anchors to maintain them. Make your dreams a reality with diligent preparation.

For example, you may want to meet and associate with famous people. Although this may happen, there will be no substance to sustain these relationships without good preparation of your purpose for being in their lives. This planning should include a good management of your schedule, time, and disciplines and the development of your knowledge base of the circles in which you desire to circulate.

It helps you to connect with purpose when you dedicate yourself to a place. Without this very important link you could miscarry your purpose because you have no place to deliver or ground you and no one which to be accountable. This place could be your local church, spiritual leader, or mentor. Regardless of who or where this person is, they are a very important part of the healthy delivery of your purpose. This person will act as a mid-wife to your dreams. Choose this person wisely because this person is critical to the success of your destiny delivery. You will need to feel confident as well as comfortable enough with this person to share your heart's deepest desires.

In addition, be sure that this person is experienced in your area of purpose and knows how to handle the delicate nature of the delivery of destiny. This person must be qualified to gently lead you to a place in which they are familiar and have journeyed themselves. Avoid leaving your destiny in the hands of amateurs. Too often we take the risk and make the mistake of putting our destiny in the hands of those who are incompetent and unskilled and have no clue about what it means to help advance in our purpose. Although there are a lot of many well meaning people, it may not be a wise to give this very important task into the hands of family, friends, or casual acquaintances. This is how many dreams are aborted and, like a stillborn child, have no basis for which to sustain life.

If you do not have the type of people in your life to help position you for your purpose, then it will be difficult for you to move forward in purpose. If you do not know anyone personally doing the things that you desire to do, then do your homework and begin to research people who have succeeded at what you want to do. Become intimately familiar with their lives. Become acquainted with their strengths, weaknesses, and patterns. This will help get you out of the realm of fantasies and into the realm of reality and unlimited possibilities regardless of how impossible they may seem. If you are in need of additional help in this area, you may contact me at www.TheDoctorOfDestiny.com and let me know how I can serve you.

It is important to remember that your purpose is unique to you. We each need someone to help guide us and give us direction. We also need mature people in our lives to help us gain an understanding about where we are headed. Destiny is not a solo act. We are meant to live in relationship with one another for the purpose of improving the human condition in the world but every journey toward destiny is unique to the individual.

> *If you can believe as well as belong, and if your maturity can be measured by your lifestyle, and if you can use your gifts to serve others, then your purpose will begin to show.*

It is also critical that we are accountable to someone as it relates to our purpose. It is true that we must be accountable to ourselves but we must also have someone in our lives that helps us to develop character and maintain integrity. If we are not careful, we will forget that the gifts, talents, and abilities are given to us to not only help us but to benefit others. If we all understood this, everyone in the world would be sufficiently blessed because we would be about the business of using what we have to improve our world. There are many things that you can do for yourself but you must recognize that there are some things that you need others to help you do.

For example, only you can decide to participate with God and take personal responsibility for the direction of your life. Only you can make the choice to position God as a priority in your life and truly worship and praise Him. No one can do this for you. Only you can choose your object of worship. Some people choose to worship their mate, their job, their car, their family, their status, their money, their abilities, and even themselves. But whatever you choose to worship will ultimately determine the outcome of your destiny so be sure that your worship is properly directed toward God and God alone.

But then there are things that you need others to help you do. You need others to help you see what is happening all around you. To prove this, try looking all around without turning your head. You realize that there is so much that you cannot see. You need others to help you through life with encouragement and assistance or most of the projects you undertake would be left undone. You also need others to love and accept you. This is what makes you feel that you are part of something great and gives purpose and meaning in life.

And just like in a natural pregnancy, you are afforded the privilege of bragging rights only when you know that you have prepared and nurtured your destiny process in a way that produces a well-defined purpose…one that will bless the world.

THE SECOND TRIMESTER

It is when you purpose starts showing that you enter into your second trimester and very soon you will be prepared to deliver the purpose that you embody. As you prepare, you feel confident because you have done everything in your power to create a beautiful life for yourself and everyone around you. We become the proud parents of a purpose that honors God and our reason for being alive. This time is where we begin to see some real significant changes in your body, soul and spirit. We begin to crave the truth like never before and want to read every book that we can get our hands on. We want to mentally prepare ourselves for what is about the happen. We also begin to change the places that we go and the people that we were connected to and begin to spend more time in prayer and devotion. This is when we begin to get a vision of the great things that will be and you become desirous of revelation that will bring about a safe delivery. This is also a time that we reject all things that are harmful to our destiny.

We should also use this valuable time to develop the skills to deliver our destiny. Because this may be a new experience, delivering purpose may be unfamiliar. This is an important opportunity for you to learn new delivery skills. You must be teachable in order to learn new ways of being and doing. Finally, in order to avoid the stillbirth of purpose, you must be willing to apply what you have learned. Too often many gain information but fail to apply it. This application of revelation helps you to be successful in the delivery of your purpose. Many mothers take Lamaz[43] classes to learn how to how a safe healthy delivery. Breathing is a very important part of this training and helps to ease the pain that comes with delivery. We too must learn how to allow the breath of the Holy Spirit to ease our anxiety and pain that accompanies the delivery of purpose. The reason why so many people fail at producing their purpose is because they begin with uneducated enthusiasm. It takes more than enthusiasm to fulfill your purpose in life. It takes knowledge, wisdom, and a plan. It has been said that if you fail to plan, that you plan to fail. This may be the reason why you are reading this book is because you want to gain insight and direction. You are to be commended for your interest. Your yearning will prove to bring physical, emotional and spiritual benefits into your life and everyone around you.

THIRD TRIMESTER

In the third trimester of producing purpose, we must get in position to deliver. But it all starts with the question: "What is my purpose for being?" The first answer should obvious: to do and be something good. And just as in a natural birth you may not know exactly what gender the child will be and what the child will look like, you will not necessarily know all of what your purpose is going to be. But you must begin to visualize the limitless possibilities for your life. You must begin to see the potential of purpose. This vision strengthens us to look past where we are to the possibilities of what can and will be and get us through the difficult labor pains that come with birthing.

---

[43] http://www.lamaze.org/

Other questions that we should ask more often are:

- What should I be doing right now?
- Who should I be doing it with?
- Where do I belong?
- Who will best love me?
- Who will accept me?
- Who will help me to fulfill my divine purpose?

If you are serious about seeing your life grow in purpose, then you must be willing to challenge much of the way that you are used to doing things. You must find more effective ways to fulfill your purpose. You will begin to see the product of your purpose, but you must persevere and be persistent. You initiate this process with prayer. Pray for perseverance. Pray for persistence. Pray to have the right perspective about your purpose. But most of all, seek to make God proud of you. Seek to make God happy, and you will never go wrong.

This is the beginning of finding your purpose. If you live long enough, you will quickly find that tying to do things in your own strength and power has tremendous limitations. But when you find people who can support the delivery of your purpose as well as your personal power and potential in God, you will be unstoppable.

SET UP FOR PURPOSE

When it comes to purpose it is important to know that God uses whom God chooses, when God chooses and for whatever particular purpose God chooses. King Cyrus was the human instrument God chose to accomplish God's divine purposes on earth[44] to serve as the deliverer of God's people from their oppression and bondage in Babylon. As the scriptures points out, Cyrus was anointed for God's mission and was specifically selected and set apart at a particular time in history to fulfill a specific purpose.

---

[44] 2 Chronicles 36:23 NIV

But contrary to popular belief, although Cyrus was used mightily by God, Cyrus did not choose God. God chose him as the conqueror of Babylon who issued the decree of liberation to the Jews. Cyrus was the celebrated King of Persia. A conqueror by trade but it was God who set him up and caused him to conquer many kingdoms. Although Cyrus had his own plans, it was God who caused him to succeed. Because God was preparing him for purpose, God assured his success. It is important to note that even before Cyrus was born, God decreed through the prophets Cyrus' impending accomplishments. Neither the king nor the Persian Empire existed when the prophecies about him were foretold. And yet God reveals the details of his victory with remarkable precision.

The Bible details how God would hold Cyrus's right hand, a symbol of strength, power, and authority, and cause him to subdue kings. It was God's intended purpose to use Cyrus to do God's work to bring down those who oppressed the children of Israel. And God will use us to accomplish great things in the world for the purposes of God's kingdom. Even if we feel incompetent or unworthy, it is the Mighty hand of God that gives us the power to accomplish great things. When we think about how intimately we are known by God, we can be assured that every detail of our purpose is known by the Omniscient One. Surely, before we were born, God knew in God's mind what we would become. I cannot imagine that vision being anything other than great.

The Bible declares that God will break down doors for Cyrus[45]. This is important for us because there are some doors that we cannot go through and we need God to break down for us. God promises to remove every obstacle, obstruction, and opposing force for God's purpose! The doors of bronze were a symbol of the human flesh that God would greatly overcome. The doors of iron were a symbol of human strength that God would overthrow. God's promise would open doors that would bring new opportunities, new resources, and great wealth. God said that He would also open a double door signifying an outpouring of abundance. The book of Revelation speaks of a door that Christ will open which cannot be shut.[46] This means that God is in complete control, and that we do not

---

[45] Isaiah 45:2 KJV
[46] Rev. 3:8 KJV

have to manipulate our way into opportunities. It is critical for us to learn how to wait for the right door to open to for us at the right time.

God said He would make the crooked places straight for Cyrus. In other words, God would bring all things in Cyrus' life into alignment with God's purposes. When we surrender to the purposes of God, it is critical that we understand that our lives must align with the intended purpose for which we were created. This means that every area of our lives is up for scrutiny. When we judge ourselves, we will not need to be judged. When we align ourselves with the purposes and plans of God, we are positioning ourselves for destiny.

> *We must always remember that God is not intimidated by an economic crisis nor is God overwhelmed by our need. For every vision God has, the provision has already been*

Interestingly, the name Cyrus means "as miserable" or it could also mean "as heir." This is a fascinating contradiction of terms. Like Cyrus, we are miserable when we do not fulfill the very purposes of God for our lives. Because we are heirs to the promises of God, we can take our rightful place of purpose in God's plan.

What is even more amazing is that God said He would reveal secret treasures in hidden places to Cyrus. This means that God would give Cyrus a supernatural level of revelation. Cyrus would have the ability to see treasures he did not know were there. But it was for Cyrus to understand that the purpose of the prosperity was so that God's people would prosper. God will reveal where the resources are for us to be successful and then give us the power to obtain them. God has command over the resources of the world.

AN ENCOUNTER WITH PURPOSE

This particular passage has always spoken volumes to me. I have always identified with King Cyrus in my calling to serve God. I think it may have to do with the fact that God chose Cyrus when he did not know God. As I look back over my life, I see the powerful hand of God shaping my life and experiences. I marvel when I reflect on the chain of events that brought me to the place of yielding God's remarkable plan for my life. Although I have always seen myself as competent, I don't know where I would be had it not been for the powerful grace and mercy of God.

I had not been the pastor long before I discovered that the church needed to have more than an ordinary agenda to sustain itself; it needed to have a sense of purpose. Like many churches getting started, it seemed as if the only aim for getting new members was for paying the overwhelming expenses needed to sustain our facility. As a matter of fact, the sole focus of getting people to church became so that we could raise money. After awhile, this became a burdensome assignment. As one called of God to advance humanity, it was difficult for me to embrace this mission of recruiting people solely for the purpose of sustaining the church budget. People need to be set free from the bondage that plagues them daily.

I had to shift and regain my focus on our true corporate purpose. Then, one day at a leadership meeting, I gently reminded the group that our primary purpose was not to be a fundraising organization but to help care for people's souls. I encouraged them to understand that if we truly focused on our mission, God would surely provide. From that point forward, we never talked about recruiting people to help us pay our bills again. The focus became building lives and nurturing souls. As the spiritual leader of the church, I needed to reset the agenda toward the purpose of our church's existence. Our mission to become more concerned about people's souls was the turning point in the life of our church and the broadening of our ministry.

In addition to shifting our thinking about why we recruited members, we also needed to rethink the purpose that God had for our ministry. At that time, we were just a Sunday church. We had the tradition down to a science. We knew exactly what we could expect every Sunday. But in order for us to realize our purpose, this was not enough. For the most part, much of my sermons felt like I was "preaching to the choir" and that the message needed to reach a larger audience. Although we were a caring congregation, at the time there was little visible evidence of concern for those outside of the church. Then God spoke to me and said, "I want you to grow the church from the outside in." I was not sure what that meant, but I would soon find out.

I approached the church leadership at the time about what God had said concerning reaching out to our community. I explained to them that we must develop new ways to bring the community into our 30,000-square-foot facility and share our resources in ways other than just the worship experience. These ways had to be centered on a sincere concern for their well-being rather than just for what they could do to help us financially.

Our first idea was to host a homeless shelter for women and children. After attempting to have this program for two years, we were unsuccessful. We learned that we were unable to appropriately handle the population of persons that came to live at our church facility. They were very experienced in the system they were a part of and knew how to maneuver in it in a way that abused our trust as well as our resources. Then some of their practices, which were out of our control, began having a negative effect on the church rapport with the community. Although it was important work, we had to recognize that this was more than we could handle, and this work was out of our league. Although we had a desire to help them, we did not have the necessary network in place to accommodate all of their needs in a way that would make a lasting impact. We asked God to give us wisdom and a better way to serve our community that was more suited to the unique culture of our church ministry and context.

This is when we discovered our niche. After our previous experience, we knew that we had to do our homework. Instead of trying to guess or assume what God wanted us to do, we surveyed our community as a way to know first-hand what were the needs in the community. But we had to first understand that we were called to address the unmet needs in the community. After we received responses back from our neighbors, we discovered that the essential need was focused upon children. Shortly after we began to address these needs, our ministry began to blossom in an entirely new direction.

Soon we had children swarming our campus on a daily basis. At one point we became so successful that it was more than we could handle. We had so many youth coming to our Youth Night Program held on Friday evenings, but we did not have enough adult supervision. We had to discontinue the program because we could not ensure the safety of all the children on our campus. Although we solicited help from the parents who were sending their children, they were unwilling or unable to support the program with their much-needed presence. We decided that it was best to stop the program and, after careful planning and with the involvement of parents and community, begin again. But out of that effort grew a vibrant pre-school and afterschool program. The Cathedral Learning Center and Motivational Achievement Program serves over 100 families daily.

Recently, our church underwent a similar process of re-visioning for our corporate purpose. We spent several weeks in study and deliberation. The members participated in strategic planning sessions looking at our demographics, history, as well as our potential. We spent a significant amount time studying "The Purpose Driven Church" by Dr. Rick Warren.[47] Out of that time was born our new sense of purpose which is embodied in our purpose statement: "As we purpose to build relationships, provide relevant ministry, and release the power of God through revelation and real worship we will reap the harvest and a rich reward." Now we have a new sense of purpose for being in our location. We are energized as we seek to reach out to new people groups with the message of the Kingdom of God. We are constantly seeking to know God's purpose for our lives.

These experiences have also affected my personal ministry. I know that God has created me for the expressed purpose of encouraging, equipping, and empowering those in need. Anytime I try to do anything other than what God has called me to do, I am unsuccessful and unfruitful. I have learned to operate in my gift as transformational speaker and a motivational teacher. I feel very effective at helping leaders to rethink their level of involvement in community ministry activities. This purpose is also revealed as I work with many individuals as a life coach helping them to be their personal best and develop a personal sense of purpose and meaning in their lives.

I am energized when I operate in my gift of administration. This gift empowers me to creatively serve God's people, God's church and God's kingdom. I enjoy

---

[47] Warren, Rick. *The Purpose Driven Church: Growth without Compromising Your Message and Mission.* Grand Rapids: Zondervan, 1995.

creating and developing programs that advance people's lives. It is important to me for things to flow in a particular order and I am intentional about operating in excellence with everything I do. Although I may be pulled in other directions, wisdom tells me to remain aligned with my purpose given to me by the Purpose Maker so that I can experience supernatural success. I have always believed that God would use me to do great things and so I have prepared my life in every possible way to be ready and available whenever God wants to use me.

What is most intriguing to me about the story of Cyrus is that God would reveal hidden treasures in secret places. Sometimes we don't realize that God often reveals treasures that are hidden inside of us that are available for God's use. God will also help us to discover the personal treasures of hidden gifts, talents, and abilities to accomplish God's Goals. But all too often we seek after fortune and fame for our own purposes and we become disenchanted. For this cause, we should always seek to glorify God with whatever gifts God is mindful to invest within us.

> *God will also help us to discover the personal treasures of hidden gifts, talents, and abilities to accomplish God's Goals. But all too often we seek after fortune and fame for our own purposes and we become disenchanted.*

Throughout my over fifteen-year career in professional ministry, I have witnessed the treasures that God had invested in me. But these treasures and gifts were not revealed to me most times until I had gone through periods of pressure, testing and trial. We must be willing to broaden our thinking to include these valuable experiences and not reject them simply because they are shrouded in times that may make us uncomfortable. It is at these times that God desires to excavate the treasures within us so that we can successfully fulfill God's purposes. I realize now that I have become a better vessel because of the many trials that I have had to face in life. I have a deeper sense of empathy with others involved in the various issues of which I am intimately familiar.

When we appropriately use what we have already been given by God, we are proven trustworthy to release the resources that are hidden in us, but mainly for God's purposes. This trust is based upon our faithfulness regarding what we do with what we have been given and what we have at our disposal. We must not use these treasures for our own selfish agenda.

I have always appreciated the fact that God called Cyrus by name. This signifies that God knew Cyrus intimately. When God calls you by name it signifies that desires to maintain an intimate relationship with you and help you fulfill your unique purpose. Cyrus did not know God. But God knew everything about him. We should make every effort to allow God to give us a name rather than try to make a name for ourselves. We should not seek to be recognized solely on our own merits. We should acknowledge that without God's Help we could do nothing of any real eternal value and that our personal success is only temporary.

What is even more profound is that God used Cyrus, a non-Jew, to accomplish God's purposes. This is a very important observation because Cyrus had a prophetic purpose, God chose to use Cyrus and God granted him all of the resources necessary to accomplish his purpose. As believers, this should bring us tremendous encouragement. How much more will God use those who have voluntarily aligned themselves with God? When we take the opportunity to get to know God beyond just the surface and develop a true level of intimacy, we are assured that God has us on God's mind. It is good to know that God wants to use us to see His purposes fulfilled in the world.

One thing is certain: you will never realize the full purpose for your life if you don't prepare yourself. God is not going to drag you into purpose. By an act of your will, you must be willing to align yourself and get into position. Cyrus was a King, and he was at the top of his game. He was at the height of his life. He was his absolute best when God chose to use Cyrus to accomplish God's purposes. God can only use us to the degree to which we are prepared. But regardless of the direction you desire to go in life, you will never be successful without some level of preparation and accountability. Accountability is directed toward God, and preparation should always be in the direction toward your known purpose.

There are many people who start second careers because they were unsatisfied in their first career or it did not work out as they planned. This is probably due to the fact that they have matured to discover their true passion in life and they set out, once again, to pursue it. It is not often that people plan their careers with the desire to fulfill God's purposes. This may be the reason why there are many people who have college degrees that have prepared them for an occupation they cannot stand! Perhaps if we begin to focus our talents and abilities towards our purpose in the world and marketplace, we may see a higher level of fulfillment, satisfaction, and joy and even more job security.

To find your purpose, it is important to know the Purpose Giver. To understand how to live out your purpose, you should seek directions from the One who created you. As you expand your thinking to include that you were created for a purpose then you will be more intentional about fulfilling God's purposes and ultimately find satisfaction in life. Regardless of the circumstances that arise in your life, don't despair. Remain composed with the blessed assurance that God created you with a great purpose in mind.

When you understand prophetic purpose, you come to realize that it is all a set-up. Prophesy is a decree spoken over your life that discloses your destiny. Most people fail because they subscribe and submit to the derogatory statements that are spoken into their lives and those words become self-fulfilling prophecies. But just like Cyrus, God wants to speak a word into your life that will cause you to prosper in such a way that transcends all negativity. The Bible supports God's desire for you to, "prosper and be in health, even as your soul prospers"[48]. God declares, "I know the plans that I think toward you: Thoughts of good and not evil; to bring you to an expectantly good end."[49] God created you for a purpose, to get you to purpose, and God does it all on purpose!

Sometimes people experience difficulties in life and lose their sense of purpose and give up. But we can learn from Jesus who knew that He had a purpose. Even though he faced tremendous opposition, Jesus pressed on and obtained His power. We have access to that same power that allows us to prosper in our walk toward purpose. The word that God desires to speak into your life will bring calm to every calamity and bring peace to every storm. Even though some things might be painful, God's intended desire is that you walk out your divine purpose.

---

[48] 3 John 1:2
[49] Jeremiah 29:11

When we have a purpose that is connected to God's purposes and a plan that is deeply rooted in God's plans, we are bound for success. We need to persevere and trust that God will give us the strength to accomplish those things God has called us to do. We will no doubt obtain enough power to fulfill our purpose from the Purpose Giver.

Jesus prepared for His purpose. For forty days he was in the wilderness and was tempted but he persevered toward his purpose and became popular and gained many followers. But then Jesus' purpose turned to pain as His message became unpopular with the religious leaders of the day. But Jesus persevered through to purpose and overcame the pain and crucified His flesh, Jesus' purpose gave Him power and continue toward his destiny which included being our Savior.

To believe that just because we experience opposition or defeat that we no longer have purpose is far from the truth. God has a destiny pathway designed just for you. That path is filled with doors of trials as well as victory but they are all designed to give you a sense of possibility, potential, and purpose. If you persevere, you will be positioned in power. Like Jesus, you embrace your reason for existing and receive the unique ability to be driven to make a positive difference in the world.

DECODE
YOUR DESTINY
REASON

Developing Your New Divine Mental Diet is the key to fulfilling your destiny. Your life will be literally transformed as you begin to get a better understanding about where you are right now. Then you can determine the direction that you need to take. Open

THINK ON THESE THINGS - your destiny dialog by honestly answering the following questions about your reason for being. Think honestly about what you believe to be your purpose in life as you continue your destiny dialog.

1. In what ways can you cultivate the destiny messages that are taking shape in your life to bring you closer to your purpose?

2. What are some destiny clues that are helping you to come to these conclusions?

3. In what ways do you think that you can prepare yourself to fulfill the purposes of God?

4. What are some of the ways that you can get past the obstacles that keep you from fulfilling your purpose?

5. What are some of the ways can you share and celebrate your new-found purpose realities?

DIVINE DESTINY DIRECTIONS FOR YOUR REASON

Now it's your turn to chart the course on your destiny roadmap as you take the information that you have learned to plot out your location. Go back and read about King Cyrus. Locate the path of his journey. Why do you think that God used him at a pivotal point in Israel's history? Determine when was the first time you knew that God had plans for your life. Now chart your course to where you are today. Calculate how far you have come.

GOING TO THE NEXT DIMENSION FOR YOUR REASON

As you go through the doorway to purpose you must gain a level of understanding that you were created with an intended purpose and that you cannot stop until you fulfill it! Use this Divine Destiny Declaration to help you press toward the fulfillment of your purpose.

DIVINE DESTINY DECLARATION

"I understand that God created me with a very unique purpose. My desire is to please God and fulfill the intended purpose for my life. Everything I need to fulfill my purpose and my calling is hidden treasure within me. I overcome every obstacle because I have the mind of Christ. I outthink all opposition by focusing upon my goal and positively moving toward my purpose. I let go of everything from my past and those things that do not serve me. I acknowledge that all things work together for my good because I love God and am called according to God's Purpose. I am keenly aware that the events of my present are designed to prepare me for my destined future. I take nothing for granted and recognize every serendipitous moment created to get my attention to keep me on the path of purpose. I also acknowledge that even when I experience painful experiences in life, I have an assurance that I am divinely positioned and therefore I persevere. I am fully alert, fully awake, and fully alive. My future is phenomenal because I have a wonderful purpose and I am determined to fulfill it. It is my time to fulfill my reason for being on the earth!"

WRITE YOUR OWN DESTINY DECLARATION FOR YOUR REASON

Personalize your Divine Destiny Declaration to accommodate your unique situation by writing your own below. Be sure to include the vision you receive from the destiny dreams that you see in your heart. As you nurture them by reviewing and saying them daily, you give your dreams the power to materialize. This is a living document so feel free to update it regularly.

DIVINE DESTINY DIARY:
USE THE SPACE BELOW TO WRITE YOUR THOUGHTS ABOUT YOUR DESTINY REASON

Many people have a wrong idea of what constitutes true happiness. It is not attained through self-gratification, but through fidelity to a worthy purpose. —Helen Keller

A good friend is a connection to life—a tie to the past, a road to the future, the key to sanity in a totally insane world. —Lois Wyse

Think about the connections and associations in your life. Think about whether or not those relationships add to or subtract from you. Are they assets or liabilities? Think about how well they encourage you on your journey toward your destiny. Now imagine how refreshing a mutually loving, caring, and cherishing relationship could be. Get ready to make covenant connections and walk in covenant agreement. Write your thoughts in your *Divine Destiny Diary* at the end of this chapter.

"New doors opened - Mercury"

8. The Secret Key
to Your Relationships
"Making Electric Connections"

I once knew a couple who I believe proved what it truly means to be in love. Even though neither of them was ashamed to show visible signs of affection, it was obvious there was something deeper that held them together. Their passion was so electric that it sparked a new dimension in their relationship which was realized in a crisis. One day the wife became so ill, even to the point of death. But

161

the husband did not take this lying down. He became the strength of his wife and began fighting the fight of *"her"* life searching out the best possible care, help and support. Needless to say, his hard work on her behalf paid off. After several surgeries, her road to recovery was celebrated each day as they are thankful each moment that they still have to share together. They live their lives much differently now. And they both agree to live each day as if it was their last.

When we think about connections, marriage, dating, and courtship relationships are probably the first that come to mind. Although these are not the only forms of connections that we can have, they are very important to the fulfillment of our destiny. But there are also friendships, business colleagues, and family connections that can make an indelible impression on the direction of our destiny. I want to make it very clear that who we interact with has a direct impact on the direction of our future and we should never take these connections lightly. I believe that as you read and incorporate the truths found in this material that you find yourself making better choices regarding your relationships.

THE FAMILY CONNECTION

When I think about a family that has connections, I think about the Kennedy family, in particular, John F. Kennedy. Born in Massachusetts in 1917, he became the thirty-fifth president of the United States and inherited a myriad of problems relating to foreign crisis. But it was his strong family relationships that gave him the tenacity to persevere even in the most difficult seasons of his life and leadership.

He was reared in an intensely competitive environment that fostered healthy sibling rivalry both physically and intellectually. This also was the foundation by which he acquired his multimillion-dollar fortune in business. After John F. Kennedy join the navy and barely escaping with his life, the political expectation of his father fell upon him when his brother died in the war. Although he planned to pursue a career in journalism or education he moved forward in the political aspirations of his father. He did not allow his intense physical pain from a back injury stop him despite three surgeries to alleviate it. He pressed past his hardships to a strenuous but successful life in politics. But it was the foundation of his family connection and upbringing that supported him throughout his political career and continues throughout the Kennedy family even until this day.

TAKEN FOR GRANTED

All too often we take for granted the people we choose to share our lives. But there are also times that we assume that our mate, or family members, will respect our potential and support our dreams and the direction that our lives are headed. This not always the case as we can see from the high divorce rates in America. Two people may be married but are moving in two distinctly different directions. Over 50% of all marriages end in divorce. I believe that there is an important reason why so many marriages are unsuccessful. One reason is that two people have consciously entered into an agreement or an arrangement but not necessarily a covenant. A covenant means that you are making a commitment until death. Many times people get married with a back-up plan "just in case" things don't work out. This is the first sign that there is no true covenant. If there is an alternative plan in mind, there is obviously no clear understanding of how deeply binding the covenant is that they are about to enter. There is also no real clarity about the expectations of the commitment. The focus is only upon the present needs. Too often these types of marriages are not prepared to go the long haul to navigate the circumstances that come with being human.

We should always focus on being the best mate possible and give our best effort rather than wondering whether or not we have found the right mate.

Another reason that many marriages fail is because the people involved lack the understanding about what is needed to maintain a healthy marriage and therefore lack necessary the skills. Recently, I witnessed a wedding on a beach in Mexico. The person officiating told the couple that marriage is not about marrying the right person but it is about being the right person. What a revelation. There is a story about a man who asked a gentleman friend why it was that he never married. The gentleman said it was because he never found the right person and one day he did. Surprised at the response the man asked the gentlemen why he didn't marry her. His response was because she was looking for the perfect man.

We should always focus on how we can be the best mate possible and give our best effort rather than wondering whether or not we have found the right mate. We increase the likelihood that we have given the relationship our best effort to see success because we are not always searching for a better option.

Yet another reason many marriages fail is because of the high percentage of dysfunctional relationship models for marriage. Because of the dearth of good relationship models, we need to be prepared to acquire the knowledge necessary for maintaining a healthy marriage from professional and relationship education sources. There is much to learn about being in a long term covenant relationship. We should never assume that we have all the answers.

Now more than ever before it is more necessary for a couple to receive pre-marital counseling to learn how to maintain a healthy marriage because there is a high probability that they have never witnessed one. In most cases, each individual person will base how they will relate in the marriage have to rely on personal experiences. If their personal experiences were bad, they have little information about how to maintain a good one. If their personal experiences were good, then they run the risk of trying to duplicate or relive someone else's experience. This is not possible because they possess a scenario of two distinctly different persons with a completely different set of circumstances. The bottom line is that too many couples enter the marriage covenant lacking a true understanding of what they are really getting into.

THE INGREDIENTS OF A TRUE COVENANT

Now let's turn our attention to the origin of a true covenant. True covenants are rooted in love. The Bible tells us that, "We know how much God loves us, and we have put our trust in him. God is love, and all who live in love live in God, and God lives in them."[50]. Jesus said, "For God so loved the world that he gave his

---

[50] 1 John 4:16 NLT

only Son, so that everyone who believes in him will not perish but have eternal life." [51]From these verses, we can see the origin of true covenant is love in connection with God.

Too often people fall in love but have no desire to be connected to the source of true love. Therefore they do not possess the real power to stay in love. In order to understand true love we must be clear that love is an activity. God loved the world and performed an act of love by giving God's son. This act of giving proved that the love God felt for humanity was tangible. By using this model we can also understand what unconditional love is in spite of what may others do. Jesus died for people who have no intention of following him. Jesus died for those people who discredit him. Jesus even died for those people who denounce him. That is unconditional love.

It is quite amazing the number of hours we spend receiving state mandated education in subjects that seem irrelevant to real life circumstances. This is why many students drop out of school because they sense that what they are learning is irrelevant not to mention the fact that they feel out of place. When given the opportunity, they do not return but instead, they settle for an education in the school of "hard knocks"; which has a powerful as well as an effective pedagogy. We can learn a great deal from our experiences. This is why on-the-job training is so effective. It has been said that education is expensive. Either way, it will be paid for. Unfortunately, there are those who never learn, and the price becomes too high, especially when it comes to learning how to have good relationships.

The sad truth is that there is little or no educational preparation regarding healthy relationships and students are left to teach themselves and often do a poor, if not brutal job of it. Hence, these poor models are carried over into adulthood. This tragic circumstance, as well as many others, adds to the reason why more than half of all marriages are unsuccessful. It is important to note that this rate is equally as high with those who call themselves Christians. But I believe that this failure is not due to a lack of faith, but rather a lack of skill.

---

[51] John 3:16

> *It is this spiritual essence that becomes the foundational bedrock that can sustain all human relationships: respect, responsibility, and cooperation.*

Many of us helplessly pattern ourselves after the dysfunctional relationship models that we see in society. Often the nuclear family units in which we were raised suffered from a high level of confusion because people just don't know what to do. Believing that these patterns are normal, many follow suit and only produce more of the same dysfunction, if not worse. So then what are we to do? Where can we turn? When we look to the educational systems of the world, the expectation is that relationships will just happen as children develop in the most crude and sometimes cruel environments. When we look to society, the pervasive self-centeredness paradigm seems to permeate every level.

Even more unfortunate is when we look to the church and find similar characteristics. Everywhere that we look our world teaches us how to look after, to, and out for ourselves. Therefore it is imperative that we look beyond the realm of the natural world into the supernatural world to find the essence of what truly makes for lasting relationships and how we should appropriately relate to one another.

When we look at how the Godhead is presented in Genesis, we see a unit that functions in complete unity. The Father, the Spirit, and the Son can be seen as a family that is interdependent. Each personality of the Godhead works in total harmony with the other and respect for one another's role. As we look at the Creator, we see the male fatherly persona. When we look at the Holy Spirit, we see the female persona. We see this more clearly when we look at this root word in the Hebrew, which happens to be a feminine noun. We can also deduce the feminine qualities to the Spirit when seen hovering in Genesis[52], and brooding like a mother over her children.[53] Then we see the Son, who can be seen as the offspring who symbolically proceeded from this perfect union.

---

[52]Genesis 1:2
[53]Deuteronomy 32:11

When we examine this Holy Family more closely, we see that there are identified roles and responsibilities with each being separately distinct yet interconnected and interrelated. We see a sense of holy cooperation as well as divine distinction. It is this spiritual essence that becomes the foundational bedrock that can sustain all human relationships: respect, responsibility, and cooperation.

I have spent countless hours in premarital counseling with couples who are about to be married. I believe that it is important to help people understand what it means to be truly committed as they prepare to enter the marriage covenant. It never ceases to amaze me how differently two partners view this new relationship. This is why it is vital for the couple to spend quality time helping the couple to communicate about what their commitment to each other will look like. This clarity is the critical foundation for them to spend the rest of their lives together. This will also avoid an enormous amount of confusion as they prepare for a lifetime of enjoyment together.

Many couples have a high level of naiveté when they come into my office for counseling before they get married. They seem to have no clue of the seriousness of the estate they are about to commit. Neither do they realize the magnitude of the sacrifices that they will need to make in order to sustain a healthy marriage relationship. But these relationship investments are well worth the effort for a lasting and fulfilling partnership. Some come to the table with two completely different ideas about what it means to be married. But the Bible asks a very important question, "How do two people walk together if they don't agree?"[54]

I typically take the couples on a minimum of a six month journey of discovery discussing various topics such as defining true love, examining their genealogical background, discussing roles and responsibilities, and healthy relationship models. And, most importantly we discuss the subject of faith, which I believe to be the bedrock of all relationships. These types of dialogs are necessary in light of the fact that our society has shifted so dramatically as to what it means to be married. Therefore it is critical that as many aspects of the relationship as possible be discussed to assure clarity and cohesion.

---

[54]Amos 3:3 NIV

Having been involved in a twenty-seven year marriage myself affords me the designation of an expert. Being now divorced raises my level of expertise, because I understand what makes a marriage work as well as what causes it to fail. It goes without saying that relationships are complex and should never be entered into unadvisedly. But more often than not, the marriage covenant is entered casually. People just assume that everything will work out. Unfortunately, more than assumption is needed to experience relationship success.

Hence, in today's society there is a lot to learn or relearn about what it means to love and be in love. An occasion that has become important as it relates to people practicing and showing their love for one another is Valentine's Day. Although this holiday is celebrated every year on February 14th by many people throughout the world, there are still those who don't know what to do on this day. In the West, it is a day on which lovers express their love for each other by sending Valentine's cards, flowers, or candy. Although this should not be the only day that lovers do this, I want to emphasize that this day is still extremely significant.

The importance of this day is proven when we take a look at the estimate from the U.S. Greeting Card Association that approximately one billion valentines are sent each year worldwide, making the day the second largest card-sending holiday of the year, after Christmas. It is also interesting to note that approximately 85 percent of all valentines are purchased by women. Conversely, the association estimates that men spend approximately twice as much as women in the United States of America.[55] This is a real indicator to the imbalance of the diverse expectations among couples.

These figures also show how important the day is to many people. Some people experiment and opt out of this day because of its obvious connection to commercialism. But I believe that this is a grave mistake. Many people make this decision because they do not realize that this day can be easily celebrated without falling into the trappings of commercialism. It is important to see this day as yet another opportunity to express love and therefore should not be overlooked.

---

[55] http://en.wikipedia.org/wiki/Valentine's_Day

This needs to be said because there are some who make the blunder of opting out and regret it for years to come. This lack of participation in one of the most important days to show love of the year undermines the very fabric of a lasting love relationship. Whether you realize it or not your actions are saying "today, I don't care that the whole world is celebrating love relationships, I'm not!" Take heed and think clearly before you decide to opt out of this day and disappoint the most important person in your life. When you are thoughtful enough about someone else's feelings, it is an act that you will never regret. After all, if in fact your reason is because you celebrate every day, then surely you don't want to miss Valentine's Day.

> *Be enthusiastic and take your time to make a thoughtful selection and you will reap the benefits for years to come.*

When attempting to show someone just how important they are to you, it is critical to develop a plan. Think about what suits your personalities and relationship. And remember that the simpler and more heartfelt the plan the easier it will be to pull it off. Allow your passion to motivate you. Whatever you decide to do, make sure it includes time and space for just the two of you to develop your love language and strengthen your level of intimacy and thereby strengthen the relationship.

This is where many couples miss the mark. They seem to forget that the same things that caused the relationship to grow and flourish in the first place are the same things that will sustain the marriage. Too many other distractions, like jobs, children, friends, and even other family members, are allowed to get in the way of this. There are few things in life are more important than special moments. After the chocolates are gone, you will still have great memories but only if you create them. Leaving things to chance could soon prove to be fatal to the relationship if you have not properly prepared for the outcomes that you would like to see. If there something special you want to tell your lover, then make the time to think it over. You want to be able to focus on your lover's response and not have to worry if you are saying the right thing. What do you really want to tell the most important person in your life? Say honestly what is in your heart and take the time to write down something really meaningful. Seeing it in writing seems makes it more real because you can look at it again and again. Besides how can your loved one let others know just how much they are loved by you if they don't have the tangible proof?

It was Maya Angelou who said that people will forget what you said and what you did, but they will never forget how you made them feel! When you want someone to know that you love them, you have to show them. Presenting your significant other with flowers is a sure way to get a positive response. And if you want to score extra points, know his or her favorite flower. It is interesting to note that men like flowers too! If you want to make his chest stick out at work, send him flowers, and all of his co-workers will turn green with envy. Please don't wai until the last minute to buy a card when the selections are slim. By doing this, you are unconsciously sending your mate a message that they are not important enough for you to take the time to show you care. Be enthusiastic and take your time to make a thoughtful selection and you will reap the benefits for years to come.

There is only one way to show somebody you love them and that is with loving actions. Assumptions just don't count! If you ever had to say, "I thought you knew how much I loved you," you are probably not putting enough effort and energy into the emotional bank account to sustain a rich, loving, lasting relationship. But this does not have to be left up to chance. Only when you make continuous deposits, can you make the continuous withdrawals, especially when you need them the most. Don't make the mistake of having an overdrawn emotional account. In the banking industry, if this happens too many times, it is considered abusive neglect and warrants closing the account. Similarly, if your emotional relationship status is consistently overdrawn, you will eventually face the closure of your relationship. Don't be surprised because just as the bank sends several warning notices before it takes action so will your mate, so please pay attention!

You can intentionally take action to assure a great relationship. You can do this by taking care of yourself physically. It wouldn't hurt to dress up for him or her every once in a while. I know this sounds really basic, but it would mean a lot for men to shave, get a haircut, and wear really nice clothes. It would be even better to wear a tie that she bought for you. Let her know that what she likes really matters. Likewise, it would be wonderful for women to dig out that dress he gave you last year that he likes to see you in, even

> *Destiny is about the decisions that we make to live our absolute best life. Those decisions include who will share our life.*

if you don't particularly like it. What is important is that you make the effort to show you care.

It is also important to know that single people also have the need to feel and give love on this day and should not be omitted. So the following information is for singles with love. Singles can enjoy Valentine's Day without worrying about the pressures that often come with this holiday. It is important not to define yourself by your relationship status. Don't make the mistake of making your relationship status your identity. And if you have experienced a recent loss give yourself permission to allow this to be a day of grieving. Do not feel like you have to pretend that it isn't difficult. But be assured that you get the support that you need. Also be sure not to allow this grieving time to last too long.

If you plan well in advance you will not find yourself in a place full of cooing couples on Valentine's. Rather get together with people who you know love you and the people who already have meaningful relationships with you. But if you're single and really don't want to be, think about how you can create the relationship you want. Focus on becoming the person your dream partner would like to fall in love with. It is when you live your life to the fullest that you will probably be the most attractive to a potential mate. But if you are single now and you like it, then affirm your choice. It is a proven fact that just because you do not choose to date or marry or marry right now, you can still have close, loving, and intimate relationships and lots and lots of fun.

RELATIONSHIP ASSESSMENTS

At an earlier part of my life, I thought that casual relationships were harmless. As I matured, I came to the understanding it is wise to be careful about the kind of people that you allow in your personal space. Everyone has the potential to benefit you but also to harm you. Doing your homework, in advance, helps you to making educated relationship choices before entering into a casual or lifetime commitment. We take tremendous risks when we cause ourselves to be vulnerable in relationships. But this is what true love is all about. What is most unfortunate is that the same people who bring us joy are the ones who can also cause us the greatest pain.

As I made an assessment of the people who I have allowed into my own life, I find that many of them have hurt me in some way. But this is to be expected as people are human and prone to make mistakes. But I found that it is what we do after someone hurts us that is the most critical. We must be willing to take responsibility for our own choices and behaviors and not blame others for them. We must also be equipped with the power to choose and choose again if necessary.

It is vitally important to recognize that the selection of a mate is critical for the successful fulfillment of our destiny. It is more critical, now more than ever, that we make relationship choices that advance the progress of our destiny. This is as important for casual acquaintances as it is for the more committed relationships. Regardless of the level of commitment, these relationships can impact our lives for better or for worst.

Destiny is about the decisions that we make to live our absolute best life. Those decisions include who will share our life. But the fact of the matter is that we need God's wisdom to help us find the right mate, business partner, and friendships to avoid wasting precious time and energy. This is critical to realizing the fullness of our destiny. We better understand this concept when experiencing difficult times in our relationships. We find ourselves running to God to fix our problems. But rarely do we take the time to seek the Lord to determine what we really need before we get into the relationship. Instead, we give God our laundry list of things we want and then we go after the first thing that tickles our fancy and expect God to run off like an errand boy. Is it any wonder why so many relationships are unsuccessful?

Sometimes the last thing we want to think about when looking for a mate is God! The thing on most women's mind is that they want to fall in love with a flesh and blood man, while most men want to be physically involved with a woman. In either case, neither gender may want to think about God while looking for a mate because this competes with all the other fantasy thoughts of what they will do with the person of their dreams.

A good exercise would be to ask God to show us His will of the mate that would truly and deeply bless our lives. This is sometimes risky, because it may contradict with what we think we want, so often we are afraid to ask. Then when we do ask and God shows us God's will we determine that he or she just "can't be the one" because they don't meet all of our required qualifications. We must remember that just because something looks good to us, it may not be what is best for us. What we really need is what is most important and that may not be as obvious. What we need, therefore, is a Supernatural Matchmaker to help us become more discerning to make good relationship choices.

In addition, we must resist the temptation to complain during the difficult times of singleness because it may be during these times that God desires to speak to us about improving ourselves and this is the perfect time to do it. This is a good opportunity to assess what is really important and what really matters in life. Times of questioning can be turned into times of wonder as we take a deeper look and evaluate our relationship with God. It is a great time to discover the best qualities of the One who would lay down his life for us, and we can use this as a guide to determine the best qualities of a true lover and friend.

I am of the belief that if we learn to fall in love with Jesus first, this will aid us in our preparation for experiencing a truly satisfying, remarkably healthy, loving union with that special person. I believe that our deep authentic encounter with Christ is our best example of what a good relationship can be like. If we have a healthy relationship with Christ we have a better idea of what it means to have a healthy relationship with our potential mate.

Conversely, if we have a haphazard relation-ship with Christ, this typically plays itself out though all of our relationships because just as we are unwilling to make a true commitment with Christ, we are unwilling to commit to anyone. Falling in love with Jesus first can have some marvelous benefits when it comes to seeking and preparing for a mate. Take a moment and consider the following ideas.

If you are not sure why you continue to attract a particular type of person, you may want to do some serious soul searching with regard to things in you that you may not be aware.

If you are in love with Jesus, you automatical-ly set a standard for yourself. You prioritize your spirituality. Many relationships break down because people are unequally yoked. Even if both partners are Christians, they may also be severely disproportioned in the strength of their faith. Sometimes when a weak believer connects with a marginal believer, their faith in Christ tends to wane almost immediately because they do not have the spiritual stamina to fight when tempted to lower their standards by their mate.

On the other hand, if one partner has a very strong faith and the other does not, there can be a struggle as contention builds around the level of spirituality. This can ultimately create personal insecurities or feelings of unworthiness. Either way, both of these scenarios must be handled sensitively if a fruitful relationship is to produce. When a partner appreciates and understands where you are in your faith, there is an intrinsic sense of respect for your unique person. There is a tension that comes with wanting those we love to be where we are spiritually while simultaneously allowing them the freedom to have their own personal journey of faith.

When you fall in love with Jesus, you have the glow. People in love carry a certain presence. They smile and beam outside what is resonating on the inside of their heart, and this is attractive! As a matter of fact, this glow is especially attractive to the opposite sex. I am constantly amazed whenever I walk down the street how many people smile at me. What I have come to realize is that they are smiling *back* at me. Because I feel a sense of love in my heart, I am in awe of His love every day. This love radiates outwardly and is received by others. This is also true when looking for a mate. People in love look lovable. They don't look desperate. Desperation is an invisible mate repellent. Neither gender appreciates it and most people run to avoid it.

However, when we are connected to Christ in a healthy way, we feel His love and we can express that love, freedom, and peace to those who we are in relationship. You have a sense of security and feel free to be yourself. We attract to us the type of people who we are. If you are lovable, peaceful, and are a person of integrity, that type of person will be attracted to you. If you are the exact opposite, get ready to meet your twin mate! If you are not sure why you continue to attract a particular type of person, you may want to do some serious soul searching with regard to things in you that you may not be aware.

When you fall in love with Jesus, you are empowered with the certainty that you are already in love. You feel a sense of confidence knowing that somebody cares, knows your name, and is concerned for your welfare. You inherently know that somebody has your back and will be there for you when you need them. This confidence attracts others because it says that you will not be a burden or a drag but an asset to the relationship.

One of the biggest problems in finding the right mate is when people carry so much baggage from relationship to relationship. It is not often that people take the time to heal and de-bag the issues they encountered from a previous relationship. There is a tendency to transfer old stuff on to a new promising relationship. People who do this subconsciously sabotage their own success because they always expect the worst based upon what has happened before. This is the biggest blunder we can make when preparing for a new mate. It is imperative to give yourself and your potential mate the benefit of a fresh start by bringing closure to all previous relationship fallouts in the healthiest possible way. Therefore, once you are free of the entanglement and even drama from a past relationship and have found happiness within yourself, you can give someone the privilege of truly sharing your joy!

Give yourself time to clear the air in your life so that you can see how God is directing you to recognize that special someone when they appear. Always seek out the unique things about this new person and resist the urge to make comparisons. Be as kind, gentle, and forgiving of yourself as you need others to be. Never rush into a relationship to get over a bad one. If you have ever found yourself asking, "Why does this keep happening to me?" it is probably a good time to stop and reflect about how your own decisions and actions help to create the cycle of these undesired outcomes. Give yourself time to analyze the choices you made and why you made them so you can prevent this cycle from happening again.

If we take responsibility for our choices, then we can make the adjustments necessary to ensure better outcomes. For example, if you find that relationships move too quickly and sizzle out, it may be as a result of your feelings of insecurity. You may push things forward too quickly out of fear of losing the relationship. If you know you do this repeatedly, intentionally slow the next relationship down. Discipline yourself to not continue repeating the same vicious cycles. Make the decision to not call or visit so much early in the relationship. Pace yourself so that you can better identify self-sabotaging behaviors and perhaps enjoy a more sustainable relationship.

Reflect on the aspects of the relationship that you really like or dislike and determine not to settle. Settling is a setup for failure later on. If things are not the way you would like them to be now, they will not be any better a week, a month or a year from now. Why enter into a relationship that you already know is not going anywhere. The responsibility and choice is yours. You are not as helpless as you may want to believe. You can change the outcome with your choices and decisions. Remember, there is no perfect relationship, but there are many good ones.

Never enter into a relationship believing that if the person is not all you want them to be that you can eventually change them. You will never be able to change anyone but yourself. It is what you effectively model that may inspire someone else to change but if you cannot model it then you should not expect the same behavior from someone else. Sometimes we expect more from others than we are actually willing to do ourselves. This is not only unfair but also unrealistic. And never allow anyone to try to change you. You are wonderfully made by God. And the same goes for the other person. You should always lovingly accept people as they are. If necessary, make gentle suggestions about loving ways for improvement. You should also decide what it is that you are willing to deal with in a relationship because no one is perfect and everyone will come with their own set of personal issues.

Finally, falling in love with Jesus should be the most satisfying experience of your life because Jesus is the perfect example of the perfect mate—always there, always understanding, always forgiving. He would give his life for you. What more could you ask for? With all that Christ has to offer, a potentially bad mate doesn't stand a chance!

Learning to fall in love with Jesus, while preparing for your destiny and a relationship, is an excellent approach to aid you in becoming a better candidate for a sincerely loving, spiritually confident, and genuinely authentic individual. Because you are in relationship with Christ, you should already feel a sense of care, concern, and confidence. Before you enter into another relationship, this sense of wholeness should be a common thread throughout your life whether you are single or married.

When you set a standard, feel loved, and are experiencing a sense of spiritual satisfaction, your life becomes rich and full and complete. When you are delighted in the Lord, God give you the desires of our heart. You feel happy in life regardless of your marital status. If you can fall in love with Jesus in this way, when someone comes to share your life, it is an absolute bonus!

MY DIFFICULT DISCONNECT

After recently suffering the loss of a marriage relationship in my life, I know full well what it means to fall in love with Jesus. I was so broken that it was difficult for me to put the pieces of my life back together. It was also hard for me to understand why my former husband, who I had spent half of my life with, no longer desired to keep our marriage covenant. We spent an enormous amount of time with him and he completed my world. I was determined to make it work and to help him see that what he was doing was wrong but after two years of watching myself self-esteem, self-value and self-worth deteriorate, I decided to leave with my dignity. But this had enormous effects upon my vision for the future. I was devastated and I could not see how God was going to cause me to fulfill my destiny dream. The truth of the matter was that I at the lowest point of my life.

I now had to make serious adjustments to my lifestyle but this gave me the space that I needed to determine what was really important to me. I had to surrender to the reality of the loss but this became the launching pad for the much needed changes in my life that I was not aware I needed. In particular I had to rethink the way I selected those with whom I formed close relationships. I had to take responsibility and recognize the poor choices that I had made. I needed to learn new relationship skills. I realized that I also needed to rethink the priorities in my life.

I had to update my thinking, form new habits, and develop a new personal mission statement. I determined that I would be better and not bitter. I decided to reinvent myself by seeking to be my personal best, do good works, and glorify God the Father. The result is that my life is richer and more satisfying because I allowed God to fill every painful void in my life and use my trials to transform me into a vessel that would make a unique difference in the world. I have a stronger personal foundation and I am the happiest that I have ever been in my entire life.

This newfound reality was the turning point in my life because the truth of the matter was that the problem had started many years earlier. I could not understand why things were so confusing and problematic. Although I felt I was a good housewife, a great housekeeper, and took excellent care of my children, there were enormous demands placed upon me to perform like others in the generations that preceded me. I was facing an inordinate amount of familial opposition because it was felt that I was not performing up to par and meeting traditional expectations. I had made a decision to spend ten years at home with my children so that I could help to teach and shape their young lives. Still, this did not seem like it was enough. I always seemed to be viewed as inadequate, which put an unusual amount of stress on me and my marriage. I was distraught and confused. To be truthful, I was desperate. My modus operandi of "try harder" did not work, and I became overwhelmed with exhaustion, and filled with distress.

Around that time I was invited to a prayer meeting where a well-known prophetess was ministering. As she preached, I was so distracted the difficulties of my own life that I could not focus on her message. Nevertheless, there was a very important reason why I was there. I became alert when she asked if anyone needed prayer. A line quickly began to form. Because this was a new experience for me, I found my way to the back of the line. As she began to pray for people, it was as if she had turned on a television and begun to see the story of their lives. She began to tell them what she saw and what God was saying about it. People were amazed, weeping, and overwhelmed with gratitude.

As I started to get closer to the front of the line, I began thinking about my situation and all of the things I wanted God to speak to me about regarding my relationship and family dilemmas. Every issue and circumstance began to cloud my mind. Suddenly I realized that there was no way I was going to be able to tell her everything that I needed prayer about so I surrendered to the moment and whispered to God, "Please tell me whatever it is I need to hear right now, I am hurting and I need answers."

The minute I reached the prophetess, she began to speak, "In the Holy of Holies is the Ark of the Covenant, and in the Ark of the Covenant is Aaron's rod." The place she described was the place where Aaron's rod had budded as a symbol that God had chosen him for service. She was making a connection to a biblical story but at the time these words were unfamiliar to me. At that moment, I felt that what she was saying was irrelevant to my life, but I would soon find out how her words, as she spoke them from God, would radically change the course of my destiny. As a result of allowing her to speak a prophetic word into my life regarding my future, I began to see how God desired to have first place in my life over and above any relationships that I was involved. I then realized that I had to reprioritize my life because I was putting the whims of people over the will of God.

Even though I had felt rejected in my circumstance, from that point on I felt that God had received me and had chosen me. This experience from God became the anchor of hope for my future and caused me to forge a deeper connection with God. Now, because I have a deep relationship with Christ, I have learned not to allow others define me or set the agenda for my life—only God gets the privilege of doing that.

MY DESTINY DEVELOPMENT

As my whole world began to fall apart, I began to feel like my life lost all sense of direction. Although I was enrolled in a great doctoral program, because of the difficulties that I was experiencing relationally, life began to lose its meaning and my future looked bleak. This is when I began to question as to whether I had a destiny and purpose in life.

Thankfully I found the answer when I was watching one of my favorite Bible teachers on television, Dr. Mark Chironna. His words during that time touched my heart and made me feel like there was hope. His message of destiny spoke to my spirit and I knew that they were not only timely but prophetic. He announced that he was holding a conference on the subject of destiny development and I just knew deep in my heart that this was my only hope to gain a sense of direction for my life. I am not sure how I found the money to get there but I am not sure where my life would be if I had not attended.

The truths that he discussed during those times would transform my life forever. It was then that I was assured that I did indeed have a destiny and that it was firmly fixed in the mind of God. This was when I would formally open up my destiny dialog with God. Dr. Mark, who then became my life coach, began to help me chart the course of my destiny. I am grateful to have been personally mentored by him. He was there when I desperately needed direction for my life. He helped to guide me safely in the direction of my destiny with his wisdom and fatherly love. This was when my life would begin to realign and change for the better.

From all of what I have been through relationally, I have learned is that it is impossible to make someone else happy. People have to decide what they need to do to be happy and to share their happiness with someone else. This is why it is important to never expect anyone else to make you happy. You have enough great qualities to be happy within yourself to last you a lifetime, you just need to access them. Although I was once terrified of being alone, I have learned to become happy within myself and to enjoy my own company. I love to spend quality time alone now, especially during my personal times of devotion and prayer. As God gives me the desires of my heart to have loving, lasting covenant relationships, I am satisfied, happy, and content with the state that I am in.

Because I have already set a standard of love for myself, I don't feel as though I need someone to complete me. I am already in an authentic relationship with Christ and I have the "glow" of someone who feels loved. And because I am already in a relationship, I am not searching for what I already possess. I have everything I need in my life to feel complete. Anything else that comes along is an absolute bonus.

As destiny would have it, my former spouse became ill and partially incapacitated. Because I had done my emotional homework when God had prompted me to resolved my issues, I was able to become his primary care giver until the time of his passing. I decided to become better instead of bitter and see him as a child of God who was capable of making mistakes. I made a decision to harbor no ill will against him and to assure that his soul was ready to be with the Lord. I found that when I forgave him, I was liberated from the debilitating emotions that come with hatred. I had come to the realization that any negative emotion toward him would only truly hurt me, inhibit my present dealings and cloud my future destiny. Today, I can honestly say that I am a free woman in every sense of the word.

Maybe you have found or one day will find someone who is willing to fight for you as well as with you. What is most important is that you gain a sense of wholeness within yourself before seeking to be in a relationship with someone else. When two people are whole emotionally, mentally and physically, then they have a better chance at having a wonderfully wholesome relationship. This can happen for you to as you allow your destiny to drive you towards those who will share in your journey of a lifetime.

DECODE
YOUR DESTINY
RELATIONSHIPS

Developing Your New Divine Mental Diet is the key to fulfilling your destiny. Your life will be literally transformed as you begin to get a better understanding about where you are right now. Then you can determine the direction that you need to take.

THINK ON THESE THINGS – Open your destiny dialog by honestly answering the following questions about your relationships. It has been said that you are only as good as the company you keep. Think honestly about your current relationships and answer the following questions. You may want to have this portion of your destiny dialog with a significant other or close friend:

1. How healthy would you say your relationships are right now?

2. Do you feel nurtured and safe enough to share your true self with the persons with whom you are in relationship now?

3. What is the difference between how you feel when people support you and when they do not?

4. If you are in relationship with people that you do not feel safe around, why do you think that is?

5. What are the types of people that you need to add to or remove from your life?

6. Are the people that you find yourself connected doing the things or supporting the things that you want to do? How can you surround yourself with genuinely caring people to support the vision and mission for your life?

7. How are the people with whom you associate encouraging you to fulfill your destiny dreams?

DIVINE DESTINY DIRECTIONS FOR YOUR RELATIONSHIPS

Now it's your turn to chart the course on your destiny roadmap as you take the information that you have learned to plot out your location. Look at the life of Jesus. In what ways can you identify with his destiny journey with his companions, the disciples? In what ways can't you identify? Now look at the life of your favorite couple. What things about their relationship that you admire? What are some things that you don't like? What are things that you can learn from them? Can you imagine yourself traveling their path? What similarities can you see ahead for your journey toward destiny and the connections that you will make?

GOING TO THE NEXT DIMENSION FOR YOUR RELATIONSHIPS

You must be completely whole and satisfied within yourself before trying to connect with another person. You can never get these things from someone else. In order to maintain a healthy, happy relationship with someone, you must possess the same qualities. Use this Divine Destiny Declaration to affirm your desire to have great relationships that advance your divine destiny.

DIVINE DESTINY DECLARATION

"I attract honest, loving loyal relationships. I thank God for the covenant connections in my life and I carefully protect and preserve them. I know that God has great plans for my life. I also know that those plans include mutually beneficial covenant relationships whether it is with a mate or friendships. I know that God wants to give me the desires of my heart as I delight myself in the Lord. As I prioritize God's kingdom, I will love, honor, cherish, and respect my mate and reserve my worship only for the Most High God. I will enjoy the company of my covenant partner and spend quality time in prayer separately and together. Until the time comes for God to send my mate to me, I will spend my time being my personal best, doing good works, and glorifying God the Father. I thank God for my season of preparation to discover what really matters in life. Even if I choose to be single, I already feel satisfied, complete and loved. I position myself for healthy friendships. It's my time for great relationships!"

WRITE YOUR OWN DESTINY DECLARATION FOR RELATIONSHIPS

Personalize your Divine Destiny Declaration to accommodate your unique situation by writing your own below. Be sure to include the vision you receive from the destiny dreams that you see in your heart. As you nurture them by reviewing and saying them daily, you give your dreams the power to materialize. This is a living document so feel free to update it regularly.

DIVINE DESTINY DIARY:
USE THE SPACE BELOW TO WRITE YOUR THOUGHTS ABOUT YOUR DESTINY RELATIONSHIPS

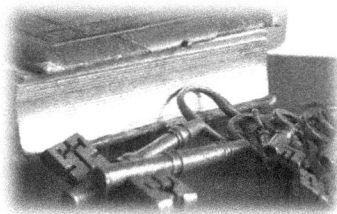

When we get too caught up in the busyness of the world, we lose connection with one another—and ourselves. —Jack Kornfield

PART III
REGENERATION

The best thing about the future is that it only comes one day at a time.
—Abraham Lincoln

Think about your distant future. Now, think about some of the things you would like to see happen in your life in the near future. What do you see? Now determine which conditions are needed to manifest your future success and best life ever! Write your thoughts in your *Divine Destiny Diary* at the end of this chapter.

"Accelerating the Future - Infiniti"

9. The Secret Key
to Your Results
"The Vehicle of the Future"

Many times we cannot successfully move toward our future and get the results that we are looking for because we get stuck in the past. For the most part, when our lives have been problematic and we experience a series or cycles of bad circumstances, we make a determination that this is the way things will always be. We give up the fight to have a better future and surrender to our current conditions.

191

Life becomes pitiful when we experience one setback after another. Eventually our outlook becomes pessimistic, and we wonder if there will ever be anything else of which to look forward. It has been said, "There is very little difference in people. But that little difference makes a big difference. The little difference is attitude. The big difference is whether it's positive or negative."[56]

In order to get to the promise of our future we must learn to adjust our attitude and experienced and intentionally overcome the difficulties of our past. This is accomplished as we redirect our thinking in a way that does not allow our past to contaminate our present. We must be able to extrapolate the messages from the mess that we have been through and discard anything that does not serve us to get to our future. This is difficult to do because we have a memory that continues to play scenes from the past, giving the illusion of an eternal drama that has no end.

IMPACTING THE FUTURE WITH RESULTS

If there was ever an international figure who has had a major impact on the world it is Albert Einstein. Born in Germany in 1879 to a father who was a salesman as well as an engineer, his father founded a company that manufactured electric equipment that eventually failed. Although they were non-observant Jews, Albert attended a Catholic elementary school when he was five years old only until he was ten. But he was introduced to information in science, math and philosophy by a poor Jewish medical student from Poland, who eventually guided Einstein in his educational interests. Even though he had a speech impediment, he became a top student. He had a talent for math and enjoyed building mechanical devices. After moving to Italy, in his attempt to study electrical engineering, his brilliance clashed with the educational authorities there regarding strict rote learning. He eventually wrote his first scientific work regarding magnetic fields.

He went on to study in Switzerland and Zurich and graduated secondary school at the age of seventeen enrolled in the math and physics program at the Polytechnic where he would eventually graduate but not before meeting the love of his life. After graduation, he was frustrated because he could not find a job for

---

[56] Napoleon Hill in *Think and Grow Rich*

almost two years but with his father's help got a job at the Federal Office for Intellectual Property as an assistant examiner for the patent office. His job was to evaluate electromagnetic devices. Much of his work led him to radical conclusions about the nature of light and the connection between space and time as well as other findings that would bring him the notice of the academic world. He would soon become recognized as a leading scientist and was appointed lecturer, then later a professor. His theory of relativity would grant him international acclaim and he was awarded the Nobel Peace Prize in Physics.

In 1955 he experienced internal bleeding cause by an abdominal rupture which had been previously reinforced by surgery, he was preparing for a television appearance commemorating the State of Israel's seventh anniversary. He took a copy of his speech with him to the hospital. He did not live to complete it. Einstein refused surgery, saying: "I want to go when I want. It is tasteless to prolong life artificially. I have done my share, it is time to go. I will do it elegantly." Einstein died in Princeton Hospital at the age of seventy-six. He continued to work until the end. Einstein was cremated. His ashes were scattered around the grounds of the Institute for Advanced Study, Princeton, New Jersey but during the autopsy Einstein's brain was removed for preservation. This was without the permission of his family. But the neuroscience department hoped that they would be able to discover what made Einstein so intelligent. What a powerful story from the past that speaks to us about how we should prepare in our present for what we want to see in our future. This way we can die without regrets and a sense of fulfillment that we have made our mark on the world.

DON'T GET STUCK IN YOUR PAST

There is a story in the Bible about a lame man sitting by a beautiful door.[57] The man could not go through the door because he was physically paralyzed. The man's friends laid him by the gate daily so that he can beg for alms. For some, this scenario could look a lot like our past: we lived a dull lame life that begged for attention. The door represents the opportunity to enter as rich and beautiful future, but we are unable to go through it. But this story can also look a lot like

---

[57] Acts 3:1-10 NKJV

our present. We should never put ourselves in a position to depend on others to help us become better beggars. We should be driving our own destiny. But how often do our friends "carry us" as they listen faithfully as we rehearse the same lame problems over and over? They gladly oblige us as we beg them to listen as we focus upon our pitiful past. We may be unaware that this practice is exactly what keeps us stuck in our condition. When we rehearse our past, it zaps our strength and makes us feel lame. We can get a sense of feeling stuck and filled with hopelessness; we see no other options but a life sentence of begging. Alone and without assistance, you can feel as if there is no real way out. This book is a vehicle designed to help accelerate you into your destiny. As you complete the end of the chapter exercises will be able to move forward with a sense of clarity about your life. Your future will become amazingly clearer and brighter.

> *In order for us to live successful lives, we should be able to think clearly about our future free from the stresses of worrying about the past.*

When Peter and John showed up, the man expected the usual handout. But what he received instead was a hand up! They took him by the right hand, which was a symbol of power, and raised not only his body but also his expectations for himself. He was without strength in his ankles, which represented the shaky foundation of his life. At the moment these men saw more for him than he could see for himself, his foundation was strengthened, and he proceeded to walk out of his past, leap past his present, and run into a new future!

THE PAST OF THE PRESENT AND OUR FUTURE

When we explore the idea of the past, present, and future, you should also recognize the connection between the three components of you—your body, soul, and spirit which has a direct impact on your destiny. It might interest you to know that just as your mind holds your memory; your body also has a memory. This is easily recognized after we have experienced physical trauma. In a moment when things get uncomfortable mentally or emotionally, our mind thinks that it is back at the time when it experienced the trauma and triggers our body to physically constrict muscles, organs, and tissues. This causes a substantial amount of pain.

I know this because once I had a terrible fall and hurt my back. For years, my back muscles would involuntarily constrict themselves whenever I got cold or uncomfortable. This would cause me a great deal of pain throughout my entire body. My body contracted itself because it remembered the trauma of the original fall and did not know how to stop attempting to protect itself. I sought medical treatment, but the condition persisted for years. I eventually found a specialist who treated the pain in a very unique way. He introduced a needle into the pockets of pain and broke up circuits while injecting a painkiller. The treatment was successful, and the pain never returned. Miraculously, I was also blessed to have a nurse in the same doctor's office that prayed for me and assured me of the success of my treatments and my eventual healing. This in itself made the experience very beneficial and effective.

Science shows us that negative stress induces toxins that ultimately advance disease in our bodies.[58] It has also been scientifically proven in a study on spirituality and children that our mental health has a direct impact on our physical well-being.[59] That is why it is important that we learn to resolve negative thoughts and memories as quickly as possible. We must learn how to break the vicious cycles that keep us in an unhealthy emotional state. In order for us to live successful lives, we should be able to think clearly about our future free from the stresses of worrying about the past. When we understand that our attitude determines our altitude, we realize that we must remain positive about our present and reduce the negative feelings of anxiety over what has already happened in the past. Because we cannot change the past, it would be in our best interest to imagine the resolution of such matters and the promise of a new day, and move on.

Whether we realize it or not, we have the power to change the outcomes in our lives. Our thoughts are like seeds that when planted grow into the fruits of

---

[58] http://www.sciencedaily.com/releases/2007/10/071009164122.htm
[59] http://www.newswise.com/articles/view/549952

our lives. We are what we think about.[60] If we have a great life, it is mostly due to a great thought life. On the contrary, if we have a great deal of negativity around us, it is in all probability due to the fact that we sowed seed thoughts of negativity in a past season, and now we are reaping a negative harvest. Most times it is the results of our thoughts and words. We should take precautionary measures and determine what prevents a good harvest and address the source of the problem. Then, we can determine to plant better seed thoughts in the future and anticipate better crop. When we learn from the mistakes of our past and know what to do to reap a better harvest in the future, then we must embrace the understanding of the need for improvement in every area of our lives. If we are stuck in the past, then we are blinded to the reality of the potential for change in our future.

Just as your body reacts to trauma, your soul is also deeply impacted by it. Your soul comprises your mind, will, and emotions. When your mind contains bad memories, your will reacts to fear of potential reoccurrence of past trauma and becomes suspect of everything – even the good things. Then, your emotions are recaptured from previous experiences and yearn to express themselves again by taking you back to feeling the moment of your trauma. This restrictive pattern inhibits growth and future progress and can even develop into paranoia.

I have learned how deeply the memory of my soul operates when I fall into challenging circumstances. If I am not careful, I will find myself involuntarily falling back into typically self-protective patterns in my soul. But these patterns keep me from fully realizing the blessing of living in the moment. As I take a deeper look at those self-defeating behaviors and become more conscious of my own attitude, I become more determined to think fresh thoughts and not to allow my past to contaminate my present or ruin my future.

When you train yourself to be more aware of these negative thought patterns, then you can begin to maintain high levels of promise in any given situation. As you and pay close attention to your thoughts and behaviors, you can intentionally arrest the forces that try to sabotage your future. Make the destiny decision to refuse to allow your current limited circumstances to determine the outcomes of your future. With God, the sky is always the limit. I have heard Dr. Cindy

---

[60] Proverbs 23:7

Trimm say, "You are one decision away from living the life of your dreams."[61] Make a destiny decision to think your way into a better future – today.

PORTALS OF THE PRESENT

The Bible says that to everything there is a season[62]. Many times we find ourselves dissatisfied with our body, disenchanted in our soul, and disoriented in our spirit. When we feel this way, we must make a qualified decision to acknowledge that our current situation is not permanent but only a temporary state. Although many of our circumstances may be beyond our control, we are not as powerless as we would like to believe. We do have the ability to positively influence the outcome of our lives. But it's all a matter of how we approach it that will ultimately affect how we navigate through the dimension of our future.

I have discovered that I can decide how depressed, despondent, and diseased that I will be. Even though I have been depressed, I became conscious of the fact that I had the choice of just how depressed I was going to be. I knew exactly the moment that I could give myself over to my emotions and when my mind would begin its downward spiral. One day I made a decision to take control and stop being depressed. Afterward my decision, I did everything in my power to proactively avoid this deadly emotion. Although I was not on any medication, I decided that I had enough. I would read a great book or listen to uplifting music. I would go around encouraging people. I would do anything that I could to reverse these negative feelings – and it worked. Soon, I was out of the emotional danger zone and back into positively safe waters. I work hard every day to maintain my positive thoughts because I am determined to see positive outcomes in my life.

---

[61] http://www.cindytrimm.com/
[62] Ecclesiastes 3:1

There are times when I have been sick and I made decisions that would ultimately affect how sick I was going to get. I quickly move into action to take advantage of every possible remedy available to me. This is especially true when I feel the symptoms of a cold coming on. I am intentional at the first sign to take action immediately. I keep natural remedies handy just for moments like this and I am typically one hundred percent successful in warding off the cold. In addition, I maintain my mind in a state of prayer and wholeness which is also very effective. Even science has proven that the power of prayer can have on illness and be effective in linking the well-being of the body and the spirit.[63] In other words, I think myself well! To support my thoughts, I eat well and incorporate a good routine of exercise in my life.

> *You are fearfully and wonderfully made by God. You have the right to an absolutely wonderful life. Determine to start that life today.*

When we are consciously in the portal of the present, then we can make a determination to carefully consider where we are in life, and take control of the direction of our thoughts and ultimately our lives. It is when we do not live in the present; that we are not consciously in control. After we have experienced trauma, we tend to "zone out". We subconsciously cannot deal with what is happening in our minds. When we find ourselves in a daze, we think that this state is harmless and even enjoyable because it gives our mind rest from painful activity. But when we are fully conscious of what is going on around us and in us, we can then be in a better position to determine where our lives are going. We must take full responsibility and intentionally be sober, present and alert at all times.

When we honestly assess the status of our lives and determine how many of our own choices led us to where we are, we can use the same decision-making power and choose to change. Once you do this, you are empowered and no longer fall victim to your circumstances or the actions of others. Blaming others is a waste of time and robs us of too much precious time and energy. In many cases,

---

[63] http://lkm.fri.uni-lj.si/xaigor/slo/znanclanki/prayer.htm

you made a decision to allow their action to affect your life and you can make another powerful decision to begin the process to disallow them.

Next, we need to make a determination that we are going to define our purpose for the future. We must not focus on the mistakes of the past, or they will deter us. But please understand that we will be in for the fight of our lives if we want to live a more fulfilled life. Fulfilling one's destiny takes work but you must remember that failure is not an option. You are fearfully and wonderfully made by God. You have the right to an absolutely wonderful life. Determine to start that life today. Begin to visualize what that better life will look like. See your future fulfilled. Begin to sense what that better life will feel like. Taste it! Smell it! Hear it!

You will also need to develop an action plan and strategies that bring your life into alignment with your vision. Develop disciplines that will sustain you in the difficult times in life even when it does not look like your future will manifest as planned. Disciplines such as consistent prayer, inspirational reading, good diet and exercise are great places to start if you are determined to live a better quality of life. It is your disciplines that will help you to hold on and persevere in the difficult times. When you are disciplined, you are stable. You are not swayed by every circumstance that confronts your life. Refuse to bend in the direction of failure because you have something so much better to do—like succeed.

Ways that you can begin to strengthen yourself is to accentuate your proficiencies and answer the questions: "What am I really good at?" and "What are some of the things that I have done right in my life?" Start a list of your best qualifications and add to it daily. By accentuating the positives in your life, your life moves more in that direction. Likewise, when you focus on the negatives, your life moves in that direction as well. You may need to shift your lifestyle and polish your image in order to project what you truly want to manifest. This will more likely attract what you really want to see in your life. In case you haven't noticed, your discouragement actually repels positive outcomes while your encouragement attracts them. Try it and you will see tremendous results.

PREPARING FOR THE FUTURE

I know a lot about preparing for the future. In 1998, shortly after developing and instituting the mission of outreach for our ministry, I received a call from the Eastern Baptist Theological Seminary, the local seminary from which I graduated. I was invited to accept a professorship to teach about community-focused ministry and I marveled at the invitation. I was honored that I was considered for the position. After aligning myself with vision I saw for our church in serving our community, I was now considered the expert! I learned that God will endorse your work of faithfulness because God sees your heart.

I developed and taught a course to help church leaders understand the need to connect their ministries to the community as a way to fulfill the Great Commission of the Church. To date I have taught this course for over ten years and have inspired hundreds of leaders to take their church ministry beyond its walls. This opportunity has opened many other doors for professional teaching, preaching, and transformational speaking opportunities. But it was my preparation that opened up the possibilities for my future. Had I not prepared myself mentally and academically, this door for my future would not have been an option for me. I have discovered that you can only go as far as you know and that you can only give what you truly have. For example, it is highly unlikely that a professional educational institution would hire someone to lecture in its highest level programming without a degree. But they would more likely seek out the most qualified candidate. This is true of any institution who wants to effectively advance its mission. If you have in mind a place where you want to be, then prepare yourself for it. Always remember that you must prepare if you want to fulfill your destiny dream.

When we recognize that one destiny door often leads to another, we will be more careful about how we prepare when we approach them. Too often opportunities come that we are sorely unprepared for. The best strategy is to always be ready. Personal improvement and advancements help turn dreams into reality. Always plan to be your personal best and make every effort to practice positivity regardless of the circumstance. Always strive to improve your performance without anyone prompting you or telling you to do so. Be self-motivated and your own self-starter.

Be highly accountable to yourself. This all-important disposition sets you up for a greater future as well as keeps a positive focus on you.

REALIGNMENT TO THE FUTURE

The Bible declares, "Now faith is the substance of things hoped for, the evidence of things not seen." [64] That which is hoped for is future tense. If your future seems uncertain, you will feel a sense of powerless and hopelessness. One strategy is to change the way you look at your future and give it substance. The apostle Paul wrote a powerful passage that can help to undergird your thinking for a better future: "And now, dear brothers and sisters, let me say one more thing as I close this letter. Fix your thoughts on what is true and honorable and right. Think about things that are pure and lovely and admirable. Think about things that are excellent and worthy of praise." [65] This is a powerful strategy by which to adjust our thinking. There is obviously no room here for focusing on your problems if your mind is filled with thoughts of good things.

God has good outcomes in mind for you! Knowing this should make you confident with the assurance that no matter what you may be going through right now; God has great plans for your life

God says, "For I know the thoughts that I think toward you, says the Lord, thoughts of peace and not evil, to give you a future and a hope."[66] Another translation says, "...to bring you to an expected end."[67] I like that. God expects you to have a great future and a good ending. But more importantly, this is what God thinks for you! God wants good things for you! God has good outcomes in mind for you! Knowing this should make you confident with the assurance that no matter what you may be going through right

---

[64] Hebrews 11:1 KJV
[65] Philippians 4:8 NLT
[66] Jeremiah 29:11 NKJV
[67] Jeremiah 29:11 KJV,

now; God has great plans for your life so you may as well align yourself and seek to fulfill them.

Because there are so many forces that attempt to keep you from realizing these promises, you must aggressively lay hold to these promises if they are to materialize. Proverbs says, "In the same way, wisdom is sweet to your soul. If you find it, you will have a bright future, and your hopes will not be cut short."[68] Wisdom knows what to do and when to do it. If you are going to apply wisdom, do so with hope and expectation to see positive results. That is the whole point of having wisdom and using it. Believe God for a great future and anticipate that it will manifest and align with God's perfect will for your life.

This anticipation will strengthen your spirit because the spirit is not bound to the past or present but is tied to the eternal. Your spirit yearns to see the manifestation of God's promises. The Spirit most always seeks to restore, realign, and renew all things to the will of God. Just because you may not see certain promises fulfilled in your life right now, know that the spirit realm is limitless. These promises can and will be released on your behalf. They are there for the taking. But you have to be willing to transformed and move from where you are and be prepared for where you are going.

A BEAUTIFUL DOOR

The mere fact that you are reading this book is a sign that this is the season for your transformation. You stand at a beautiful door of opportunity. It is filled with richness and power. This book is like an extended hand to raise your expectation for your future so that you can begin to leap in the fulfillment of your divine future. In order to go through the dimension of your future you need a transformational experience similar to that which the lame man received. Although his transformation initiated outside of himself, it was when he connected with the vision of the apostles that his miracle manifested.

Like the lame man who leaped out of his past to revive his life, you too can receive a revival into your life. His life was restored and it changed the future of

---

[68] Proverbs 24:14 NLT

everyone around him. His present became the launching pad for something great. His miracle started an entire movement of faith. But his past had to first be put to rest if he was going to realize the possibility of his new future.

THE SECRETS TO YOUR FUTURE

Jesus told a story that is a good illustration of how to see an abundant harvest for our future. Jesus knew that the people lived in an agricultural society and so he told them the stories packed with prophetic messages, in the context which they could relate. So he told them story is about how seeds germinate differently in different soil conditions.[69] To aid him in his storytelling, Jesus used a parable. A parable is a short allegorical story designed to teach a truth, religious principle, or moral lesson.

Jesus masterfully created a fictitious narrative that described the nature of people and the things of God. He particularly used nature in conjunction with God's kingdom. In other words, he used an earthly story to convey a heavenly message. After he told the story, the first question that is presented to Jesus does not relate to the story at all but his methodology using parables. The disciples wondered, "What's up with the deep stories, Jesus?" His response was probably more than they anticipated.

He responded to them with, "to you it is given the understanding of these mysteries, but to *them* it is not given (emphasis added)." [70] He explained to them that he speaks in allegory because they are already given the ability to know the mystery of the stories but he makes it clear that this privilege of understanding the mysteries of the Kingdom of Heaven is not given to everyone. There is a similar connection to the people who really understand the mystery about what God is preparing them to do in their future because everyone is just not going to get it.

But this exclusion of people should prompt us to wonder and ask a second question, "Who is exactly is *them?*" We immediately must also determine that we do not want to be like *them* because we want to be completely informed about our

---

[69] Matthew 13:1-9 KJV
[70] Matthew 13:1-9 KJV

future and about how to live in the Kingdom of God. We must also determine that whatever it is that *they* are doing, we don't want to do it! Why? Because Jesus tells us that *they* are not given the same privileges. In order for us to fulfill our destiny and prepare for our future, we need to have an understanding of the mysteries and unlock the secrets that bring meaning to our lives. Based upon Jesus powerful story, we already have access to this understanding.

Jesus told this story in ancient times but it is equally important for us today. One reason is because there are people who love to hear a good sermon or message but would rather not exert the energy it takes to extract and use the wisdom found within it. In this parable Jesus says, "To those who are open to my teaching, more understanding will be given, and they will have an abundance of knowledge. But to those who are not listening, even what they have will be taken away from them." [71] In other words, he wants us to see how important it is that we are open to his teaching and listen to what he says so that we get it! Why? Because whoever gets it (the secrets of understanding), will get access to more secrets. But whoever doesn't get it, what little they have, even that will be taken away. Sounds shameful but isn't that the way it always is? Another way to look at this is with you IQ, or intelligence quotient. You may have a high IQ today but if you continue to do things that to not use your intelligence, like watching a lot of television, drinking excessive amounts of alcohol or abuse drugs, your IQ has a good chance of lowering substantially.

Jesus explains to his disciples why he speaks to them in parables: because *they* have eyes but don't see and ears but have no understanding. He reaffirms that this fulfills Isaiah's age-old prophecy that people will "hear and not understand and see but not perceive."[72] But Jesus makes it clear that this limitation is more about desire than ability. Here Jesus proves to be an economist. He refuses to waste the "goods" on people who have consciously decided not to receive it nor on those who have deliberately hardened their hearts and closed their ears and eyes to the truth.

But that is *them*. This does not have to be you! You can make a conscious decision not to be like them by hearing the words of truth and gain an under-

---

[71] Matthew 13:1-9 NLT
[72] Matthew 13:13 NLT

standing about the wisdom presented with the power to propel you into your future. Jesus describes this methodology as one to use if you desire to be a person that receives the revelation of the mysteries. He simply says that we need to hear with a conscious understanding. If not, then the wicked one will come and snatch what was sown in our heart.[73] This often happens when we hear wisdom from an experienced teacher or sage and don't listen. When we ignore it, we soon forget what was said and reap the consequences of our poor choices.

This leads us to a third question: If the wicked one has the ability to steal the wisdom and revelation that has been presented to us, then what is he doing with it? I propose that he uses it like an assault weapon of confusion against you! He takes the truth and alters it and then uses it to confuse you. Remember, the Bible shows us that this was Satan's strategy in the Garden of Eden against Adam and his wife Eve. He also used this strategy against Jesus in the wilderness. And I am sure that you can agree that at some point he has even used this same strategy against you too!

You can make a conscious decision not to be like them by hearing the words of truth and gain an understanding about the wisdom presented with the power to propel you into your future.

One of our enemy's major strategies that he uses against us is "to steal, kill, and destroy."[74] Therefore, it is critical for you to intentionally understand the wisdom that you hear to avoid being set up for destruction in a state of confusion. I have seen people in this terrifying condition. You can spot them easily. They are the ones who blame God for everything. Some are even angry with God. Others are out and out opposed to God. This condition is tragic because they have turned against their Creator and their only source of real help.

In this story, Jesus reveals that there is yet another state that is equally as tragic. This is when people hear wisdom and get excited about it but the excitement

---

[73] Matthew 13:4 KJV
[74] John 10:10

quickly wanes when they are offended by the persecution that comes with believing the word. Because these people are shallow and have no depth, they don't understand that life comes with ups and downs and everyone will not always agree with you. This story teaches us the importance of persevering in what we hear in spite of what others think or say.

Jesus explains another condition that keeps us from hearing information that would set us on a course to a better future. He describes those that receive the truth but the cares of the world choke out the word, and therefore it becomes unfruitful.[75] This is obviously a question of priorities. We get distracted by the difficulties of life and are unable to develop a depth that will sustain us. Sometimes we look at our problems and are not able to see the solution. We forget that the problem is not greater than the Problem Solver. It is critical then that we do not allow the world to come before the Word of truth. When we do so, we lose the opportunity to transcend our circumstances with liberating information, and hence, we remain trapped within them. Jesus describes these heart conditions in terms of soil conditions for planting the seed of the Word.

Our only real hope to avoid these negative soil conditions of the heart is that we follow Jesus instructions and intentionally receive the word of truth, and follow its wisdom. Jesus tells us that as we activate these keys of the Kingdom we will bear a word harvest producing some thirty, sixty, and even one hundred times over.[76] The word then takes on a reproductive function when properly received. This is when it has the potential to produce a full revelation about the Kingdom of God and a wealth of possibility for our future.

Jesus uses the analogy of someone who sows seeds to spread his message and to get his point across. In this case this is the responsibility of the prepared farmer, which can be easily interpreted as a skillful preacher, teacher, or sage. The seed is the word of God, the word of truth which is the word of life. This is guaranteed authentic by God, recorded in God's Word, and spoken by God's representatives. The soil represents the heart and its spiritual conditions. But we must understand that the heart is under the responsibility of the hearer.

---

[75] Matthew 13:22 KJV
[76] Matthew 13:23 KJV

In order for a good harvest to occur in the future, all conditions have to be good: the sower, the seed and the soil. In other words, the teacher, the word, and the heart must be good in order to produce a great harvest. When the preacher broadcasts the un-tampered Word of truth, it is guaranteed good. But it is only when the preacher lives a life pure before God can they be certified as good.

An area that individuals run into real problems is regarding the quality of the soil of the heart. It is interesting to note that seeds settle and react differently to different soil conditions. Because not all soil conditions are good. This has a direct impact on the quality and quantity of the harvest. Based upon the story, we can see at least three conditions of the soil, or the heart that Jesus does not consider good:

1. "By the Wayside"- where the hearer totally misses it!
2. "Stony places" - the heart that has no intentions to change or be impacted by the word of truth.
3. "Thorny" - the heart that allows the cares of this world interfere, distract, and deceive.

> *It is this divine determination that brings us into divine connection with God and gives us the revelation and answers we need to succeed.*

Seeds germinate differently based upon the ground that it is sown into. Likewise, if the soil of the heart is not good, then a good harvest cannot be produced. This is evidenced when a hearer has no intention to receive the truth no matter how many times it is told. Another barrier to a bountiful harvest is if the hearer intentionally does not let the word sink deep enough to develop to maturity. Finally, if the hearer does not nourish the word of truth by meditation, activation, and affirmation, it will not flourish and grow in her heart. Only the good ground of the heart, which is suitable for planting the rich word of truth, will produce an excellent harvest. It is distinguished by its fruitfulness and yields a harvest of 30, 60, and even 100 times more than what it received.

Our objective should always be to maximize whatever is received and always aim for the highest possible yield. When we understand that the harvest is always disproportionate to what was sown, then we nurture what is sown and expect to reap in abundance. In addition, we can only reap that which has been sown. You will never see tomatoes grow from cucumber seeds. Therefore, we must be careful what we plant into our lives. If we want a wisdom harvest, we must plant wisdom in our lives. We do this by receiving wise counsel. If we want a knowledge harvest, then we must plant knowledge seeds into our lives. We do this by seeking out as much information that we need from all possible sources. If we want a prosperity harvest, then we must plant wealth seeds. Another thing we must do if we want wealth, we must give out of our wealth and expect a multiplied return. "If you give, you will receive. Your gift will return to you in full measure, pressed down, shaken together to make room for more, and running over. Whatever measure you use in giving--large or small--it will be used to measure what is given back to you."[77]

This is enough reason to frequently check the condition of our hearts and the way we hear the word. If we are to succeed in our future, we should avoid having a stony, hard heart and seek to be receptively pliable. We should be careful not allow the word to go by the wayside with way out thinking with whatever suits our fancy. We should not miss it by being distracted by a thorny un-prioritized lifestyle.

We should be the kind of hearers that are determined to gain access to the mysteries and secrets of life by intentionally receptive hearing. This is how we will advance everyday and in every way into our future. It is this divine determination that brings us into divine connection with God and gives us the revelation and answers we need to succeed.

It is also important that we are intentional because Jesus said that there would be those who would have spiritual heart problems, spiritual hearing problems, and spiritual seeing problems. But thankfully, Jesus also shows us the solution to these chronic conditions. He becomes our spiritual cardiologist to give us a clean heart to understand the mysteries. He is our spiritual ophthalmologist and gives us eyes to see with distinct clarity. He is our spiritual otolaryngologist and gives us ears to hear what

---

[77] Luke 6:38

the Spirit is saying to the Church. In other words Jesus is our eye, ear, and heart specialist and he has the ability to heal all of the woes that prevent us from obtaining a great future. If we allow him, he will be our Great Physician.

But once we make a decision to go to this Great Physician, we must be willing to follow doctor's orders if we want to experience the reality of a healthy future. If we expect great mysteries to unfold then we must go a step further and obey the truths and the wisdom presented to us by him. When we give our hearts to him, Jesus gives us a new heart and replaces our stony heart that has been hardened by the world. It is also important to make regular visits to our spiritual eye, ear and heart specialist to ensure optimal spiritual health. We do this as we engage in prayer, praise, and by listening to holistic messages firmly rooted in the Word of God.

So now we see that there is a remedy for those who are labeled as *them*. Those with spiritual heart conditions can get a renewed heart if they reach for revelation, are receptive to the word and are ready to reproduce a harvest. But in order to accomplish this, they must be willing to really listen for the truth and regard the Word with high esteem. This way they are prepared for activation and multiplication and can prepare for a fruitful harvest.

Finally, the moral of Jesus story is that in order to produce a great harvest for your future, the ultimate responsibility rests on the hearer. Once the good seed of the word has been broadcasted, the farmer can only wait for the soil to do its job. You can determine the quality and the quantity of the harvest that you receive for your future. You can get a thirty-fold return if you just give a little effort and listen intentionally. You can receive a sixty-fold return if you give a good effort and seek to understand what you heard through study. You are guaranteed a one hundred-fold return when you are productive with what you heard by application and then multiplication by sharing it with others.

It all starts with the planted seed of truth that contains the potential to produce a great harvest for your future. But never forget your responsibility to listen receptively and intentionally. The sower is good. The seed is good. So be sure that your soil is good and you can guarantee an abundant harvest that is driven to produce the results of a great future and yield the fulfillment of your destiny.

DECODE YOUR DESTINY FOR YOUR RESULTS

Developing Your New Divine Mental Diet is the key to fulfilling your destiny. Your life will be literally transformed as you begin to get a better understanding about where you are right now. Then you can determine the direction that you need to take.

THINK ON THESE THINGS – Open your destiny dialog by honestly answering the following questions about the results that you are getting in life. It has been said that you are only as good as the company you keep. Think about how your past impacts your future.

1. What are some things from your past that are preventing you from enjoying the present?

2. What are some things that are happening in the present that threaten to rob you of your success for the future?

3. What is the one thing that you could do to insure that you have a better quality of life right now?

4. What would it feel like? Look like? Smell like? Taste like? Sound like?

5. What would happen if you took action steps to gain success in the future?

6. Why do you feel that it is important for you to do these things?

7.   When will you start?

8.   When can you anticipate completion?

9.   How are the people with whom you associate encouraging you to fulfill your destiny dreams?

DIVINE DESTINY DIRECTIONS FOR YOUR RESULTS

Now it's your turn to chart the course on your destiny roadmap as you take the information that you have learned to plot out your location. Consider the life of the lame man. What things make you different from him? Can you find any similarities to him? What do you think was his destiny path and purpose before his miracle? Where do you think he eventually ended up? Imagine where you will eventually end up. Write your destiny directions here.

GOING TO THE NEXT DIMENSION FOR YOUR RESULTS

"Anyone who is willing to hear should listen and understand!..."[78] "But blessed [are] your eyes, for they see: and your ears, for they hear..."[79] "To those who are open to my teaching, more understanding will be given, and they will have an abundance of knowledge..." [80] As you go through the door of your future, you must be willing to surrender the negative memories of your past and replace them with the positive possibilities of a phenomenal future. Say this Divine Destiny Declaration to secure your future and reap a bountiful harvest.

DIVINE DESTINY DECLARATION

"I expect results because the sum total of all my experiences have served to prepare me for my future. Therefore I am intentional about preparing myself for a remarkable future. I maintain a positive mental attitude in all that I do because as I think, I become. I watch what say because I know that my words are like seeds and will produce a great harvest. I think about the wonderful things that God says about me. I am wonderfully made in the image of God. I am excited when I wake up in the morning because it is represents the dawning of a new day in my destiny. I look forward to my future with tremendous anticipation. I know this new day it is going to be greater than anything I have ever seen before. Everyday my life gets better and better. My future is phenomenal! It is my time for my future and destiny to unfold."

---

[78] Matthew 13:9 NLT
[79] Matthew 13:16 KJV
[80] Matthew 13:12 KJV

WRITE YOUR OWN DESTINY DECLARATION FOR YOUR RESULTS

Personalize your Divine Destiny Declaration to accommodate your unique situation by writing your own below. Be sure to include the vision you receive from the destiny dreams that you see in your heart. As you nurture them by reviewing and saying them daily, you give your dreams the power to materialize. This is a living document so feel free to update it regularly.

DIVINE DESTINY DIARY:
USE THE SPACE BELOW TO WRITE YOUR THOUGHTS ABOUT YOUR DESTINY RESULTS

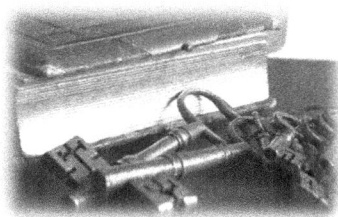

Change is the law of life. And those who look only to the past or present are certain to miss the future. —John F. Kennedy

Life…it tends to respond to our outlook, to shape itself to meet our expectations.
—Richard M. DeVos

Think about what you might be looking forward to in your life. Think about the probability of these things happening. Now, imagine being able to raise your level of anticipation to something so profound that when it comes to pass, it exceeds your every expectation. Write your thoughts in your *Divine Destiny Diary* at the end of this chapter.

"Shift expectation - Nissan"

10. The Secret Key to Your Reflection
"Feel the Difference"

There is a story about a little girl who was very ill and needed a blood transfusion. Her tough little brother volunteered to help after finding out that he and his sister shared the same blood type. While in the hospital, he watched as his blood left his body with his face squinted the entire time. When the transfusion was almost over, the doctor came over and asked him if he was in pain. The boy said no but asked, "When am I going to die?" The doctor reassured the boy that he was not going to die but his act of bravery would save the life of his sister. It is very important that we have informed expectations or else we can expect the worst when in fact the best is forthcoming. Once there is a shift in expectations, the difference in the outcomes is nothing short of remarkable.

Life is full of expectations. People have expectations about their future. Parents have expectations for their children and family life. There is an expectation about where or whether one will go to college. We all have expectations from our relationships and our friendships. We have expectations of our bosses, teachers, and mentors. A society can have a host of expectations for its people. Even the media has an expectation for its viewers and displays this with commercials every time the radio or television is turned on. As you read and incorporate the contents of this book into your life, your expectations will change and you will begin to see an amazing turnaround in your life. If you are going to achieve your destiny you must realize that what you reflect on will have a tremendous impact upon the expectations for your life.

THE POWER OF EXPECTATION

Someone who originally did not expect much out of life, is Mary Jane Blige. Born in 1971, to a nurse and a jazz musician, in Yonkers, NY, she knows all too well what it feels like not to have any expectations. She was raised in the housing projects of the Bronx where she had to fight everyday to keep from getting jumped or robbed. She often talks about how that experience makes you feel like you are constantly being "pulled down". She was determined to be a stronger woman after watching her mother struggle to take care of her and her sister and two brothers. Although she went to a performing arts school studying music, she dropped out before the twelfth grade. She worked several part-time jobs as a teen but it was her environment that shaped her musical identity.

She sang regularly in her church choir where she fondly recalls attending all night and also how good everyone was to them. She remembers how much better she felt when going to church every Sunday and how much fun it was.

She also remembers the block parties and the artists that influenced her music. But it was her father, a professional jazz musician, that left his mark on her.

But even with all of her musical influences and encouragement, she did not expect to make money singing. But as destiny would have it, she would be encouraged to raise her expectations by many R&B contemporaries to usher in a new sound where she would be considered one of the greatest singers of all times. Unfortunately, she was unprepared socially and professionally for such astounding visibility and made many costly mistakes. She was determined to get a new attitude and in doing so renewed her commitment to God and in an interview with Time Magazine said, "God comes first. If I don't love him, I can't love anybody. And if I can't love me, I can't love nobody."

She continues to raise her expectations for herself as she also continued to work on her image. Although she did not care about these things in the beginning, she is determined to be her best person possible. Once she told Ebony magazine: "I'm a young lady now; with growing up comes a lot of responsibilities. So there are a lot of things that I have to do, and there are a lot of things that I can't do anymore... I want to challenge myself more to see what comes out of it. Patience is a virtue to me". She was also quoted as saying that "Once you have self-knowledge and figure out love is the key to drawing good things to you, you glow." And glow she does and she has risen from the ashes of the projects in the Bronx to become a world music legend receiving numerous Grammy Awards as well as recording many multi-platinum albums. Her story is an encouragement to anyone who needs to raise their level of expectation to be a better person and make contributions in the world.

RAISE YOUR EXPECTATION

You may need to raise your level of expectation. When you have a clear expectant mental attitude, you have the unique opportunity to raise the potential of your dreams coming to pass. A clear attitude about what you expect will build your personal morale as well as the morale of others. You become motivated as you obtain a degree of focus and concentration. Rather than focusing on numerous ideas, you now begin to narrow down your efforts. Your rate of frustration lowers because you gain a clearer sense of direction. Frustration is always a sign that there are conflicting visions in your mind, and the one you want is not winning.

In order to begin to gain a new sense of fulfillment, it is important that you clearly communicate your expectations with regularity wherever you go— whether you are at home, in the office, or the grocery store. When you understand that you are defined and identified by your expectations, you quickly begin to organize your life around your expectations, giving them top priority. This, of course, increases the probability of them happening because you are consistently breathing life into your expectations. And when you have clear expectations, you even attract those who are willing to help you to accomplish your goals.

Secondly, just like the name of a child will ultimately be revealed, you need to reveal your expectation. The Bible teaches that you will have whatever you say.[81] When you feel confident enough to reveal your expectations, you creatively inform the world of their existence. Then the entire creation has the opportunity to collectively collaborate with you to bring your words to reality.

Thirdly, you should rejoice in expectation so that even when things are not going well, you maintain a sense of joy, knowing in your heart that things will soon change. This joyful composure has the potential to change the landscape of every area of your life. Even when darkness covers the deep recesses of your life, with every dawn, light comes. When you have great expectations, something beautiful happens.

There is a prophetic word found in the book of Isaiah that reveals the quality of the expectant Savior. This passage gives us an idea of what it means to have a royal expectation. He prophesies hundreds of years prior to the coming Messiah: "These will be his royal titles: Wonderful Counselor, Mighty God, Everlasting Father, Prince of Peace. His ever expanding, peaceful government will never end. He will rule forever with fairness and justice from the throne of his ancestor David. The passionate commitment of the LORD Almighty will guarantee this!"[82] When you raise your expectation and name your future, you can have a royal expectation. Rejoice in your expectation and call it wonderful. Reveal your expectation and see it as mighty, majestic, and powerful. Calling things into

---

[81] Mark 11:23 NKJV
[82] Isaiah 9:6 NLT

existence is a continual process of hope, faith, expectancy, and manifestation. Your future has the potential to be phenomenal! Your royal expectation gives you royal status. This causes you to walk like it is so, talk like it is so, act like it is so, and live like it is so…because in your mind, it already is!

God will destroy every enemy of your expectation by bringing your expectations to pass. The day will come that you won't have to fight any more for what you believe. You won't have to worry anymore about whether it will happen. When all said and done, you will have all that you royally expected and so much more because you have gained the confidence you needed to believe again and again and again.

AN EXPECTANT HOPE

In Greek, the word for expectation is *apokaradokia*, (*pronounced*: ä-po-kä-rä-do-kē'-ä), which means an "earnest, anxious, and persistent expectation" or an anxious longing.[83] Other meanings and variations of the word are "the act or state of expecting, anticipating something expected." [84] These definitions are more direct in that they allude to a specific objective.

Another word that relates to expectation is "hope." In Greek, hope is *elpizō*[85] (pronounced: el-pē'-zō), and means to trust, hope, hope for, or things hoped for. Other variations of the word include definitions that mean to have hope. Yet another word that is associated with expectation is faith. In the Greek *pistis*[86] (pronounced: pē'-stēs) means "faith, assurance, believe, belief, them that believe, and fidelity."

When you are in expectation, you are waiting for something specific to happen. We understand this best when we think about the times when we expect the worst. You can hope for something to happen but generally this is not as strong as an expectation. You can even have faith for something to take place but it is the strength of your specific expectations that takes hope and faith to a totally new level. In other words you must follow up your hope with faith and back up your

---

[83] http://www.searchgodsword.org/lex/grk/view.cgi?number=603
[84] http://www.merriam-webster.com/dictionary/expectation
[85] http://www.searchgodsword.org/lex/grk/view.cgi?number=1679
[86] http://www.searchgodsword.org/lex/grk/view.cgi?number=4102

faith with an expectation! "Now faith is being sure of what we hope for and certain of what we do not see."[87] Turn what you hope for into faith and turn your faith into expectation.

Fear, the enemy of faith, must be conquered before we can enter into the key of expectation and subsequently the realm of manifestation. It is there that faith can be reproduced and multiplied. It is very important to be around faith filled people. Faith is best increased when it is co-mingled with the faith of others. But the same is true when you associate with people who live in fear. Your fear and their fear will reproduce exponentially and reinforce more fear. This is why it is critical to associate with people of faith if you plan to advance toward your destiny. This is the primary purpose for joining a church or a group of believers. It is there that you should be able to find people of like minds who can support one another, especially when we are daily confronted with the effects of a fearful world.

> *Turn what you hope for into faith, and turn your faith into expectation.*

This is also true when it comes to hope. In order to produce more hope, you must conquer the enemy of hope, which is hopelessness. In order to reproduce hope, you must interact with hopeful people. Likewise, when you consistently associate with people who are filled with hopelessness, you multiply hopelessness in your life. Therefore it is vitally important that you associate yourself with people who can help to increase your level of hope and activate your faith. This is critical if you want to see the fulfillment of your divine destiny because you must have the support of others to help you to do what you cannot.

To go one step further, once you have moved from hope to faith and persevered into the element of expectation, you must persist. Settling is the enemy of expectation. It is in the place of living beneath your privileges that we can be enticed to relinquish our dreams before they come to fruition, regardless of how much faith that we believe we think that we have. Remain committed to your expectations until they come to pass. In other words, when you are fully committed to your dreams you become energized by the expectation of them coming to

---

[87] Hebrews 11:1 NIV

pass. As we wait in eager anticipation, expecting something specific to happen, we continue to believe until it manifests. This strategy will sustain you as you believe that things will happen even when things look their worst.

Having expectation is a lot like having a baby. There are things that are expected like physical changes, growth, and a change in diet, stretching, pressure, weight changes, and so on. But with a natural birth, there is also the unexpected, like a sudden kick or a sudden change in size or the surprise announcement that you are having twins! But regardless of the challenges, the mother is inspired to persevere because she knows that soon a beautiful baby will be born. Like an expectant mother, we too must persevere through the discomforts in life because we know that something beautiful is about to come into our lives.

It's even better if you take the risk of expecting something phenomenal, because then you have an even better chance of receiving the same.

When parents are expecting, they typically have thought about a name for their baby. Sometimes parents are really particular about what they will name the baby. Sometimes they select the name of their new baby based upon the meaning and connotation of the name. Or they select a name based upon ancestry—their parents, grandparents, aunts, or uncles. Sometimes the baby is even named after good friends or after great people.

Other times the child is named based upon what the parents hope and expectation for the child's future. For example, if they want the baby to be sweet, they name their baby Candy. Or if they want the baby to be smart, they name their baby Poindexter. If they want the baby to be a talented performer they may name the baby Beyonce or Brittany. If they want the baby to be athletic, they can make his first and middle names Michael Jordan. One of the trendiest names that people using today all over the world to name their babies is OBAMA! I don't think I need to say why. But I believe that the name is now associated with hope and promise.

Likewise, your expectations should be named with hopes that they will live up to your dreams. When you are expecting for your future, it is very important what you call it. If you expect nothing, what you will get is nothing, or pretty close to it. And if you expect little, you will also get little. But if you expect something great, you will most likely get something great! It's even better if you take the risk of expecting something phenomenal, because then you have an even better chance of receiving the same.

This joyful composure has the potential to change the landscape of every area of your life. Even when darkness covers the deep recesses of your life, with every dawn, light comes.

Naming your expectations is important especially when things in life are difficult. It is the actual act of expecting something beautiful that can completely change a situation. When you have something positive, locked in your mind, you therefore tightly hold onto the prospects of a good future. When you are in anticipation of something good, you have an expectant mental attitude that good will come. When you are in expectation of something great, you increase the degree of probability that something great will occur. The exact opposite is also true. If you expect the worst, there is a good chance that something bad will happen or you will be tormented, gripped with fear the entire time of anticipation. This is why it is important to be clear about what you want to see happen. Having clarity while you are waiting strengthens your resolve and makes you even more intentional about receiving what you are expecting.

EXPECTING THE UNEXPECTED

Let me interject here that it is important to be thankful that we do not receive some of the things that we asked for. There are times when what we expect to happen happens—for good or for bad, I might add. Webster's definition for expectation is, "the state or act of expecting: to wait in expectation; the act or state of looking forward or anticipating; an expectant mental attitude; the degree of probability that something will occur."[88] Typically, when we expect things to go wrong, more often than not, they do. Likewise, it is amazing how many miracles we see happening all around us simply because we expect to see them happen. But when we have negative experiences, we sometime project and expect every area of our existence to be negative. This is the nature of expectation. It impacts us for better or for worse.

To consider the process of expectation, let us look again at the story of the man at the gate called Beautiful.[89] The apostles went to the temple. A crippled man who was brought to the temple daily asked them for a handout. The man expected this to be like any other ordinary day of which the man had grown accustomed. But this day would be dramatically different because the divine power of God was at work in the apostles who just happened to show up that day.

They looked him straight in the eye and said, "Look at us!" Now, I believe this command for the man to look their way was not just because they wanted to be seen. They wanted this man to change his expectation of himself. I believe that when the man gazed at the disciples, he saw an expectation that would transform his life, and he desired to connect with it. In order for us to receive a miracle from God, we must change our outlook to believe that one is possible. If we want to see a miracle manifested, the way we currently see, think, or believe may not be big enough to contain the magnitude of God's blessing. In other words if we want to see something different happen, then we should first expect something different to happen. We should also do something different. If we do something different, then we can ultimately expect to see different outcomes.

Sometimes all it takes is for us to believe is to connect with someone who has the assurance that the impossible is possible. The man gave the disciples his undivided attention and allowed himself to shift in his expectation for himself from the temporary provisional handout to the continual anticipation of a better life. Too often we expect temporary solutions to solve our long-term problems when only a miracle will do.

---

[88] http://dictionary.reference.com/browse/expectation
[89] Acts 3:2

BEYOND WHAT I EXPECTED

If we do not shift our orientation of looking at our problems to having an expectation from the Problem Solver, we will not receive the best outcomes for our lives. We can use this concept as we look at our day-to-day lives. This idea reminds me of a time when I was searching for a much needed new car. I desperately needed a car quickly because the lease on my old one had ran out. The only problem was that I had a difficult time imagining driving a different model of car than what I was already driving. Although the model car I was driving was expensive to maintain, I had gotten so comfortable with it because it had been in the family for so long. I never expected that I would drive anything else. I did expect, though, that I what I would get would not just be newer but better than what I had.

While searching, I began to put a list together of the qualities I was looking for in a car. The top priority most important to me was to reduce the high cost of the vehicle's maintenance. This was a real area of concern for me because I put so many miles on my car. As I searched online for the car, I found a car that was acclaimed for this feature. Although it looked very different from what I was used to, it offered me what I needed. The only problem was that this car was so dependable there were very few available. After a time of searching, I found one vehicle available in my area. Although I was unaccustomed to the different look of the car, I got out of my comfort zone long enough to go see it.

When I arrived at the dealer, for the first time in my life I had a physical reaction to a car. This is because the car totally exceeded my expectations. What looked plain in the small picture looked surreal in real life. It was priced so reasonably and was so gorgeous that I found myself asking God "Is this something that I can actually have?" I was so amazed in this moment that I believe I heard angels singing! I am happy to say that this car has been the best driving experience in my life. It all started with the decision to see things differently and broaden my expectations. I will never forget the positive effects that this experience has had upon my life. My increased ability to broaden my limited expectations, take risks, and make new choices, ultimately has moved me closer to my destiny. But I could never do this without the guiding help of an omniscient, omnipresent, and omnipotent God.

The apostles told the man to get up and walk! They saw something better for him than he saw for himself. And then they helped him get up. This pastoral approach of the apostles presented to the man a new reality. The fact of the matter is that although he did not have the power to get up himself, he had to participate with them for his transformation to materialize. The miracle was not complete until the man participated with the healing. This is where our destiny begins to unlock before us as we participate with the plan that God has already designed.

Now he could have said, "Well now, you don't understand. I have been this way all of my life. I expect to be this way for the rest of my life. Please leave me alone. I don't want to get my hopes up too high." Or he could have thought that it was too much trouble. Sometimes people don't want their situation to improve because it would mean that they have nothing to complain about and that would leave nothing for them to do. Or maybe it would mean that they would now have to support themselves and this is too much work. But it is vitally important that we participate with our transformation in order to properly go through the dimension of expectation. This miracle in motion was effective because the man allowed himself to be helped while embracing a new expectation for himself. The interesting thing is that they did not just tell the man to get up but also to WALK!

> *The miracle was not complete until the man participated with the healing. This is where our destiny begins to unlock before us as we participate with the plan that God has already designed.*

Now if you have never walked your whole life, you could very well be petrified! Do not underestimate the power of fear and doubt as the culprit of the limitations in your life. Fear and faith are not compatible. They are two opposing forces. At some point you will have to get up the courage to raise your expectation and believe to see God move tremendously in your life. This bravery is an act of your will. The question that remains is, "What are the options?" The answer is either to believe and expect something different or be doomed to your current existence.

Unfortunately, too many take the second option, deciding that it takes too much effort to see change. The fear of failure is a very powerful deterrent to walking out your destiny. When you are tempted to fall into the temptation of fear, it may be a good idea to ask yourself the following question: "What is the worst that can happen if I use my faith to expect God to move mightily in this situation?" Another problem is the fear of success which involves work and responsibility. These are two things in which some people just don't want to engage.

The Bible declares that "instantly" the man's feet and ankles became strengthened. This man's experience helps us know that we too can instantly have the same life-changing experience if we can only raise the expectation of possibilities for our own lives. When God has moved in a way that we cannot, we need to instantly respond with praise! And by an act of his own will, the man participated with his miracle and jumped to his feet and began walking, leaping, and praising God! We should also remember not to lose heart because miracles are not always instantaneous but come as part of a process. But that does not make them any less dynamic.

Because the man changed his expectation for himself, he now is able to express his feelings about it in a whole new way. How many times have we seen God move and remain arrogantly emotionally untouched? This man's total active participation: body, soul, and spirit, is evidenced by the man's jumping, leaping, and praising. This overflow is confirmation that a true miracle has transpired, and transformation has taken place.

The change of this man's expectation for himself created a supernatural chain reaction of events that spilled over into other people's lives. This "miracle in motion" caused the man to go places where he had no prior access—into the temple courts. When all the people saw him walking, leaping, and praising God, they were filled with wonder and amazement at what had happened to him. What an awesome witness and testimony. When we are miraculously transformed because of our raised expectations, it causes others to stop, look, and listen and perhaps even desire what we have—a renewed mind, a renewed hope, and a renewed life.

What is amazing is that when Peter saw this reaction from the people, he said to them, "Men of Israel, why does this surprise you? Why do you stare at us as if by our own power or godliness we had made this man walk?"[90] In other words, Peter wanted to make it absolutely clear: We have done this with no power of our own. The disciples immediately identified where their power came from as they declared, "In the name of Jesus Christ of Nazareth . . ."[91] They were careful to specifically attribute all of what happened to the power of Jesus Christ.

This is where we sometimes run into a problem. We often look to people and expect them to solve our problems. We were taught when we were children to go to others for help, which we should. But there are people who expect others to fix their problems. Although we should be able to rely on people to aid us, we should never depend on the arm of flesh to do it for us. The tragedy is when we look to the arm of flesh and expect people to do what only God can do. We look to others as the source instead of being a mere conduit. What is even more tragic is when those same people allow others to look to them as the source of miraculous power. Peter wanted to be sure that God got the glory for what God had done! His declaration makes it clear that it is by his faith, which is founded upon his hope and expectation in the name of Jesus that made the miracle possible.

In addition to raising the man's expectations, Peter himself had to have a spirit of expectation. The miracle worker had to have some impression that the miracle was possible or he would have kept on walking past this lame man without incident. God had to speak to Peter in such a way that caused him to have an expectation in his heart and reach out to the man and give him hope. Like Peter and John, we are put here on this earth to make a difference in people's lives and to be a blessing. In the times we are living in, if there was ever a time that we needed a renewed expectation, we need it now. This world does not contain the power to heal itself without the Healer. This world does not have the power to have peace without the Prince of Peace. This world has no power to save itself without the Savior. The sad truth is that it will take a miracle to get the world out of its current condition. We can help to positively change the world and walk in this expectation.

---

[90] Acts 3:12
[91] Acts 3:6

THE MAKING OF NEW EXPECTATIONS

When we realize that we become what we think about, we will be more careful with what we allow to enter and entertain our minds. We would also not think so casually about the images that come across our televisions, computers and other forms of media that we are bombarded with everyday. As a practice, I am very cautious about the entrance of these images into my space and safeguard against their existence. When an unsuspecting image comes, I quickly delete it, disarm it or destroy it, rendering it powerless and ineffective to my psyche.

People who have a history of abuse and discouragement often have dismal outlooks and see no hope in their current circumstances or their future. Negative images that they see in movies, films, and reality only reinforce this pessimistic orientation. In order to shift out of this vicious cycle, it is therefore critical to intentionally maintain a positive attitude and focus our mind on new perspectives and flood it with positive images and stories.

This was Jesus objective when he preached his first sermon[92] filled with revelation about the hopeful reality of the Kingdom of God. Jesus' development of the beatitudes message helps us to understand that a good attitude as the best way of life and has the potential to produce intrinsic goodness in all things. The attitudes that Jesus describes in the Beatitudes are distinctly different from those commonly practiced in that day. They are as different as light is to darkness, and as different from the Kingdom of Heaven is to the kingdom of hell. Instead of putting everyone in the same category, Jesus makes a clear distinction and teaches his disciples how to be different.[93] In the Beatitudes, Jesus is calling the disciples to a higher level of thinking and existing. Likewise, his message speaks to us today.

The Latin word for blessed is *beautus,* means the supreme blessedness or exalted happiness. Because he knows that most people want to experience heaven, he goes on to show them what it would take to experience this blessedness. He describes the character of the people of the Kingdom of God. He describes the specific characteristics of those who would inhabit that kingdom and the process for obtaining them.

---

[92] Matthew 5 KJV
[93] Matthew 5 KJV

Jesus fully understands the difficulties that come with life, but he shows how they can be transcended by focusing on the direction of our thinking. He declares that those who weep will be comforted and even laugh. But this is only possible as the person shifts their perspective to receive the encouragement. His message also points us in the right direction when he says, "You're blessed when you're at the end of your rope. With less of you, there is more of God and his rule."[94] Here Jesus shows us where we can get the assistance that we need in order to maintain our composure in life. In other words, if you come to the end of your rope, this does not mean that it is completely the end of life but merely the beginning of a life that trusts, leans, and depends on God.

This is a direct reversal of the way we have become accustomed to thinking when things do not go the way we planned. Instead of thinking the worst, we can see the best that life has to offer regardless of the circumstance. This becomes even clearer when in the same passage Jesus says, "You're blessed when you feel you've lost what is the most dear to you. Only then can you be embraced by the One most dear to you."[95] In other words, it is only when you have lost it all that you gain everything!

It has been said that it is your attitude, not your aptitude that determines your altitude.[96] Your expectations are very important to your quality of life. Gratitude is another important attribute that helps us to receive what is best. When we appreciate what we have, where we are, and how far we have come, we set ourselves up for more good to come into our lives. Likewise when we are ungrateful and discontent, life seems to dwindle away. When we adjust our expectations to be thankful for even the little things, then we can expect the best. This type of thinking gives us the latitude to dream bigger than we have ever dreamed before and frees us from the narrow restrictions that keeps us from seeing the best of outcomes.

Therefore, it is vital that we expect the best in order to see the best. We must think the best if we want to experience the best. In order for this to happen we must possess an expectation for a great change and move of God in our lives. Enter the dimension of expectation and allow yourself to reflect on God's best for your life and soon you will be on a direct course to collide with your destiny!

---

[94]Matthew 5:3 Message
[95] Matthew 5:4 Message
[96] Zig Ziglar

DECODE
YOUR DESTINY
FOR YOUR REFLECTION

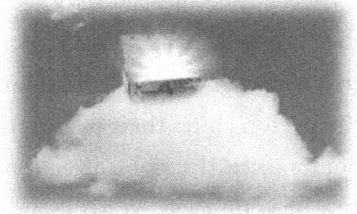

Developing Your New Divine Mental Diet is the key to fulfilling your destiny. Your life will be literally transformed as you begin to get a better understanding about where you are right now. Then you can determine the direction that you need to take.

THINK ON THESE THINGS – Open your destiny dialog by honestly answering the following questions about the quality of your reflection in life. It has been said that you are only as good as the company you keep. Thinking about how your past impacts your future and honestly answer the following questions:

1. What are you hoping to see happen in your life right now? Why do you want to see this?

2. What goals are expecting to accomplish in the near future?

3. How do your expectations align with God's?

4. In what ways do you need to raise your expectations to meet God's?

5. What is your expectation about your ultimate destiny?

6.   What is your plan to get there? Write it here.

7.   Proceed to accomplish your goals with a sense of confidence and expectation to fulfill them.

8.   When will you start?

9.   When can you anticipate completion?

10. How are the people with whom you associate encouraging you to fulfill your destiny dreams?

DIVINE DESTINY DIRECTIONS FOR YOUR REFLECTION

Now it's your turn to chart the course on your destiny roadmap as you take the information that you have learned to plot out your location. Think about and chart the destiny of either Peter or John. What were their joys? What were their challenges? Where did their life begin? Where did it end up? Now see if you can connect with their journey to get you on your destiny path.

GOING TO THE NEXT DIMENSION FOR YOUR REFLECTION

At this door you must be prepared to imagine and expect the best of everything for your life, future, and destiny. Take the initiative and intentionally expect everyone and everything to bless you! Use this affirmation to transform your thoughts and expectations and ultimately your world.

DIVINE DESTINY DECLARATION

"Because what I reflect on is good, I expect today to be a wonderful day. Tomorrow will be even better. Every day of my life will get increasingly better and better. I expect to live a long, healthy, and prosperous life. I expect to be happy and satisfied in all that I do. I know that better days are coming, and my future is bright and full of possibilities. I expect to fulfill my destiny and accomplish all of my goals. I expect that God will give me the very desires of my heart as I delight myself in the Lord. I expect God to bring me every blessing that God intended for me to have from before the foundation of the world. As I position myself for God's best in my life, I know God will fulfill the words spoken over my life as it relates to my kingdom success. I expect all things to work together on my behalf and in my favor. It's my time! I expect the best, I think the best, I do my best, and I receive the best."

WRITE YOUR OWN DESTINY DECLARATION FOR YOUR REFLECTION

Personalize your Divine Destiny Declaration to accommodate your unique situation by writing your own below. Be sure to include the vision you receive from the destiny dreams that you see in your heart. As you nurture them by reviewing and saying them daily, you give your dreams the power to materialize. This is a living document so feel free to update it regularly.

DIVINE DESTINY DIARY:

**USE THE SPACE BELOW TO WRITE
YOUR THOUGHTS ABOUT YOUR
DESTINY REFLECTION**

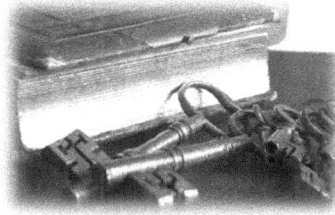

---

*Don't lower your expectations to meet your performance. Raise your level of
performance to meet your expectations. Expect the best of yourself, and then do
what is necessary to make it a reality.* —Ralph Marston

There are two ways to live: you can live as if nothing is a miracle; you can live as if everything is a miracle. —Albert Einstein

Think about a time that you may have experienced a miracle, regardless of how insignificant you thought it was. You just know that there was at least a time that God did something in your life that you knew was out of the ordinary or defied natural laws. Now imagine that every day you can have breathtaking experiences that leave you in awe and wonder. Write your thoughts in your *Divine Destiny Diary* at the end of this chapter.

"Like nothing else - Hummer"

11. The Secret Key to Your Revolution
"Driving is Believing"

On one Christmas evening while driving home from visiting family in New York, a friend and I were met by the sight of headlights facing us on the highway. To our surprise, an overturned tractor trailer was strewn across the road blocking traffic. Before I knew it, my friend stopped the car, and like superman ran out to see if he could help in any way. Sure enough, the driver was in distress because

239

she was trapped and could not get out of the cab. He was able to help her out of the truck but she was miraculously unscathed.

I have heard countless stories similar to this where the people involved escaped impending danger unharmed and the only explanation could be that it was a miracle. These people knew that they had lost power over the situation and could in no way control the outcomes. They knew that only a power greater than themselves, had miraculously afforded them a special opportunity to be alive. They were not only grateful but soon became believers. It was clear that the radical shift that they experienced drastically revolutionized their lives. As you read this book, you will experience a revolution that causes you to see far-reaching changes that deeply affect and reform your thinking and behaviors. You will become increasingly aware of where and when they are happening. You too will be able to gain a sense of the miracles that are happening all around you…most that are out of your control.

PARTICIPATING WITH A MIRACLE

Oftentimes when we think of miracles and the miraculous, we think about those things that are beyond our control. But I believe that we can participate with miracles that are happening all around us. The story of Helen Keller always strikes me as miraculous! How she was able to become an accomplished author, activist and exceptional leader without the ability to see or hear is nothing short of miraculous! What is even more remarkable is that in addition to writing almost a dozen books, she also went to college, and travelled worldwide. She personally met twelve presidents from the United States and probably did more than and seeing and hearing person in her lifetime. It is clear that although she could have easily given up, but rather she participated with the miraculous power to transform her existence and her world. She refused to allow her disabilities to hinder her progress as a viable, contributing person in the world. Although she was not born blind or deaf, she became so after a serious illness before she turned two years old. She became very frustrated but with the help of a tutor, Anne Sullivan, she was able to master the new sightless, soundless world that she had silently become a part. She learned how to talk and read French, German, Greek and Latin in Braille. She was born with tenacity for life and became the forerunner in the cause for deaf and dumb people. At twenty years only, she entered Harvard University's Radcliff College for women. She raised money for organizations for the blind and she went around the world giving speeches about the experiences of blind people visiting approximately thirty nine countries. I could go on but the point is that not only was this woman amazing, her story inspires us to go to new levels of greatness that taps into a power that is greater than ourselves. But sometimes this super power is only realized when we are faced with crisis.

THE REVOLUTIONARY CHRISTMAS MIRACLE

When I think of miracles what comes to mind is the miracle of Christmas. In today's society Christmas means different things to different people. For some Christmas means a holiday and spend quality time with family and friends and be thankful for the birth of Christ. For others, Christmas is strictly a time for giving and receiving gifts without any religious connection. And yet for others Christmas means a free for all excuse to "shop-till-u-drop" spending spree.

At the time of this writing, the holiday season retail spending is over $430 billion. That is a lot of money to spend on Christmas when we think that only sixty-six percent of Americans celebrate Christmas for religious reasons.[97] What is even more interesting is that although ninety-five percent of Americans celebrate the Christmas season, only an estimated seventy-six percent of American adults identify themselves as Christian.

Traditionally, Christmas is a time to gather with family and friends to share good times as well as an opportunity to create some really great memories. But because of the dwindling percentage Christian perspectives, it is important to determine exactly what the significance of Christmas is in our society today? We may get a reliable answer if we go back to a significant moment just before Christmas and look at some of the pre-Christmas events. To get a more in-depth answer, we may want to ask a pivotal question like, "What did Christmas mean to Mary?"

---

[97] http://www.foxnews.com/story/0,2933,580462,00.html?test=latestnews

The Bible tells us that an angel was sent to a young woman named Mary who lived in Galilee who happened to be in the right place at the right time.[98] This is the first part of the miracle because it is a sign that involves a divine message from a higher power. Mary did not invoke this message nor could she resist it. Interestingly, the word *angel* in this passage in the Greek is *aggelos,* which means "a messenger, envoy, one who is sent, an angel, a messenger from God."[99] This angel was ordered to go to an appointed place at an appointed time to give a message to an appointed person. This appointment is a miracle because Mary neither requests nor can control the visit from this representative from heaven. The angel is on the obvious assignment to prepare Mary for the birth of Christ and give her a very important message about her future.

Now we have to believe that when the angel appeared to Mary he was in a state that she felt comfortable with or else she would have been scared out of her mind. It is not often that we would naturally feel comfortable talking to "other beings" that are "other worldly", and so Mary must have felt comfortable with the way that the angel presented himself and therefore was inclined to listen to his message.

This is a very important detail in this encounter because sometimes we expect that because the angel came from heaven, this was a spectacular event. But the opposite must be true, or Mary would have ran or passed out from the shock. The reason why it is important to recognize the casualness of this meeting is that this is often how our miracles often present themselves to us. And we can miss some of the greatest miracles in our lives if we are not sensitive to the small still voice of God speaking ever so softly about the great things that are about to occur in our lives.

What makes me so sure that this was a quaint intimate meeting was that Gabriel's assignment was not just to Mary but specifically to her womb! His assignment to her was to prepare her to be open enough to reproduce spiritual things. It was critical that she would be receptive if this holy plan was going to work. Therefore his message had to make the connection with her innermost being so that she could naturally cooperate with the process.

---

[98] Luke 1:30 KJV
[99] http://www.searchgodsword.org/lex/grk/view.cgi?number=32

The angel gives her salutations and salutes her with "Hail!" which means "to rejoice, be exceedingly glad; to rejoice, to be well, to thrive." [100] When used as a salutation it means, "I have good news." He tells her, "you are highly favored," which means that she is graceful, charming, lovely, agreeable, and one to be honored with blessings. Another miracle was that she was blessed above all other women and did not even know it! The angel had to reveal this to her. She is obviously humble and surprised because she asks herself, "Why is he talking to me this way?" This shows her humility. For a brief moment, Mary is afraid. This shows her humanity.

But the angel proceeds to comfort her by letting her know that she has found favor with God to miraculously conceive a son who she should call Jesus. Mary would have to conceive the miracle in her mind before she delivered a child from her body. Although Mary was afraid at the angel's salutation, she is overwhelmed by the angel's revelation to her. But this does not stop her thinking process because she responds to the angel with a very intelligent question: "How will this be, since I am a virgin?"[101] This shows that Mary is smart! Mary is thinking on her feet. She is fully confident that she is not involved in activities that would warrant a pregnancy and so poses the question of the methodology of her pregnancy.

And we can miss some of the greatest miracles in our lives if we are not sensitive to the small still voice of God speaking ever so softly about the great things that are about to occur in our lives.

Mary could not comprehend the possibility of the angel's words in her mind. This was because what she was hearing was above and beyond her natural comprehension and originated from the supernatural world. Then the angel explained to her that the power of the Holy Ghost would come upon her and overshadow her. Therefore as a result, the miraculous thing that would be produced by the experience would be called the Son of God. It is important for us

---

[100] http://www.searchgodsword.org/lex/grk/view.cgi?number=5463
[101] Luke 1:34

to understand that the birth of Christ was preceded by the conception of Christ...in Mary's mind and heart.

In other words, before the Holy Spirit could exert creative energy upon the womb of Mary and impregnate her, he has to give her information that she must first receive in her mind and then in her heart. The angel discloses to her that the Holy Spirit would "overshadow" her. The use of this word can be connected to the idea of when the Spirit hovered over the darkness in Genesis. This was to symbolize the immediate presence and power of God that would be accessible to Mary. In order for this to be successful, Mary had to be prepped to participate with this miraculous experience with God.

This miracle story of a common girl helps us to understand that anybody can have the opportunity to have access to the miraculous and cooperate with God to reproduce his glory. It shows us the capacity that we all have to receive the impartation of holy things to be impregnated by the Holy Spirit in the womb of our hearts. But it is important that we live our lives in a way that we are considered blessed among others. We should ask ourselves a similar question as Mary, "Am I considered highly favored? Would God see fit to send an angel my way?"

We should wonder how we can position ourselves to activate God's promises, power and miracles in our lives. We should also wonder how we can prepare ourselves for a visitation from angels and fulfill God's purpose and the destiny for our lives. Are we the kind of people who warrant a visitation from an angel? Do we exemplify a life that warrants that we hear that we blessed and highly favored? Are we prepared for our lives to be interrupted and overtaken by God's purposes? Are we positioned to be miraculously overshadowed by the Holy Ghost?

The first thing that we need to do is to follow the example of Mary and posture ourselves to get impregnated by the Holy Spirit. Now that we know it is possible, based upon Mary's story, we too can allow God to give us the very special gift of impartation. If we are receptive, we too can give birth to something great that can save humanity from its collision course with destruction. We must present ourselves to say like Mary, "Behold, the hand servant of the Lord; be it unto me according to thy word."[102] But in order for this to become our reality, we too must be in position, postured and prepared in order to receive the greatest

---

[102] Luke 1:38 KJV

miracle of all: Life. The best gift that we could give to God is the gift of ourselves over to the Holy Spirit for Divine Purposes. As we receive the gift of the Holy Ghost, this is the best gift that we can give to others. This gift and miracle of life is one that we can give and then re-gift over and over again.

In order to go through the dimension of miracles, we must first learn to identify miracles when they happen. We must be careful not to ascribe the powerful acts of God as coincidence or happenstance. God is continuously at work in our lives. We simply need to recognize the miracles when they happen no matter how big or even how seemingly small.

THE REVOLUTION OF THE RESURRECTION

Now we can move from the birth of Christ to the death of Christ. Once he was dead, his disciples prepared his body to be buried. Embalming the body of a dead person with spices was a customary act in ancient Hebrew times. It was a necessary ritual, or else the body would stink profusely. In that day, dead bodies were placed in tombs above ground, if the body was not embalmed, the foul odor could permeate the air. Once I smelled the place where a person had died. This odor is indescribable. The ancient art of embalming used spices to neutralize odor.

Although I believe that the idea was ingenious, it also helped me to understand how important this valuable this process is because sometimes life stinks, and we need a remedy. When we can't find one, we come to a place of disenchantment and begin to believe this is just the way life is. It becomes familiar to us. It's all we know and what we become accustomed. But this kind of life can also become predictable. We prepare for it. We gear ourselves up for it: a cruel, lifeless, dissatisfying existence. We make ourselves believe this is all there is, take it or leave it!

But then in the divine providence of God, the unexpected happens as we apply the spice of Christ to our lives. We wake up one morning and something has changed. The uncontrollable! The unpredictable! The unimaginable! Something unexpected takes our breath away, and we can no longer live life the way we have been. There can be no more business as usual. The furniture of life is not where we expected it to be, and we trip over it!

This is what happened to the women who found that the stone that was covering the entrance to the tomb where Jesus was laid rolled aside. When they went into the tomb and they couldn't find the body of the Jesus, they were shocked to find that it was not there. The expected didn't happen.[103] There are times when the expected things in life don't happen. Although we are prepared for the worst, it doesn't happen. I have heard that about forty per cent of the things that people worry about never happen. Then there are about thirty percent of the things we worry about that have already occurred and therefore are not subject to change. Yet much time is wasted on worrying about what cannot be changed.

As crazy as it seems, when the things we worry about don't happen, we get perplexed. We get confused and even disoriented. We don't know what to do! We simply react without thinking. The temptation is to do what we are accustomed to doing. We easily shift into typical modes. But when God moves in a way that is beyond our expectation, it is no longer possible to maintain the status quo, so we search for answers. When the expected doesn't happen, we should see this as our opportunity to shift and miraculously transform our thinking!

When crisis hits in our health, relationships, and finances, we go into survival mode. Although I have done this repeatedly in the past, I have discovered there is another dimension into which we can shift. A miracle mode! In this mode we are completely helpless but this is where we learn how to depend on the power of God! We surrender to the fact that all things are no longer under our control and we are forced to believe that with God all things are possible. We anticipate that God will move in our situation in a way that we cannot. And suddenly, things change!

In this story, two men clothed in dazzling robes, appear to the women. Some valuable lessons can be learned from this resurrection experience. First, when things look impossible, look for an angel! An angel is a messenger from God sent to fulfill a specific purpose. I believe in angels. I depend on them. They are sent to minister to us as heirs of salvation.[104] The angels that the women encountered were on a very special assignment to bring a message of clarity about this confusing moment. These angels asked a very important question, "Why are you looking in a tomb for someone who is alive?"[105]

---

[103] Luke 24:1-5
[104] Hebrews 1:14 KJV
[105] Luke 24:5 NLT

This is an excellent question because sometimes we look for life in dead places. We go to the cemetery of our lives looking for any sign of life when we know otherwise. Yet because those places are familiar, we find ourselves there. We look to the same people, who do the same things, and yet we expect to see different results. Albert Einstein called this behavior insanity.

It is equally insane to expect the expected to occur when God has already dramatically changed the outcome. It would have been equally as foolish for the women to ask the angel to return the body and thus allow them to continue with their plans of embalming him so they could get on with their ritual of mourning. Yet that is precisely what we do when we continue in our despondency when deliverance is at our doorstep. We miss it when we shift into our emotional automatic pilot and go back to our usual mode of handling life. We become unaware that God has already transformed the outcomes. This is just as bad as when we do not believe God's Word. God makes promises and because of our unbelief we cannot take advantage of them.

Another lesson that we can learn from the resurrection is to take the time we need to seek God for a strategy to resolve our dilemmas. We need to be intentional to resist operating in our typical modus operandi. We should give God the opportunity to transform us so that we can see and do things differently. We should ask God to open our eyes so that we can recognize the change when it comes. We can begin this transformational process by asking a very important question, "Why am I looking in a tomb for someone who is alive?" God has moved. The circumstances have changed dramatically. We must be willing to change our direction and way of thinking to accommodate the miraculous.

One answer to the question—"Why am I looking in a tomb for someone who is alive?"—is possibly that we cannot imagine life ever being any other way than what it is: dead! But we must allow our imagination to run wild with the possibility that maybe, just maybe this crisis, this tragedy, and this circumstance has arisen to bring about a change great enough to move us in the direction of our destiny! The angels answered, "He isn't here! He has risen from the dead!" He is not here! He is alive! Similarly, our situation and circumstances have resurrected regardless of how lifeless they appeared.

> *There will always be something that will change in our lives that will be unexpected and out of the ordinary and we must be willing to respond with unshakable faith.*

There are times when life becomes impossible: You are betrayed into the hands of sinful men and even crucified. But when this happens remember the words Jesus said, "I will rise again!"[106] Another lesson that Jesus' resurrection helps us to see is that in spite of how tragic our circumstances become, if we can expect miracles, death can be changed to life. Even from the deepest pit, we can rise changed and transformed full of power and resurrected with victory.

A song I enjoy, entitled "Still I Rise,"[107] sung by Yolanda Adams, contains this prophetic promise and reminds us of the possibilities of rising triumphantly from even the darkest of circumstances. It speaks about the ability to rise above life's problems and never giving up. This is the resurrection! This is the Life! Jesus said that he came to give us life and that we would have it more abundantly.[108] But all too often we live in everything but abundance.

When Jesus was resurrected, it was early on the first day of the week, he appeared first to Mary Magdalene, out of whom the Bible says he had driven seven demons. In her gratitude, she anointed Jesus feet with oil while he was alive, preparing him for his death on the cross. Her faithfulness afforded her the first resurrection encounter. When she went and told those who were mourning about his death, that Jesus was alive and that she had seen him, they did not believe it.[109] Sometimes we don't believe things when they sound too good to be true. We naturally resist because it is out of the norm. But what is even worse is when we refuse to believe that better is possible without any investigation. When we think this way, we can miss some truly marvelous opportunities to see God at work in our lives. Kurt Vonnegut has said that, "Hell is locked from the inside."

---

[106] Matthew 27:63 KJV
[107] Written by Percy Bady),recorded by *Yolanda Adams" Still I Rise","The Best of Yolanda Adams"* compact disc, Copyright © 2000-2007 Verity.
[108] John 10:10
[109] Mark 16:9-11 NIV

There are times when we choose to lock ourselves in our own prison of our own minds and throw away the key.

But our faith is challenged when we are confronted with changing circumstances. This is true in technology, fashion, relationships, and society. We must be able to decide, at any given moment, which direction we will move especially when the landscape has changed. Into every life will come the unexpected, the uncontrollable, the unpredictable, and even the unimaginable! Will we move in the direction of faith or in the direction of fear? We must learn move in faith as we see these dramatic experiences as the divine providence of God.

Yet another lesson that we can learn is that God uses crisis to allow us to see our lives from a different perspective. Have you ever considered that some of the circumstances arise in your life to strengthen our faith? Can you embrace the idea that God wants to get you to a place where you can believe that there is something better for your life regardless of where you are right now? We must grow past a faith crisis and move on what we believe. There will always be something that will change in our lives that will be unexpected and out of the ordinary and we must be willing to respond with unshakable faith.

Most times when we fear the unknown, we get perplexed, we get confused, and we even get disoriented because things are unfamiliar. We are at a loss for strategic action. The temptation is to immediately resist the change and maintain whatever we have been accustomed to doing. But that is no longer possible now. Something has changed, and we can't undo it! We must accept the fact that God allows these radical changes on purpose. We can use these opportunities to shift and activate our faith and do something radically different to align us closer to our destiny.

The story goes on to say that, "afterward Jesus appeared in a different form to two women while they were walking in the country side. They returned and reported it to the others; but they did not believe them either. Jesus rebuked them for their lack of faith and their stubborn refusal to believe those who had seen him after he had risen."[110] Jesus' followers quickly settled in with the reality of Jesus' tragic death. They did not know how to believe for a different outcome. They did not know how to believe that circumstances could improve. After all,

---

[110] Mark 16:12-14 KJV

Jesus was dead! It would take a miracle to get them to shift from their typical mode of thinking outside the realm of known possibilities! And it did.

THE ANATOMY OF A MIRACLE

At times in our lives we get comfortable with the way things are. Regardless of the possibilities, we just can't believe things can get better. What is even worse is when we don't believe that we deserve any better. That is when we really need to be transformed by the renewing of our minds.[111] The Bible teaches us to have faith in God to do anything. This kind of faith believes the impossible, feels the intangible, and sees the invisible. This kind of faith can overcome anything. For the disciples, the resurrection experience altered their worldview. Their lives were dramatically changed forever. God sets a course of action to make things happen for us. We simply need to cooperate with the Lord.

Like Mary, we can continually posture ourselves with a discipline of prayer and obedience. I learned the value of this important discipline when I was wrongfully accused by one of my students. Spending time in prayer helped me to handle what could have had an ugly outcome. I had no choice but to humble myself and yield to whatever outcomes God had in mind. Things did not go quite the way I planned, but I had to surrender the situation to God and seek the Lord before I acted. But I was only able to do this because I was prepared for this experience as I heard the assuring voice of God that what would happen to me would not hurt me but help to refine me and produce character in me that would remain with me for a lifetime.

Because I was willing to submit to the process of character development, I was able to see the fruit of it in my life. That is not to say that I have arrived or even that I am perfect but it just means that I understand the importance of being teachable and available for God's use. When we do this wholeheartedly we are able to say like Mary, "Be it unto me according to your word."[112] Although the experience seemed like it lasted a lifetime, it was not long after that the student returned with an apology for their actions and misunderstanding my objectives.

---

[111] Romans 12:2 KJV
[112] Luke 1:38 KJV

THE AFTERMATH OF A MIRACLE

There will be times when those around you who, although they witness the miracles in your life, will try to convince you that what you experienced was just a figment of your imagination. Therefore, when you receive a miracle, you must be armed with faith and prepared for the aftermath of the miracle. When we look back at our story from the book of Acts, Peter and John had just performed a miracle at the gate called Beautiful healing a crippled man who sat at the gate begging everyday of his life. He is then seen leaping and praising God for the blessing.[113] But not everyone was happy!

Firstly, the priests, who offered the temple sacrifices and were involved with general sacred rites, were not pleased with this miraculous activity because they could not get the credit for it. The priests of the time fabricated formulas and rituals for the people to get to God. These priests possessed a works mentality and mandated that these rituals be followed in order to please God. They wanted to control believers' behaviors toward God for their own selfish purposes.

God is setting you up for a miracle, but you must stand firm and maintain your faith! If you stand your ground in belief, God will activate a supernatural cycle of miracles in every area of your life that you will be able to easily recognize.

Matthew teaches us that unless our acts of kindness have holy underlying motives that connect us to the Father, we will face the ultimate disappointment and hear Jesus declare, "Depart from me . . . you never knew me,"[114] regardless how great of a work we have done. Matthew shows us that doing good for the sake of being praised by others puts us in danger of judgment because it appeases the flesh and declares, "Look at what I have done for God!" This mentality keeps the focus on the doer rather than on whom we are doing it for – God.

---

[113] Acts 4:1-4 Message
[114] Matthew 7:23

We must contend with those so-called holy people who want to dictate how God should move. God is not bound by such limitations and can heal outside the organized rules and regulations of institutionalized worship. Sometimes it is these rituals that keep us from receiving the blessing of the precious presence of the Healer. We need to understand that what really matters to God is that we have an authentic loving relationship with him.

Sadly, the captain of the temple guards was also unhappy with the miracle of the lame man. As the commander of the Levites who kept guard in and around the temple, he represented a militant controlling spirit whose chief duty was to maintain the status quo. He probably believed that he was controlling things for God. But what he did not realize was that only God is truly in control, and God's miracle working power does not need to be patrolled. God will do what God wants, when God wants, and with whom God wants!

Lastly, the Sadducees, which in Hebrew means *the righteous*, was a religious party among the Jews during the time of Christ. Filled with legalism, they denied that the oral law was a revelation of God to the Israelites. They also believed that the written law alone was obligatory and the divine authority. This party represented the self-righteous spirit that has a form of godliness but denies the power of God. What made matters worse is that they denied the doctrines of the resurrection of the body, the immortality of the soul, and the existence of spirits and angels. The Sadducees wanted to be the last word in the things of God and put a halt to all other godly expressions. They wanted to keep people in the superficial realm of the natural while aggressively shutting down any supernatural activity except what they could control. This is so "sad-u-see!"

Miracles are taking place all around us. When certain people can't stop them from happening, they try to refute the results. Although Jesus was undeniably resurrected, these religious people refused to allow this fact to reform their thinking. They could not change their old beliefs to fit this new paradigm and shift into a new worldview. Though the healing of this man could not be denied, they chose to stay in their realm of unbelief and out of the realm of faith, unable to embrace new possibilities. In their indignation about the healing, they arrested, questioned, and threatened the apostles. Only Satan hates healing because it takes the afflicted out of his grip. If we are not careful, we could find ourselves falling into this trap of agreeing with religious and demonic spirits. We must arrest, cancel, and rebuke these spirits and continue to confidently move forward focused in faith, believing that with God all things are possible.

The apostles represented a fresh wind of spiritual anointing on the religious scene. They exercised their kingdom power and authority over evil spirits, sickness and disease. They were arrested but not stopped. They were questioned but they had the answer—Jesus! Although they were threatened, they did not get out of character and try to defend themselves because they were confident in whom they believed. They were filled with the Holy Spirit. They were filled with courage. They turned to God in prayer and, as a result, many believed!

This miraculous moment caused a cascade of other miracles. But although there was a miraculous move of God—religious, legalistic, and controlling spirits came to arrest the movement. When this happens in our lives, we need to follow the example of the apostles and activate fervent prayer. As a result of their perseverance, they were able to witness more miracles, signs, wonders, and a unified corporate agenda.

We must remember that miracles come in many forms but we must learn how to recognize miracles. In order to recognize miracles, there has to be a time of preparation in God's presence, an expectation of God's purpose, and an anticipation of God's power. This participation with God's plan will always bring glory to God and transformation to our world. God is already working miracles in your life. It may start small, but it is only to prepare you for greater manifestations regardless of who doesn't like it!

God is setting you up for a miracle, but you must stand firm and maintain your faith! If you stand your ground in belief, God will activate a supernatural cycle of miracles in every area of your life that you will be able to easily recognize. Although dissenting spirits will try to stop the move, your fervent prayer will arrest those forces. Like the apostles, your holy boldness will be a witnessing tool that will cause multitudes to believe. In addition, you will experience no lack, as the disciples had all things in common. This set the atmosphere for a flow of miracles, signs, and wonders to continue. It's your time for miracles. When God begins to bless you supernaturally, there are those that will try to manipulate you out of your blessing because they liked things just the way they were. Don't let anyone try to stop you, block you, or rob you of your miracle! It's yours and it has your name on it! Remember, it's your miracles that keep you on course with your divine destiny. It's the small still voice of God that gives you the confidence to continue moving in the right direction.

I was recently watching a conference where a minister by the name of Sandie Freed[115] was teaching about the meaning of the word *hail*. She explained that hail means something good is about to happen—to rejoice, to be glad and rejoice exceedingly, and to be well and thrive. She reminded us of the biblical account when the angel came to Mary, the mother of Jesus. The first thing that he said to her was, "Hail." He announced to her that she was blessed and highly favored and because of that, something great was about to happen to her. She was chosen to produce the Son of God, the Savior of the World.

Freed went on to explain that God wants us to know that something good will happen for us, too and that God wants to do the miraculous. Then she asked the audience: "Do you believe that something good is about to happen?" She said, "If so, then your response should be, "HAIL YES!" You need to believe that something good is about to happen for you. And just as the angel came to Mary, the angel will also come to you and say, "Hail! I declare that something good is about to happen that will revolutionize your life. You are about to rejoice and be glad! You are about do exceedingly well! You are about to be well and thrive!" All you need to do is get postured, get prepared, and get in position to be driven by your destiny! Your future is revolutionary and nothing short of a miracle!

---

[115]http://zionministries.us/Zion/index.php?option=com_content&view=article&id=45&Itemid=57

DECODE
YOUR DESTINY
REVOLUTION

Developing Your New Divine Mental Diet is the key to fulfilling your destiny. Your life will be literally transformed as you begin to get a better understanding about where you are right now. Then you can determine the direction that you need to take.

THINK ON THESE THINGS – Open your destiny dialog by honestly answering the following questions about where you are on your life's journey. Continue your destiny dialog and think honestly about how you feel about miracles by answering the following:

1. Where do you need God to perform a miracle in your life?

2. Is this something that you can do yourself or is it something that only God can perform?

3. What will it look like when your miracle happens?

4. What are you doing to prepare yourself to recognize the miraculous?

5. How much time do you spend postured in God's presence in preparation for a supernatural move of God in your life?

6. Are you ready for your miracle?

DIVINE DESTINY DIRECTIONS FOR YOUR REVOLUTION

Now it's your turn to chart the course on your destiny roadmap as you take the information that you have learned to plot out your location. Imagine yourself in a room with Mary. Ask her about her early life. Ask her how she felt to be the mother of Jesus. Ask her about her first experiences and her encounters with the supernatural. Now put yourself in her place and see if you could walk in her shoes. While you are there see if you can find destiny clues that are indicators for your own destiny path.

GOING TO THE NEXT DIMENSION FOR YOUR REVOLUTION

As you go through the dimension of miracles you must learn to recognize whenever God has miraculously moved regardless of how big or small. Use this Divine Destiny Declaration to help you prepare for the miracles that are surely coming your way.

DIVINE DESTINY DECLARATION

"My life is one great big miracle! From the time I was born, I have experienced one miracle after the other. When God created me, God planted a seed of greatness in me and intended for it to produce. Therefore, the germination of miracles is activated in every area of my life. I am responsible to nurture and water the seed with my faith and believe that with God all things are possible. I know that God is omniscient and therefore knows exactly what miracles it will take to get me to my destiny. I understand that God is also omnipotent and has all the power to make miracles happen to me and through me. I know that God is omnipresent and is able to be present in every area of my life to make great things happen on my behalf. It's my time to fulfill my destiny! It's my time for a total revolution to occur in my life!"

WRITE YOUR OWN DESTINY DECLARATION FOR YOUR REVOLUTION

Personalize your Divine Destiny Declaration to accommodate your unique situation by writing your own below. Be sure to include the vision you receive from the destiny dreams that you see in your heart. As you nurture them by reviewing and saying them daily, you give your dreams the power to materialize. This is a living document so feel free to update it regularly.

DIVINE DESTINY DIARY:
**USE THE SPACE BELOW TO WRITE
YOUR THOUGHTS ABOUT YOUR
DESTINY REVOLUTION**

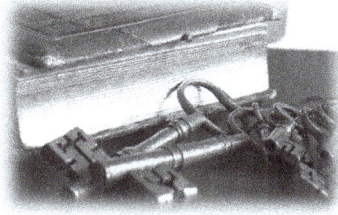

---

*When we do the best we can, we never know what miracle is wrought in our life
or in the life of another.* —Helen Keller

It's choice – not chance – that determines your destiny. — Jean Nidetch

Think about something in your life that makes you more aware that you have a very real and unique destiny. Think about a course of events and themes that helps you to understand the special direction for your life. Now, imagine that you see more clearly the greatness of your inevitable future . . . and walk right into your divine destiny. Write your thoughts in your *Divine Destiny Diary* at the end of this chapter.

"The ultimate driving experience - BMW"

12. The Secret Key
to Your Reward
"Travel Well"

My grandmother, who was born in Barbados, West Indies, was an extremely industrious woman. As often as she could, my mother would send us from New York to visit her. I remember how she would wake up very early in the morning and tend to her farm animals giving them feed and water. Then she would water her plants and look after those who she hired to help her with her farm. I remember her spending a good portion of the rest of her time reading spiritual

261

books. She spent a lot of time in silence. There were times that she would talk on the phone or with her neighbors and she would give out a loud screeching laugh. It not only surprised me, but also was a delight to hear her, knowing all that she had been through. It made me feel like everything was going to be alright. She had quite a journey in life but it was clear that she had travelled well. Ultimately, she overcame the things that could have overcome her. I am reminded of her every time I hear myself laugh.

It is interesting to wonder what my grandmother had to laugh about when her mother died at an early age. She became the stepdaughter of her father's second wife. She had a lot of trouble with her older brother who was extremely jealous of her. She moved to the United States only to work very hard to try to earn money to help her father. Then she married an abusive husband and had three children. Later on she moved back to Barbados and became a farmer. Life for her was difficult to say the least but she was a hard worker and continued to persevere. When her father died, because he trusted her more, he left all of his acres of land and possessions to her and not to her older brother. She was suddenly a very wealthy woman. After all of her hard labor, she had received her reward. She sold some of the land and built the biggest house in her community and spent the rest of her years enjoying the fruit of her labor. She died at the ripe old age of eighty eight leaving her children, grandchildren, and even great-grandchildren with the remainder of her wealth. Life has a way of turning some very interesting corners. And history has a way of repeating itself.

It was my gift and pleasure to know her. And when I think about it, I am a lot like her—hardworking, spiritual, dependable. I think that I inherited my unique laugh from her as well as many other qualities. But more importantly, her life inspires me especially when I am experiencing my most difficult times. I am reminded that as her life took some very interesting but unexpected turns, my own life has and will do the same. But I know that all things will work in my favor in the end because she showed me how it is possible.

A FREED CAGED BIRD

Another woman's life that inspires me is that of Maya Angelou. She was born to parents who divorced when she was only three years old. They sent her and her brother to live with their grandmother in a legally enforced, racially discriminating town in Arkansas. Fortunately, she had the benefit of her grandmother's deep rooted faith and old fashioned courtesy of the traditional south to sustain her. But while back visiting her mother in Chicago, she was sexually molested by her mother's boyfriend. She was only seven. She ashamedly confided in her brother who told his uncle, who killed the man. The shock of knowing that her words caused her attackers death caused her to go into silence and for five years she did not speak. Maya never uttered a word until she was reunited with her mother at thirteen. And she has been profoundly speaking ever since. She won a scholarship to study dance and drama and was exposed to progressive ideals. She quit school only to return there but became pregnant in her senior year graduating a few weeks before the birth of her son.

She left home at sixteen and supported herself and her son working as a waitress and cook but thankfully, she never gave up on her dreams for dance and drama. She had a short term marriage to a Greek man but still never gave up on her dreams. It seemed as though she became a national figure overnight with her writings that drew an international audience. Angelou has been invited by successive presidents of the United States to write and serve in various capacities. She is a highly sought after professor, actress and director. Regardless of all of the setbacks that she experienced in her life she forged forward toward the fulfillment of her divine destiny to intensely impact the world.

GOD-INSPIRED DESTINY

Your divine destiny relates to all that is God-inspired regarding your future. I believe that we are all imprinted with God's divine destiny dream the time that we are born. Allow your unique fingerprints be a constant reminder of this fact. Whatever God dreams will be God-driven and will happen for you! This is why you should become more aligned to what God dreams for your life because God will go to great lengths to make things happen to fulfill your divine destiny—and we all know God's record for making things happen.

Your divine destiny is fulfilled when you make the destiny decision to follow the dream that God has designed for you regardless of how impossible it seems. Knowing that God has a destined purpose for your life should be enough to help you to want to press into your destiny and overcome every obstacle. This knowledge should inspire you and give you the strength to scale any mountain, cross any river, or leap over any gulf to get to your divine destiny. You should be prepared to participate with whatever it takes to make happen what is already considered a reality in the mind of God. As you align with this reality, you become driven by the powerful vision of your destiny. After you are exposed to it, nothing can stop you.

I love the Bible story of Esther who once an orphan eventually becomes a queen.[116] This fairy tale type story offers us all so much hope as it relates to the fulfillment of our divine destiny. It also helps us to see that it really doesn't matter where you come from or where you start. What really matters is where you end up!

In spite of the loss of her parents and the difficulties that come with adopted life, this orphan becomes a queen. I am not sure if she dreamed about it or even planned it. But what I do know is that it was all planned in the mind of God. It was everything that God dreamed that it would be. Even though every odd was stacked against her, only God could have opened such a wide door of opportunity to her.

Your destiny journey may seem strange, and there may be times that you do not understand why only you have to do and go through certain things. I once received a card early in my ministry with a caption that read: "Others can, you cannot!" When I first read this I became angry because I did not understand why I was being singled out. Then I learned that because our divine destiny is integrally connected to God's purpose for our life, we must follow the individual path that God has uniquely laid out for us. Therefore there is no need to advance using our own power. We cannot possibly fulfill God's plans without relying upon God's power to drive us in our destiny direction. We do not need to make destiny happen. We merely need to flow with it.

---

[116] Esther 2:7-9 NIV

Know with all certainty that from the time that you were conceived in the mind of God, God already imagined your life would be a complete success. And we know that whatever God imagines has the powerful ability to materialize. But in order to obtain this glorious future, we must be prepared to strategically realign, reinvent, and re-create our lives to look more like the destiny dream God has for us. Coming into a right relationship with God is the first step to the recovery of what your life should be. The Bible makes it clear that a right relationship with God is to believe that God loves you so much that God sent God's Son as the savior of the world to die for a sinful humanity. But the good news is that Jesus did not just die but also resurrected. If we embrace this truth, then we can be saved from our sinful nature and be given the opportunity to live again a new life in a new reality. The moment we commit our lives to Christ, we are on our way to fulfilling our divine destiny. Anything outside of this reality is questionable. It is foolish to take chances with your destiny with whims and ideas that are not rooted and grounded in the Word of God.

This is because our destiny is founded in God, the Master Architect. God has artistically fashioned a fabulous schematic for our lives and because it is God's design, we need to check with the Creator for the instruction on how best to operate it. And because we are a God idea, all things work together according to God's divine purposes. Once we surrender our lives to God, then we can perceive the highly detailed design that belongs to each of us.

And because we are a God idea, all things work together according to God's divine purposes. Once we surrender our lives to God, then we can perceive the highly detailed design that belongs to each of us.

You need to embrace the fact that every detail of your life is created as part of a larger pattern whose final graphic presentation is nothing short of astounding. It is when we come to the realization that we are God's workmanship and his divine project that we can appreciate every motif and flourish that God creates to bring depth into our lives. When we understand the fact that every object strategically placed in our lives will work in our favor, then we will fully embrace the masterpiece of our destiny.

If we are to fulfill our destiny, our only hope is to cooperate with God that has already divinely designed it. More importantly, we also need to realize the necessity to align with the power of God before our destiny can be fulfilled. It is pointless to think that you can fulfill your destiny and not submit to God. I have found that destiny can only be fully realized as you make the very important decision to cooperate with what God has already created for your life. This decision will help you redefine your choices and decisions and set you on your destiny path.

One only has to live for a short while to discover the complexities of life. These layers often cause our destiny design to become distorted. This is proven especially when we look at the dysfunctions that have become prevalent in our society. When we understand that our lives are multidimensional and multi-layered, then we can see how things can intensify over a period of generations. But we must reclaim the destiny that God has already created for us. Although sometimes the vicissitudes of life can cause us to take destiny detours, we simply need to realign and embrace what already is and reclaim what is rightfully ours: a destiny that is divine.

> *But when we are enlightened to see the direction of our destiny, it becomes more difficult to return to wastelands of darkness.*

Too often we desire to accelerate towards destiny because we feel like things are not happening as fast as we would like. More often than not we expect instantaneous blessings. One thing that we should be clear about in this microwave society is that the discovery of destiny is not immediate. Because it is rooted in the eternal nature of God, it is critical for us to rest assured that the process it takes to be transformed into the new creation of our destiny will not be rushed. This process is experienced on many levels in your life. It takes time for old things, in particular dysfunctional habits and patterns, to be reversed and overturned to get us back on the path.

Sometimes we don't realize when unhealthy behaviors have developed in our lives. These vicious cycles will take some time to undo. The difficulty comes in determining exactly what dysfunction is, because everything in our lives revolves around what we believe is normal. But it is also important to note that when we make the arduous journey toward the wellspring of wholeness, it takes a full-fledged effort to unravel from what is keeping us from fulfilling our destiny. But when we are enlightened to see the direction of our destiny, it becomes more difficult to return to wastelands of darkness.

Thank God that we can make a u-turn in life when we come to those significant junctures. When we mature in our understanding that our complete cooperation with a corrective course of action is needed, then we can begin to advance in the journey toward wholeness more swiftly. We must be careful to develop healthy protective mechanisms and learn new skills in order that we do not find ourselves frustrated and worse off than before. It may be the drive of your life but, if you persist, the journey is worth the trip.

Sometimes we believe that our destiny is accomplished by using the world's formula for success. Although some of these methods are not all bad, if they become the absolute focus, it could become spiritually detrimental. This spirit of ambition may be the result of hidden insecurities that cause us to overcompensate and is a clear indication that there is an underlying problem. If there is a constant need for one's ego to be stroked, this may be a sign of low self-esteem or the lack of feeling loved and accepted. This unhealthy existence can inhibit a truly authentic relationship with God and the revealing of destiny if not properly handled.

If we are not held in personal accountability to God and significant others, there is a good possibility that we will get distracted from our course. We see this being played out with highly visible leaders who fall due to improprieties. I believe this fall is a result of the lack of people with integrity strategically positioned in an inner circle to counter the crowd of "yes" people who are so easily inclined. In these instances, God must mandate a stripping process of unhealthy behaviors to become people of integrity ready to fulfill God's destiny.

We need God's supernatural assistance because when we are caught up in these types of situations, we cannot always determine what is best neither can we always comprehend which direction God wants us to move. So the moment things get a little uncomfortable we can get easily convinced that we are out of the will of God. But this is not always the case. God may be at work. And when we are unsure about God's plan for our destiny, we cannot tell when it arrives, therefore our destiny vision is blurred.

God may be asking you to examine your life right now. There may be things that come to mind you know that you are struggling with, such as bitterness, malice, and anger. This negative disposition will surely impede your vision path to destiny. But you are the only person who can address and change areas in your life that are working against you achieving your destiny. You must willfully submit to the process God allows for change. God will not do for you what you can do for yourself. You can ask God for help, but until you willfully and sincerely participate with the Father, your deliverance is futile.

Then there are things in your life that only God can do. For example, only God can give you a true revelation of yourself. Only God can show you your desperate need for God's power in your life. We soon realize that this is something that we cannot always identify on our own. Sometimes there are some subconscious deep-rooted issues that keep us from moving forward in our destiny and seeing our future. These are some things we are unaware of and have no control over. As a result, we fall into the bondage of frustration in need of a Mighty Deliverer to help free us. It may be an addiction that runs through the family line or a problem with maintaining employment. It could even be issues of sexual promiscuity and other vicious cycles that are detrimental to one's physical, mental, and spiritual health. In any case, there are times that we are powerless to free ourselves, no matter how hard we try. We stand in desperate need of a deliverer, and God is there.

As you prepare to approach this dimension of your destiny, think critically and carefully about the steps you are about to take. Recognize the inevitable process that comes with realizing one's destiny and be determined to persevere. My objective here is to help empower and equip you with the tools needed to get you in touch with yourself and in touch with your dreams. If you feel you need more help being guided in this area, you may contact me. I have experience in successfully coaching people in their destiny direction. Please visit my website at www.TheDoctorOfDestiny.com and let me know how I may serve you.

The power lies within you to set sail in a new direction toward your destiny. Once you decide to begin your journey, you must be aware that there will be obstacles. But I want to encourage you to set your sights and vision high and press toward the mark, because as you are driven by your destiny, your life will never be the same.

DESTINY DRIVEN

As one who is familiar with the many difficulties of life, I feel compelled to position myself to discover the design that God has for my divine destiny. Because of this, I have sat at the feet of many mentors. I understand that I cannot arrive at my destiny solo. I need the help of seasoned individuals, who have treaded out the course before me, to show me the way. With their guidance, I have purposed to readjust, reinvent, and redesign my mental world as the mechanism to come closer to the destiny picture that I see in my heart. These people push me to greatness. I have embraced the vital understanding that it is the choices that I make that create many of the outcomes in my life. I am no longer a victim of my circumstance but a victor with a powerful destiny. As I connect to the vision that God has for my life, I make destiny decisions that lead me in that direction.

I remember when God opened the door for me to go back to continue my post-graduate education. I knew that this was a destiny move because I had this overwhelming sense that God was not through working with me. I felt driven to prepare myself for the road ahead and that time was of the essence. It seemed as though the minute I enrolled and got accepted into the doctoral program at Palmer Theological Seminary, overwhelming turmoil struck my life. I was devastated. After all the trials I had already experienced, I felt sure that it was time for my life to improve.

But I would soon find out that this would be the most difficult, yet crucial, part of my journey toward my destiny. Destiny roadblocks developed every step of the way. During my time of study, everything that could go wrong went wrong in my life. Loved ones died, my marriage fell apart, my children went astray, and my ministry was challenged in every way imaginable! I lost everything that I held near and dear. I had every excuse to give up, yet because I have a destiny image in my mind, I persisted. Sometimes all I had to hold on to was the knowledge that God had a plan for my life. This thought alone was what drove me.

Through all of these trials, my studies became what I call a holy distraction. I needed something in my life to keep me focused on my destiny direction, and God provided it. I have to honestly say that this was also a true proving ground for the fulfillment of my destiny. My character, faith, and stamina were all tried in the fiery furnace of purpose. I realized that there were so many things out of my control and that I needed a power greater than myself to keep me from getting off course. I soon discovered that all I had been going through was part of God's divine design and began to gain a sense of peace and assurance even in the midst of turmoil.

Too often we want to arrive at a destiny destination and fail to understand the critical need to prepare for it. Many people want to go through streamlined processes and then want to be considered experts. All of the purchased degrees in the world will not give you what only experience can teach you. The unfortunate truth is that this is a waste of time because only time and experience will prove the level to which you have attained. Regardless of the titles that are coveted, you simply cannot give people something that you yourself do not have. The bottom line is that you cannot take people where you yourself have never been. If you find yourself merely desiring is a title, once you get it will leave you with a sense of dissatisfaction from what you thought that it could provide for you. Because once that is achieved, there is still more hard work ahead.

There are no shortcuts to destiny. What we should ultimately crave are the tools necessary to make an authentic, long-lasting positive impact on society. When you find yourself coming up short, this is the time to go back to the drawing board, and obtain the integrity that only time and hard work will afford you. I know many disheartened people who regret wasting time and money because they took short-cuts. Late in life, they are finding themselves having to start all over again. I still say, better late than never.

After five years of study, attending a nationally accredited institution, I completed my academic requirements. I was intentional about submitting myself to a process of refinement that could help shape me to be a person of solid character and integrity when I was completed. The day came when I would be awarded a Doctor of Ministry degree. Something beautiful happened to me on that day that I will never forget. As I stooped down to be draped in my doctoral hood and receive my degree, it was as if I was being crowned by the Spirit. I could almost hear the Spirit say, "It is finished. Now you are ready to move forward into the divine destiny that I have planned for you." Because this was a pivotal destiny moment for me, I became aware that I had finished a course, and I had kept the faith. I gained a sense that there was a crown of righteousness laid up for me because I had been obedient and finished this part of my destiny journey.

There are no shortcuts to destiny. What we should ultimately crave is the tools necessary to make an authentic, long-lasting positive impact on society.

I am sure it does not take a doctoral degree to be prepared for God's divine destiny for your life, but I will say that there is something really special about preparing for it. My preparation was in the world of academia; yours may be in the world of business or in the world of your neighborhood or even in the world of a child. All I know is that my process changed the course of my life forever.

Through all of the tests and trials that I have faced, my life is simply not the same. In spite of my many challenges, I have been conformed into the image of Christ, and I like the person I have become. My renewed level of self-confidence and self-worth prevents me from settling for less than the best of what God has for me. My desire is to please the Father and to do God's will in such a way that exudes excellence and the qualities of the Kingdom of Heaven. Although there may be many difficult days when preparing for destiny and perhaps even tears to cry, the possibility of the promise should cause us to reach for the highest heights.

The book of Proverbs tells us, "A man's heart plans his way, but the Lord directs his steps.[117] This is a crucial truth for us to embrace. We can plan as we may but we should make certain that those plans are directed by God. I am sure many of us can say that life has not always turned out quite the way we planned. This may be the primary reason why you are reading this book. Many are searching for help to understand where they are in life because of the many mistakes made. It is with a sense of self-empowerment, we feel empowered to make plans but we soon discover the many things that were completely out of our control.

As we look at the concept of having the ability to plan our lives and God's ability to bring order and direction to our plans, it is a lot like the electric current that goes into a light switch. We may have the individual switch or the socket but the plan it only works when the power source is connected. This is not something that we can do for ourselves or else we would have done it many times over. We need God to give us the power so that the switch in our lives can work so that we may see the light. We don't have to live long to see just how powerless we are when it comes to the fulfillment of our divine destiny. But this is where God steps in and equips us with the knowledge so that we can make wise choices. Our mission, then, is to align ourselves to all that God plans for us. Life is so much easier as we effortlessly enter into this flow of experiences that lead us to the dimension of our destiny. Sometimes that means going places that you could have never imagined.

A GLOBAL DESTINY

I never dreamed that my divine destiny would include being a world traveler but little did I realize that God was preparing me for exactly that from the time that I was a child when my mother would send my sisters and I to Barbados, West Indies almost every year to visit my grandmother. It was then that I became familiar with other cultures as we travelled through the airports of New York and the Caribbean. Because I lived in the New York melting-pot, it was natural for me to meet and know people from all over the world. As I was growing up, it was

---

[117] Proverbs 16:9 NKJV

normal for me to have friends from other countries. I thought that the whole world was integrated until I moved out of New York and started to travel to other states throughout America.

So I should have been prepared when years before his passing, my dear friend and brother, the Reverend Thami Mogase, invited me to come to his homeland, South Africa. We were classmates in seminary. He had come to work with me in the ministry of my church upon our graduation. Not long after, he expressed to me that he felt that God was calling him to go back home. He asked me to come to help build his ministry there. I made excuses that I did not have time, but the truth was I was fearful about traveling so far. I had been to the Caribbean—but Africa?

After four subsequent invitations from other South African pastors, I began to sense that God has something in mind. I consented simply because they felt that I would be a great encouragement to the people there. I agreed to come solely on that premise. Needless to say, after three subsequent visits there, it has been a radically life-changing experience. Since then, I have had similar experiences with my travels to the Caribbean, India, Latin America, and the Philippines. My global destiny to the nations is now being fulfilled as I have connections all over the world.

And now I have come to recognize that even holy inconveniences lead me to align with my destiny. While traveling on my all expense paid sabbatical to Latin America, I found myself in an exclusive five star hotel. Although I only booked a standard room, it was quite large and very comfortable. I was tired from a long week of studying Spanish in Costa Rica so I changed into my pajamas quickly and went to bed. Not long after my head hit the pillow I heard loud noises coming from the adjoining room. It sounded like some young people having the time of their lives. Although it was great for them, it was horrible for me. I was exhausted and desperately needed to rest. My mind was in knots from trying to learn this new language.

After about thirty minutes, I was forced to call the front desk to register my complaint. They were kind and said that they would call the room about the noise immediately. They did, because I heard the telephone ring. But after three calls to the front desk, the problem had still not resolved itself but rather had escalated. I had asked for a room change but the front desk told me that it was impossible because the hotel was completely full. Now, I could hear someone vomiting and the commotion that went along with that.

It was after midnight and I realized that the situation was hopeless. So rather than settle, I decided to do something very different. I decided to pack my things and leave the hotel. I was not sure where I was going but I knew that it was not where I was. At this point, the problem had escalated to the degree that security had been called. This was an obvious abuse of my time and patience and I had come to the place where this was no longer acceptable.

When I got to the front desk, without making a scene I told the attendant that I wanted to check out of the hotel and that what I had to endure was completely unacceptable. Suddenly, another room became available. Wow, it was that simple. The minute I decided not to settle for something that I was uncomfortable with, a new door opened. This is an important lesson for me as it relates to my destiny.

Incidentally, the room that I was offered was probably one of the best in the hotel. When I thought about it, it was where I should have been in the first place. But look at what it took to get me there. Had I not listened, I would have missed a very valuable lesson as well as an opulent experience. This is when I realized that sometimes God allows negative things to happen as an opportunity for us to move to a better, healthier place. Unfortunately, we don't always oblige because we think that it is too much trouble.

Sometimes we stay in circumstances that can be harmful to us longer than we should. I have learned that this is a violation of my conscious and that I should be gentler and kinder to myself by responding to the inner voice that is there to guide me. The moment I begin to feel uncomfortable, is the time to act to rectify the situation—not hours, days, weeks, months or even years later. It is important that you listen to yourself and be true to who you are. Do not feel pressured by what others think is acceptable for you. I believe that it takes a certain amount of humility and wisdom to recognize when you are not comfortable with what others believe you should be able to endure.

Too often we ignore our inner conscious and therefore the voice of God. God speaks clearly to us to get us to move from unhealthy surroundings that may have become our comfort zone in order to get us to a higher place of peace. This is imperative to the fulfillment of your destiny! Temporary moments of discomfort are not always designed to make you unhappy but are often signs that you should shift your destiny direction. Pain is a sure sign that you are moving in the wrong direction. It may seem like a little thing but over time, it could bring about disastrous results. For example, if a pilot's navigational instruments are off just a little, you could end up in the wrong country! Our divine destiny demands that we fine tune our perception to be carefully guided toward the plans and purposes that God has already designed for us.

DESTINY CLUES

I know God has brought me into the kingdom for such a time as this and has launched me to the nations. But I did not arrive to this place on my own. I am aligned with my destiny and everything in my life is synchronized to the timing of God. My mentor and life coach Dr. Mark Chironna has taught me how to discover and anticipate the synchronicities of life. These synchronized moments manifest themselves when you are in a prophetic flow with God. Then the entire universe cooperates with God and all things come into divine alignment. I have learned that God will to bring your divine destiny to fulfillment but you must first come into alignment with God.

The ministry of Chuck Pierce helps me to understand how to recognize the seasons of my life so that I can cooperate with the divine timing of God. In addition, I have discovered the dysfunctional vicious cycles that kept me from my destiny and have learned how to break them through prophetic decree and prayer focuses.

Dr. Cindy Trimm helps me to know that I am not crazy! I now understand that I am truly on the right track as I live in the reality of the Kingdom of God and not in the limitations of the world. Her profound ministry keeps me prayerfully focused on my goal to honor and serve with a level of integrity and excellence that exhibits the majesty of the King.

Bishop David Evans encourages me to go to another level of excellence and be about our Father's business as well as to understand the vast opportunities of Kingdom Enterprise that advances God's purposes in the earth.

Dr. Rick Warren helps me to know that God truly has an awesome plan that is filled with purpose. I see how integrally connected we all are and how God will use whomever God chooses to help bring God's plan to pass.

If these prophetic associations and connections are any indication of what my future will resemble, then I know that I am on the pathway to greatness. Their models, interwoven together, have presented me with destiny clues that are brilliant, prophetic, dynamic, and astounding. I am humbled that God would put such gifted people in my life to look to for destiny direction. These people help to push me to greatness. I need these people and others to help me to see with clarity my divine destiny.

I see my destiny unfolding each day in every area of my life. As I was concluding developing the concept for this book, in the process I have created an entire "Driven By Destiny movement". As part of the developmental stages, I wanted to brand myself so that my work would be easily recognizable. I came up with the name "The Destiny Doctor". I moved quickly to get the web domains so that I could use them for promotional purposes later. I was amazed that these were available. I also looked into the regional trademark of this brand and found that it too was free but before I committed I was inspired to check the name on an international level. To my dismay someone else had diligently done his homework and trademarked the name almost a decade ago. To say the least, I was horrified. For a moment, I was paralyzed. Even though I had the domain names, I did not feel like I could move forward because I would be limited and the truth of the matter is, he got there first.

In good conscious, I could not knowingly infringe upon his intellectual property. But then I had an idea that perhaps he was not using the name and could talk to him about transferring it. After I finally got up the courage to call him, the most cheerful man answered the phone. "You don't know me but…" started my conversation about my journey with the branding experience. To my disappointment, he informed me that he was happily using the name. At that point I did not know what else to so I offered him the domain names, all six of them, for free. He insisted that he pay for them but I told him that it meant more to me that I was able to give them to him to advance his work and as an act of admiration for his due diligence. Then something remarkable took place. He told me that he was so incredibly impressed with my integrity that he would do whatever he could to help me in my endeavors. At that moment it became clear to me that our paths were destined to cross: The Destiny Doctor" and the "Doctor of Destiny." We have forged a West coast-East coast connection that helps us both to know that it was part of our destiny to connect. Thank you Mr. Tony Magee for all that you have done to encourage me to be the best "Doctor of Destiny" that I could possibly be. This has indeed proven to be one of the best connections in the fulfillment of my destiny.

Part of the fulfillment of my divine destiny was for me to intimately share some of my journey with you in order to show you how you could discover the destiny journey that is uniquely your own. In spite the difficulties you may be facing, the purpose of this book is to raise your awareness that your destiny is intact and resides safely in the mind of God. Our stories and the challenges we face may differ but the destination is still the same . . . destiny. Who is in your life that is pushing you toward your greatness? If there is no one in your life to help support you in the accomplishment of your destiny, please visit TheDoctorOf-Destiny.com and let me know how I can serve you.

A red robin flew alongside my car today. It may have only been for a few seconds, but it was long enough for me to notice and smile. Maybe she knows that I am on my way to fulfilling my destiny and wanted to join me, even if only for a brief moment. You are on your way to your divine destiny. There are many dimensions in life that you must go through to get there. You will make discoveries and gain revelation. You will have many options and opportunities to experience renewal and transformation. You will uncover your purpose and the hope for your future. You will make connections and form relationships designed to transform your life. You can expect miracles along the way.

As God caused Esther to rise from obscurity to a place of royalty and stature, God's Plan for your success is the driving force behind fulfilling your destiny. God will divinely prepare you to move into a position of nobility and honor. God will crown your life with regal success. As you make the destiny decision to receive your reward and align with God and you receive the revelation of God's divine design for your life, you will manifest the power that will drive you right into your destiny. Now, you truly are unstoppable!

DECODE
YOUR DESTINY
REWARD

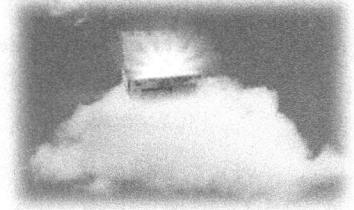

Developing Your New Divine Mental Diet is the key to fulfilling your destiny. Your life will be literally transformed as you begin to get a better understanding about where you are right now. Then you can determine the direction that you need to take.

THINK ON THESE THINGS - Open your destiny dialog by honestly answering the following questions about your life's reward. As you prepare for the fulfillment of your divine destiny, ask God to dialog with you and help you to answer these very important questions:

1.   What do you believe to be your passion in life? By exploring this, you may be able to discover the direction of your destiny.

2.   What are some destiny roadblocks that keep you from fulfilling your destiny?

3.   What are your spiritual gifts?[118]

4.   How do these gifts help you to advance toward your destiny?

---

[118] Spiritual gift inventories are readily available on line. Peter Wagner also has developed a great spiritual gift inventory tool, available at www.ChristianBook.com.

5. Develop a SWOT assessment for yourself. Determine your strengths, weaknesses, opportunities and threats.

    These are my:
    Strengths—

    Weaknesses —

    Opportunities —

    Threats —

6. What are some positive recurring themes in your life?

7. What are your levels of intelligence? Please consider more than just an educational intelligence. You may discover that you know more than you think when you assess the other areas of intelligence in your life in which you are completely competent.

8. What are your goals? What do you see yourself doing in the future? Short-term? Long-term?

9. Why did you choose these goals?

10. What is your strategic action plan to accomplish your goals over the next ninety days? Over the next five years?

11. How will you monitor your progress?

12. How will you celebrate your success?

As you answer these questions, your destiny direction will become apparent and clear. You will begin to see your unique future divinely designed by God unfold. The vision that you develop in your mind will be the driving force that gets you to a dynamic future. May all of your destiny dreams come true.

DIVINE DESTINY
DIRECTIONS
FOR YOUR DESTINY
REWARD

Now it's your turn to chart the course on your destiny roadmap as you take the information that you have learned to plot out your location. Esther had an interesting road to travel before she became queen. In what ways was her journey was like yours?

GOING TO THE NEXT DIMENSION FOR YOUR DESTINY REWARD

As you go through this final dimension to your destiny, know that you have made a substantial turnaround in your life. You have begun the all important destiny dialog that orients you to be driven in your destiny direction. Commit to stay aligned with your destiny so that your future endeavors will produce an abundant harvest.

There are many tools out there that say that they can help you to decode your destiny, but if they are not connected to the Designer of your destiny, they will ultimately lead you on a destiny detour. It is important that you remain fully engaged with God in the defining of your destiny while proactively striving to achieve your divine goals.

DIVINE DESTINY DECLARATION

"Only the God who created me could show me the blueprint of my true destiny. I have come to a better understanding about where I am in life. I have discovered more about who I am and whose I am. I have received revelation about God's plans for my divine destiny. I seize every opportunity to fulfill my purpose. I am grateful for the people and the connections that God has placed in my life to help me stay on my destiny pathway. I have an expectation for my future and therefore I am transformed and have renewed my mind to the truth of God's Word. I anticipate the miracles that will cause my destiny to be realized. I am excited because everything I do from this point forward will bring me closer to my destiny and bring absolute glory and honor to God. It's my time for me to receive my reward and fulfill my divine destiny."

WRITE YOUR OWN DECLARATION FOR YOUR DESTINY REWARD

Personalize your Divine Destiny Declaration to accommodate your unique situation by writing your own below. Be sure to include the vision you receive from the destiny dreams that you see in your heart. As you nurture them by reviewing and saying them daily, you give your dreams the power to materialize. This is a living document so feel free to update it regularly.

DIVINE DESTINY DIARY:
USE THE SPACE BELOW TO WRITE
YOUR THOUGHTS ABOUT YOUR
DESTINY REWARD.

We can make our plans, but the LORD determines our steps. Proverbs 16:9
NLT

CONGRATULATIONS!

This is to certify that:

_____

(YOUR NAME)

Has fulfilled all the requirements to be

"DRIVEN BY DESTINY"

And is hereby positioned to be a Supernatural Success!

Dr. LaVerne Adams, The Doctor of Destiny®

_____
Signature

_____
Today's Date

If you want to know more about how you can stay Driven by Destiny, please visit us at www.DrivenbyDestinyNOW.com for more information.

About the Author

Dr. LaVerne Adams is an author, certified life coach and inspirational speaker. She specializes in coaching celebrities and high powered professionals in need of spiritual guidance and emotional support. She is passionate about sharing her wisdom from years of experience and training to help people to define their destiny, maximize their potential and live the life of their dreams.

The Reverend Dr. LaVerne Adams celebrates over twelve years as Pastor, Teacher, and Vision Architect of the Cathedral of Praise Community Church, located in West Philadelphia, Pennsylvania. This church began with about 35 members who were mostly senior citizens. Today the church is thriving with vibrant worship and countless community outreach programs to youth, which is the signature of this growing ministry. Her leadership has helped the church to develop disciples and prepare leaders in the Kingdom of God.

As pastor, Dr. Adams has instituted the COPCC Leadership Academy that strengthens spiritual growth and accountability with plans underway for the development of the International Kingdom Strategy Center that will prepare leaders to strategically expand God's kingdom in the marketplace. The Net-Get-Connected Small Group Ministry was created to help keep members connected and supported. Another divinely inspired innovation was the Biggest Loser Life Changing Experience, where participants were led through an eight-week journey, shedding weight from the body, soul, and spirit. The group collectively lost almost 100 pounds as well as some unnecessary emotional and spiritual baggage. To address the needs of adolescent youth, Pastor Adams is the innovator of the Cathedral Crossroads Rites of Passage Program, offering supportive activities for youth between the ages of 13 and 18.

As Executive Director, she developed programs at the church's 30,000-square-foot facility, which ministers to over 100 families in the community daily, though the Motivational Achievement Program (MAP), a before- and after-school program which continues into a full-day Techno Arts Summer Camp specializing in the arts, media, and technology. The Cathedral Learning Center is a full-service preschool, with a curriculum that is literacy-based and includes the "I Can Read Program" to inspire infants to preschoolers to have a love for reading. These community programs employ over 30 people from the community. In the newly renovated computer lab, the church hosts a community computer program for all ages, helping to bridge the digital divide as well as prepare area residents with advanced technology skills and better employment opportunities. In its newly renovated kitchen, the church sponsors health programs and teaches nutritional cooking classes to children. These creative and innovative ministries have made the Church the center of the community as it touches and changes lives every day.

As community leader, Dr. Adams has been awarded Community Service Awards by Mayor Michael Nutter, State Representative Louise Williams Bishop, and State Senator Vincent Hughes. She has also been awarded numerous federal, state, city, and private grants to continue her work in the community. Continued efforts are being made to provide relevant opportunities to community residents—turning this once deteriorating neighborhood into a place "where God lives in the Praise" (Psalm 22:3).

As professor, Dr. Adams is a graduate of Palmer Theological Seminary with a Doctor of Ministry degree focused on the Renewal of the Church for Mission and the holistic needs of youth in church and community. She was nominated for "Who's Who in American Universities" in 1996. Since 1998, she has served as professor at the Eastern School of Christian Ministry and adjunct faculty of Palmer Seminary teaching professionally courses in Community Focused Ministry, Stewardship, and Small Group Ministry. Dr. Adams also teaches Bible and Foundations for Christian Spirituality at Eastern University's Esperanza College. She is a recognized church leader with the American Baptist Churches, USA and is a member of the Abundant Harvest Fellowship of Churches under the direction of Bishop David Evans.

As Scholar Practitioner, Dr. Adams is recent recipient of the Lilly Endowment National Clergy Renewal Program award, which gave her the opportunity to hone her Spanish-language skills through lengthy sojourns in Latin America with the expressed purpose to learn the language and the culture to minister to more effectively to a multicultural audience.

Dr. Adams is a dynamic preacher, teacher, and transformational speaker. She believes that her God-given calling is to make God truly known to every person she encounters. She is host of "A Life Changing Word" radio broadcast. As the *Doctor of Destiny* she is a life coach to busy professionals, she is affectionately known as Dr. "V". She hosts "Livin' It!"—a Web TV & web radio talk show that discusses how you can live the Christian life with victory in a post-Christian world. Dr. Adams has been seen on Fox Television and in Redbook magazine and is known for her vivacious spirit and zest for life.

Dr. Adams has world-wide apostolic influence and has been launched to the nations, traveling internationally spreading the gospel of Jesus Christ. She has traveled to Africa, India, the Caribbean, Costa Rica, Dominican Republic, Mexico, Puerto Rico, the Philippines, and Venezuela. She is host to the Christian Women's International Empowerment Conference launched in Bridgetown, Barbados, West Indies and scheduled to span to locations around the globe. We know that God has more in store for her as she avails herself to be God's choicest vessel fit for the Master's use in a new age, a new millennium, and a new world.

For more information and speaking engagements contact:

Cathedral of Praise Community Church and
International Kingdom Strategy Center
6400 Haverford Avenue
Philadelphia, PA 19151
215.474.2680 phone • 215.474.7586 fax
www.TheDoctorOfDestiny.com™
www.CathedralofPraiseInternational.org

AVAILABLE NOW!

Driven By Destiny Discovery Manual E-book

&

Driven By Destiny 30 Day Devotional E-book

You can get your copy of these
valuable resources free with your
Driven By Destiny
Proof of Purchase
For more information please go to:
www.DrivenByDestinyNOW.com

COMING SOON!

To help you continue
on your journey toward
fulfilling your destiny…

Driven By Destiny in Spanish
De la Mano del Destino

Also, COMING SOON the new
Driven By Destiny Journal
and the
Driven By Destiny Bible

ALSO CHECK OUT:
"Driven By DestinyTV"
www.Ustream.com/DrivenbyDestiny

and the
DRIVEN BY DESTINY
BLOG RADIO BROADCAST
at
www.BlogTalkRadio.com/DrivenByDestiny

For more information please go to:
www.TheDoctorofDestiny.com
www.DrivenByDestinyNOW.com

www.ingramcontent.com/pod-product-compliance
Lightning Source LLC
Chambersburg PA
CBHW062035090426
42740CB00016B/2912